THE TRAPPER'S HANDBOOK

by
Rick Jamison

D1597427

DBI BOOKS, INC., NORTHFIELD, ILL.

STAFF

EDITORS
Robert S. L. Anderson
Harold A. Murtz

COVER PHOTOGRAPHY
John Hanusin

PRODUCTION MANAGER
Pamela J. Johnson

PUBLISHER
Sheldon L. Factor

DEDICATION
Dedicated to Slim and Dorothy Gilliam, two fine people who taught me how to trap coyotes.

ISBN 0-910676-67-4   Library of Congress Catalog Card #83-072346

CONTENTS

chapter 1
WHY TRAP?

TRAPPING has long been recognized as a valuable wildlife management tool, and wildlife management, today, is a very precise, exacting science. In recent years many dedicated, caring individuals have tried their best to maintain a balance between wildlife populations and the ecosystems wildlife is dependent upon. Today, with the increased awareness of what's happening to our environment, in addition to pressures from special interest groups, there is an awareness about our environment like never before. For this reason, the general public has recently joined the sportsman and trapper in really caring about what happens to our wildlife. Conflicts arise, however, when an uninformed general public fails to recognize wildlife management as a scientific, efficient means of maintaining wildlife populations in balance with their habitat.

There are many who feel that removing individual animals from the population tends to decrease or endanger the survival of that population. In actuality, the wise and regulated taking of individual animals greatly improves the health, and even the numbers of the animal group that are able to exist.

Though these two statements may seem a bit contradictory to the average person, it's all very simple to the

Trapping can be an important income producer. The author, is shown here with two bobcats and 10 grey fox trapped during a 3-day weekend in the 1983 season.

4

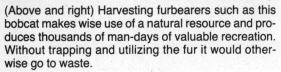
(Above and right) Harvesting furbearers such as this bobcat makes wise use of a natural resource and produces thousands of man-days of valuable recreation. Without trapping and utilizing the fur it would otherwise go to waste.

farmer or rancher. He knows that one, 300-acre pasture is capable of sustaining a given number of cattle over a long period of time. He is careful to remove cattle from the pasture at a carefully managed rate, or both the herd and the pasture will suffer.

If the cattle were allowed to reproduce without restriction or management, the cattle herd would increase, in a very short time, to a point where it would eat the pasture grass down to the roots. Not only would the grass suffer long-term effects, but the cattle would then turn to eating the leaves on the trees, followed by the bark on the trees, resulting in trees dying from girdling. Subsequently, the entire herd would weaken from lack of nutritious feed and become very susceptible to disease. Furthermore, future generations would eventually suffer due to the general poor health of the existing animals and from the inferior genetic characteristics passed on to young herd members.

As a result, the likelihood of the entire (unmanaged) herd dying off during severe winter months due to lack of food is great. In addition, pasture, as a result of herd mismanagement, would be rendered incapable of sustaining another healthy herd for some time to come.

In the case of over-grazing cattle, grasses can replenish themselves in a relatively short period of time, but not all animal species feed on the quickly-replaced grasses. Browsing animals such as deer are one example. If an overpopulation of deer are allowed to decimate a range, it may take 20 or 30 years for the range to replenish itself to the point where it could, again, support a substantial herd.

Though these facts are obvious to the wildlife manager, or even farmer, rancher or sportsman, they are not easily grasped by the general public. The sportsman has only to look at the Kaibab National Forest where all hunting was once banned, and the deer allowed to reproduce at will. The ultimate result was that the deer ate themselves out of house and home and massive die-offs occurred. It took many years for the depleted range to come back to sustain a stable population of deer. Today, the mule deer on the Kaibab are harvested annually, and careful management practices have prevented any further severe die-offs.

It doesn't matter whether it's cattle, mule deer, beaver or muskrats; animal populations that are left to reproduce at will have the capacity to destroy the delicate balance of their ecosystems. Muskrats, for example, may destroy the vegetation in a swamp which not only

(Left) Trapping is sometimes necessary to control predation. Furbearers destroy millions of dollars in livestock annually. This photo illustrates the results of a problem beaver which was cutting down all the trees around a pond, carefully landscaped by the owner.

Trapping can provide an important source of income for retired people such as Slim and Dorothy Gilliam shown here with a coyote pelt.

Trapper, Clifford Gilliam, has had a successful season, and these bobcats will provide an important contribution to this family income.

destroys their own habitat, but the habitat of many other forms of wildlife as well.

Wildlife managers use a term called *carrying capacity* to describe the maximum number of individual animals that a given area will sustain without long-term damage to the environment. If the carrying capacity of a range is exceeded, both the habitat and the population suffers. Again, habitat destruction and degradation is the real danger to the survival of wildlife, not hunting or trapping. And trapping, in many cases, has been the only efficient, practical means of removing surplus animals.

According to biological data received from the Illinois Department of Conservation, common furbearers such as muskrat, mink, raccoon, opossum, red fox, grey fox, beaver, striped skunk, weasel and coyote have the natural capacity to reproduce at a rate exceeding 50 to 80 percent annually. This means that for every 100 animals at the beginning of the breeding season, there will be 150 to 180 by the end of the season. In other words, wild animals produce this surplus naturally. During the lean months of winter the surplus is again pared back to the carrying capacity of the range. In most situations, the winter months, when food is most scarce, determine the carrying capacity of the range. It is also at this time that factors such as disease, starvation, etc., pare back those weaker animals. This type of death (due basically to undernourishment) is much more inhumane than

Trapping offers healthful wholesome outdoor recreation for these two young lads running their trapline on a cold winter morning.

(Above and below) Though the financial rewards may not be great by anyone's standards, there's little that can match the enjoyment of running a trapline for a young boy. Here, Bradley Elder reaches into a den to retrieve a just-dispatched skunk.

hunting or trapping. In addition, trapping allows the trapper to utilize the surplus rather than let it rot. At the same time he is helping maintain a healthy, viable wildlife population.

Man's influence on his environment cannot be over-emphasized. The advent of highways, cities, shopping centers, pollution, etc., has so altered his environment that he has no choice but to lend a helping hand and use any of the wildlife management tools at his disposal. Trapping permits wildlife biologists to obtain animals for examination, measurements, studies on aging, sexing, weighing and potential tagging. If an animal is tagged and released, that same animal, when trapped again, at a later date, can provide valuable information on species movement and condition. From such data researchers can determine the structure of an animal population including age distribution, reproductive success, percent of survival of the young, and the nutritional condition of breeding females. Trapping is also essential in conducting disease surveillance programs that directly relate to human health and the welfare of domestic livestock and wildlife alike.

The more crowded animals are, the more likely they are to not only contract a disease, but to spread it as well. Trapping can reduce the number of individual animals in an area which in turn reduces the chance of the others contracting and spreading a disease. Some of the

more important diseases that can be transmitted to man from animals are rabies, tularemia, plague, leptospirosis and Rocky Mountain spotted fever.

Between 1970 and 1975, over 80 percent of all documented rabies cases in Illinois were in wild animals. Recent studies of the coyote in Arizona indicate that a high percentage of these predators have plague antibodies in their blood.

A July/August 1976 issue of *International Wildlife,* an official publication of the National Wildlife Federation and the Canadian Wildlife Federation, reports that rabies cost the Province of Ontario 3 million dollars each year in documented animal losses and control expenditures. All this is not to mention the fact that a very real human threat is present, particularly in areas of animal overpopulation.

Other diseases such as sarcoptic mange and distemper not transmitted to man endanger the survival of wildlife. Sarcoptic mange is a disease of furbearers caused by a mite living in the skin. Distemper is a viral disease that breaks out when populations reach critical densities. In addition to these there are a multitude of parasitic infections which are ever present and continually threaten wildlife species. A well managed program of harvest, involving sport trapping, greatly reduces the danger of these diseases.

Another valid reason for trapping is stock, poultry, and crop depredation in addition to other forms of damage caused by wildlife. To the farmer or rancher, his very livelihood may be dependent upon the use of traps to control marauding animals. All sorts of furbearing animals (weasel, foxes, opossums and raccoons) raid henhouses. Coyotes eat sheep and calves. According to the California Wool Growers Association, coyotes cost ranchers an estimated 4.7 million dollars in 1975 by attacking newborn lambs and other animals.

A 1974 study, funded by the U.S. Fish and Wildlife Service, and conducted by the University of Montana, reported sheep losses due to *both* predators and natural mortality. The study pointed out that about 2,000 sheep were exposed to predation during the March to October 1974 period—coyotes killed 429.

Recent studies in Arizona are proving what has been suspected all along—that coyotes are the prime limiting factor to antelope fawn survival rates. A period of high-coyote population, resulting from no control, results in an antelope fawn survival rate of something in the area of 15 or 20 percent. Conversely, periods of low-coyote densities, resulting from control methods, show an antelope fawn survival rate approaching 90 percent in most areas. Again, if all animals are in balance with their ecosystems, all is well and good. To maintain this balance man must intervene by using trapping as a management tool to maintain the balance, year after year, without having periods of "boom" and "bust" cycles.

Not all of the reasons for trapping are to prevent a negative end result; there are many positive aspects of trapping as well. One such aspect is the commercial fur

Not all trapping income arises from the *major* furbearers in the United States. Much important furbearer income, for the individual trapper comes from little-known furbearers such as this ringtail cat.

trade — a fine garment for the individual. Trapping offers the means for making or having made one's own garments. In addition, the money derived from the pelts of furbearing animals is a definite asset, not only to the individual trapper, but to the country as well, for millions of dollars worth of harvested furs are exported each year.

Perhaps most important, however, is that trapping provides a healthful, wholesome outdoor recreation. Estimates made by the Illinois Department of Conservation indicate that in past years trapping provided over 374,000 man-days of recreation nationwide. In an area where the opportunity for healthful outdoor recreation during the winter months is limited, trapping makes an important contribution.

In short, trapping is fun. There is no question that it is a challenge to study an animal, its habits, habitat, and then devise a set, and somehow outwit it. One who has trapped knows that little can replace the thrill of running a trapline.

There are those who question the "humaneness" of steel traps and snares. Again, trapping, when done properly, harvests the available surplus in a manner that is generally much more "humane" than nature itself. Nearly every trapper, when trapping water animals, makes his sets so that the animal drowns upon being caught. In other types of sets, body gripping or "instant killing" traps are used which deliver a swift blow to the animal, stunning it, and killing it quickly.

Nearly all states have laws governing the frequency that traps must be checked and some limit the number of furbearers taken. Generally, the trapline, by law, should be checked once every 24 hours; so, stories of animals starving to death while being restrained by a trap are more fiction than fact. It must also be said that the serious trapper checks his line for yet another reason: A trap which has been sprung, or holds an animal, is not available to catch a second or third animal. Hence, it's not wise to leave traps set for any length of time without checking them. Nearly all trappers go through their lines as early as possible in the morning, and remove trapped animals quickly. If the animal trapped is the "target" (desired) animal, it is quickly dispatched (if necessary) and placed in the bag.

My home state of Arizona, has a law requiring the trapper to have some means of releasing undesirably trapped animals unharmed. As a result, nearly all trappers in Arizona carry "catch sticks" which are similar to a catch stick that a dog-catcher uses — a long hollow pipe (usually aluminum) with a steel cable running through its length, with a loop at one end which can be tightened or loosened by the user at the opposite end. This catch stick is used to loop an animal around its neck or body and hold it away from the trapper while it is being released unharmed.

Again, no one is more interested than the sportsman or trapper in the survival of a furbearing species. As a consequence, every measure is taken to preserve the

This trapper has brought his pelts in to a local furbuyer, B&M Traders in Mesa, Arizona. A lot of long hours and hard work have gone into the furs seen here. This meeting rewards all that effort.

quality of life for furbearers and make it an absolute certainty that no furbearer currently being trapped will face the danger of extinction. In fact, exactly the opposite is the case. Animals which are sought after for their fur, or for sport, are nearly always more closely managed and watched than are other animals which serve less useful purposes. However, wildlife management practices for furbearers and game animals generally help the non-game species as well.

Trapping is an American heritage that will indeed be passed on for years to come.

Economic Importance of Trapping

According to a recent report from the U.S. Department of Commerce more than 320 million dollars in raw fur was exported from the United States during 1981. When considering such a figure, it's little wonder that trapping is an important contributor to this country's economy. Today, the major market for U.S. fur is Europe, the United Kingdom and Japan.

Arizona isn't generally thought to be a major furbearing state. However, during the 1981-82 Arizona season, trappers netted a total of 26,000 coyotes, 28,000 grey fox, and more than 8,000 bobcats. With coyote pelts selling in the neighborhood of $25 to $50, grey fox in the $25 to $40 range, and bobcat in the $100 to $300 range, these figures deserve consideration in terms of their positive impact on any state's economy. Also, funding by trappers through the purchase of trapping licenses, permits and exportation tags supply much needed funds for biologists and wildlife managers to thoroughly study the various furbearing animals involved. For example, Arizona requires a $5 bobcat tagging fee for any bobcat trapped within the state. At the rate of 8,000 to 10,000 bobcats annually, those figures can easily pay the salary of a state game biologist. It is through such self-supporting funding that wildlife populations are closely watched and maintained today.

For states such as Louisiana, trapping is one of the top income producers for the region. That state's fur industry includes an estimated 12,000 trappers — they lead the nation, providing 25 percent of the U.S. production of wild fur. Louisiana also supplies over 95 percent of North America's nutria pelts and 10 percent of the North American muskrat pelts. The average value of furs to the Louisiana economy amounts to something on the order of 25 million dollars annually.

While there are men who earn an entire income from trapping furbearing animals, those individuals are few and far between. In fact, it's very difficult to make a living from trapping exclusively. Instead, today's trapper is from all walks of life — the factory worker, the doctor, the schoolboy, and the out-of-work-for-the-season construction man.

To the farmer, trapping not only offers a way of controlling marauding furbearing animals, it also provides him with a source of income that can be used to replace

The author's son, Kevin, is holding up a grey fox trapped in Arizona. Though trapping may be considered to an be insignificant income producer by some, the $40 received for the grey fox means a lot to a 12-year-old trapper such as Kevin.

at least a portion of the livestock lost to him. For the seasonal worker, trapping offers a valuable source of income during the lean periods. For example, construction generally booms in summer and is very slack in the winter. For fruit pickers and harvesters it is generally the same way. Were it not for trapping, the families of some of those people might suffer some additional economic hardship. For the schoolboy, trapping may offer little more than spending money, although its return in wholesome outdoor recreation may far outweigh its monetary benefits. Still, a $30 coyote, to a young trapper, is *important* income.

One of the best things about trapping is that the enterprising individual who decides to go after furbearing animals for money is not taking anyone else's job by becoming thusly self-employed. On the contrary, he's supplying work for others in the form of trapping equipment, supplies, gasoline, etc., which he purchases for his venture.

From the standpoint of American history alone, trapping stands out as an occupation that can be traced back to the colonial days. Today, trapping still provides an income for hundreds of thousands of hobbyists as well as professionals. And, it must be said that the pursuit of the almighty dollar is only a small part of trapping's *raison d'etre*. The love of the out-of-doors experience has, and will continue to be, the prime motivator. Unfortunately, too many forget that man is as much a part of the woods and streams as are the animals he pursues.

In the end, trapping has to be described as an outdoor experience that provides a source of income, helps maintain an ecological balance and serves to educate all who are willing to learn the full meaning of game conservation.

chapter 2

FOOT-HOLD AND BODY-GRIPPING TRAPS

THERE ARE basically two types of traps used for catching furbearers — foot-hold and body-gripping traps. Foot-hold traps have been the standby since their invention many years ago, while body-gripping traps have become popular only during recent years.

Foot-hold traps are commonly used on both land and under water, but body-grippers are recommended for use only under the surface of the water or up in a tree as is done when trapping marten. Many states have laws restricting the use of body-gripping traps on land. These traps kill the catch quickly, and they are not selective. If a non-target catch is made with a foot-hold trap, it's a simple matter to release the animal, usually unharmed. The same cannot be said of the body-gripping type. If a cat or dog strays into a body-gripping trap which has been improperly or illegally set, it will be killed. No matter what the law, no conscientious trapper would use the large 330-size Conibear body trap on land for it is capable of dispatching a sizable dog or even small child.

I have included a series of photos to illustrate the proper and safe method of setting both a foot-hold and a body gripping trap. Unlike most foot-hold traps, a body trap large enough to catch beaver has the potential to harm a person if handled or set improperly. The springs are quite strong and hard to depress; they must be in order to kill a beaver quickly. I suppose it's possible for a body trap to break a person's arm if the trapper were unlucky enough to trigger it accidentally; so don't go feeling around underwater for a body-gripping beaver set. Use a stick. This information is not intended to scare you, only to instill the proper respect and care when handling such tools.

Foot-Hold Traps

Foot-hold traps, for the most part, have changed very little since Sewell Newhouse invented the steel jaw trap back in 1823. Today's foot-hold traps, at least some models, bear a remarkable resemblance to those of yesteryear.

There are three types of steel-jawed, foot-hold traps in use today — the *long spring,* the *coil spring,* and the *jump* or *underspring.* The long-spring trap is the one that most resembles the old Newhouse design and consists of either one (single long spring) or two (double long spring) long flat springs extending outward from the jaws to lend speed and strength to the trap's operation.

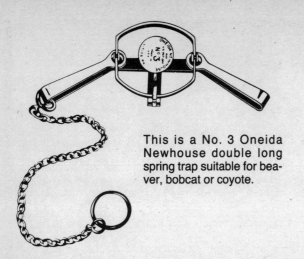

This is a No. 3 Oneida Newhouse double long spring trap suitable for beaver, bobcat or coyote.

This is a standard double long spring trap. Though it does not lie as flat or have as thin a profile as the coil spring variety, it is preferred for strength and holding power. It is also preferred for its ability to come up through a frozen crust.

The long spring has been considered the trapper's standard for years. It is reported to have speed and power second to none and is generally the preferred choice when strength is desired. For example, when it's necessary for the trap to break through a lot of cover or possibly a frozen crust, the long spring is the first choice. Coyote trappers, in particular, have long preferred the *double long-spring* trap.

The *single long-spring trap* is basically of the same design as the double long spring except that a single spring is located on one rather than both sides of the jaws. The single spring design is generally employed on traps intended for smaller animals, because not as much strength is required for closing the trap or holding the animal.

The long-spring trap is also desirable when additional trap weight is needed, say, for a drowning set. However, that same weight can be a disadvantage when it comes to carrying. Also, the long-spring trap can sometimes be more difficult to conceal due to the long spring(s). Particularly for sets on land, a larger hole

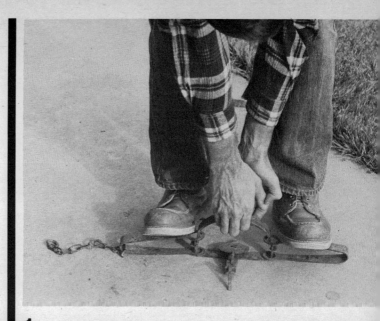

1. The springs on a Victor No. 4 trap are quite stiff so it helps if you pull up on the trap jaws while depressing the springs with the balls of your feet. Keep the chain attachment at the end of the spring, out of the way, not under it.

How to Set a Foot-Hold Trap With Your Feet

2. Then quickly swing the jaws open and hold them down with your hands. They're easy to hold in this position once they're all the way open.

3. Then place the dog over the one trap jaw and hold it in place with the thumb. As long as *one* trap jaw is held open, this keeps the springs depressed, and the jaws can't close.

This series of photos illustrates how to set a Victor No. 4 trap with the feet. It is normally done while wearing rubber gloves and boots to eliminate human-scent contamination.

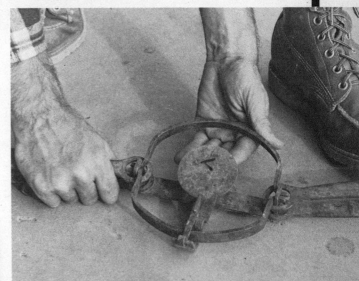

4. (Above) Keeping the opposite hand out of the way of the jaws, push the pan upward as the dog or trigger is fitted in the pan notch. Get the hands out of the way while holding upward pressure on the underside of the pan to prevent the trap from springing. Make sure that this upward pressure is maintained with a hand *underneath* the trap jaws.

5. (Left) After the trap is set, swing the springs(s) toward the dog or fly so that the trap will lie flat in its bed.

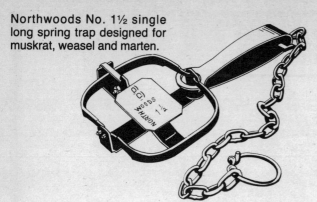

Northwoods No. 1½ single long spring trap designed for muskrat, weasel and marten.

(Right) The Montgomery coil spring trap has a very narrow treadle or pan. This requires that the animal have its foot directly in the center of the trap jaws before the trap will trigger. However, it is possible for an animal to have its paw well within the trap jaws and, instead of depressing the treadle, it may have its weight on the jaw closing and locking devices.

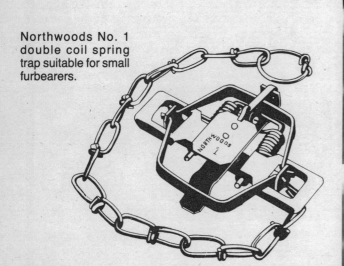

Northwoods No. 1 double coil spring trap suitable for small furbearers.

Added Springs

must be dug for bedding the spring(s) in addition to the trap jaws.

The *coil-spring trap,* as the name implies, utilizes coil springs rather than flat springs for trap strength. Because of their design, coil-sring traps are smaller and lighter. Trappers frequently prefer the coil-spring styles because the compact size makes them easy to conceal. This is an advantage when it comes to bedding a trap in ground that is hard to break through. Coil-spring traps are available in all sizes for catching furbearers up to and including coyotes. The No. 2 coil spring is probably

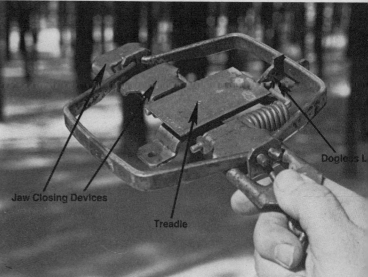

Jaw Closing Devices

Treadle

Dogless L

The Montgomery coil spring trap lies very flat, or has a thin profile, as shown here. What this means is that not as deep a trap "bed" is necessary to get it below the surface of the earth.

(Left) Trappers frequently modify traps in different manners. This coil spring trap has been modified with the addition of a second set of coil springs to increase speed and strength.

How to Set a Foot-Hold Trap Without Your Feet

This series of photographs illustrates how to set a Victor No. 4 trap when you can't place it on the ground. I've developed this method out of necessity when trapping water furbearers. Sometimes you're standing in a stream with steep banks or possibly the trap is staked in deep water, and it's impractical to find a flat, non-muddy spot to set the thing. However, this method should *not* be used when trapping for scent-wary furbearers, unless the trap will be placed under the surface of the water because you'll leave scent all over it.

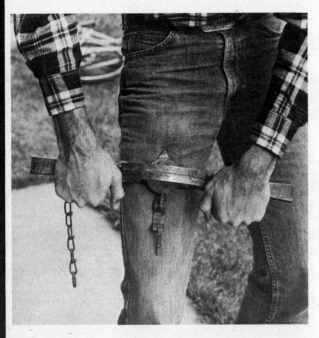

1. I simply grasp the two springs in my hands, as shown here.

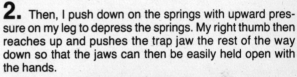

2. Then, I push down on the springs with upward pressure on my leg to depress the springs. My right thumb then reaches up and pushes the trap jaw the rest of the way down so that the jaws can then be easily held open with the hands.

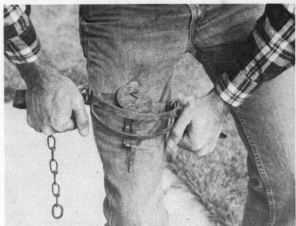

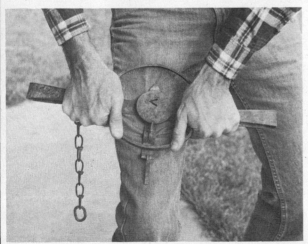

3. (Above) If you can't reach up with your thumb and swing the jaw down and open, you can hold one spring with the underside of one leg. This frees one hand to assist the thumb of the other hand.

4. The trap pan notch is now positioned with the dog or fly.

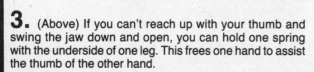

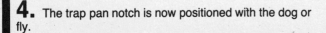

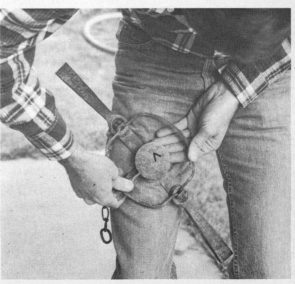

A No. 1½ Jump trap. Note jump spring (arrow) which allows a higher hold on furbearers.

The double-jawed trap prevents animal wring-outs and chew-outs. The second jaw, lying just inside the primary jaw, keeps an animal from twisting off in many cases.

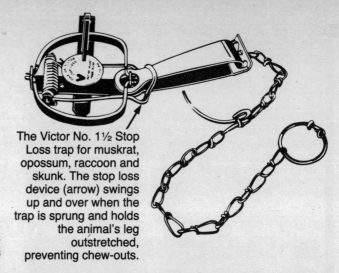

The Victor No. 1½ Stop Loss trap for muskrat, opossum, raccoon and skunk. The stop loss device (arrow) swings up and over when the trap is sprung and holds the animal's leg outstretched, preventing chew-outs.

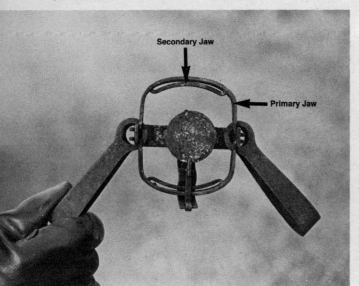

Secondary Jaw

Primary Jaw

The effectiveness of the double-jawed trap is illustrated here. This raccoon would have freed itself if the trap had been a standard single-jaw. This is a Blake & Lamb No. 1 single-spring double-jaw with a second spring added for speed and strength.

one of the most popular trap sizes for red fox.

The third basic type of foot-hold trap, the *jump* or *underspring trap,* also utilizes a flat spring. It is different from the long spring, however, in that it utilizes a piece of bowed spring steel at the base of the trap or frame in addition to a diagonal piece contained almost wholly within the trap jaws.

When the trapper depresses the diagonal spring, a bowed frame is stressed at the base of the trap, the trap jaws holding this spring down when the trap is "set." When the trap is sprung, the bowed under-frame springs quickly upward in the middle, causing the ends to flip the trap upward, out of its bed. The idea is to gain a higher hold on the animal and hopefully reduce the incidence of toe catches.

Like the coil-spring, the jump or underspring trap is compact and easily concealed, though a bit heavier than the average coil-spring trap of the same size. Underspring traps are frequently used when trapping under water where no trap covering is used. Trappers who trap on dry land sometimes complain that the end of the jump trap's spring throws debris into the jaws when the trap springs shut, thus jamming the jaws and preventing the trap from closing completely. Other trappers use the trap on dry land with complete success.

While these are the basic types of foot-hold traps, there are a number of variations existing within these basic types to achieve certain advantages for specialized trapping purposes. For example, some single spring, long-spring traps are fitted with a *stop loss* or *sure hold* device which is nothing more than a U-shaped wire with coil spring tension applied to it which holds the animal's leg outstretched and its head away from the trap once it is sprung. The idea is to prevent the animal from twisting or gnawing out of the trap which the stop loss device does quite effectively.

Another variation to the basic trap type is the *double jaw* trap. This is not to be confused with the double-spring trap mentioned earlier. The double jaw trap, as the name implies, has what amounts to two sets of jaws rather than one. In addition to the basic trap jaw, a second set of jaws are attached slightly below or inside the

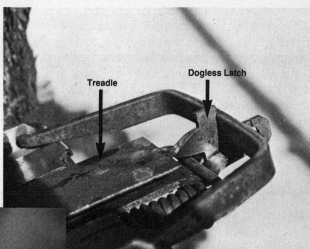

Though many consider the Number 1 too small for raccoon trapping, this illustrates the usual type of hold that is possible. The extra spring makes for added speed and strength.

(Above) This is the Montgomery dogless trap—a relatively recent design in trap-triggering devices.

Some trappers modify the dog and notch in the treadle so that the trap will trigger very crisply. In this instance, a notch has been filed in the tip of the dog with a three cornered file while the main portion of the treadle has been filed to a point that mates with the notch.

primary trap jaws. The reason for this design is, again, to prevent furbearer losses due to the animal gnawing or twisting out of the trap.

A third variation on the basic trap theme is the *offset jaw* trap which features jaws that do not completely close, just very nearly so. This trap is thought to be more humane than other types, and some states, California being one example, require the use of offset jaw traps.

Offset-jaw traps can be purchased directly from the manufacturer or, in some instances, can be made by the trapper himself. The trapper can remove the jaws from a standard frame, reverse them, and then reassemble the trap. Due to the shape of the standard jaws and where they're attached to the trap frame, the now reversed jaws will not close completely.

Some trappers produce offset jaws to stay within the law by other means. One method is to weld tiny beads of metal to each side of a trap jaw. This prevents the jaws from closing completely and, in states where offset jaws are required, this home remedy is generally per-

mitted. Other trappers, in a pinch, have produced offset-jaw traps simply by twisting a large-diameter wire around each side of the trap jaw, again, preventing them from closing completely.

Though most trap jaws are die cut, some of them are cast. Some trappers prefer cast jaws to the cut variety even though they're generally more expensive. Why? One reason is that the cast jaws are thought to be more durable and that the rounded gripping surface of cast jaws is less likely to cut into an animal's skin and flesh. The die cut jaws are quite square-edged and sharp.

The basic trap designs vary in a number of other respects, as well. For example, some traps utilize a flat piece of metal, called a dog, to restrain a jaw when it is set; others have a notch in the pan or treadle which contacts the jaw directly to serve the same purpose. There are proponents of each design and both produce excellent results. The type of trap used usually depends on the preference of the individual trapper rather than one trap being better than the other. Probably a good bet here is to talk to other local trappers for their opinions.

Body-Gripping Traps

The body-gripping traps, the most common and well-known example being the Victor Conibear, consists basically of two heavy wire or rod squares crossed and hinged at two sides. A coil spring is fitted at one hinge and is stressed when the jaws are "open." When the trigger releases the jaws, spring tension causes the two squares to reverse direction and "close" the opening.

For a body trap to work an animal must attempt to pass through the opening and touch the wire trigger to release the springs, causing the squares to close and hence clamp the animal's body or neck. Such traps deliver a stunning blow and suffocation or strangulation occurs in a matter of minutes.

These quick-killing body-gripping traps have gained rapid acceptance during the last few years. This popularity is certainly justified for the Conibear is readily adaptable to a number of trapping situations, and particularly to under-water trapping.

Because of their quick-kill capabilities, Conibears are legal in some states for use *only* under water. In other states, however, Conibears of a particular size can be used on land to trap marten. So before setting a Conibear trap on land, check your state trapping laws concerning the legal use of such traps.

The quick-killing traps have been a boon to water trappers going after animals such as muskrat and beaver. The trap can be positioned in front of a den or a run, and the trapper is almost certain to take any animal going into or out of the den entrance or run. What's more, the animal is dispatched in a relatively quick, humane manner.

One advantage to the Conibear trap is that it doesn't have to be staked as securely as a foot-hold trap. First of all, the animal's ability to fight the trap is decreased severely because the trap clamps its body tightly. Secondly, with a body-gripping trap, the animal generally dies quickly so that it doesn't have as many opportunities to escape as it does with a foot-hold trap. For this reason, particularly where there are few natural trap attachments, the trapper may find the body trap quicker and easier to set.

There are also some instances where a body-gripping trap might work where a foot-hold trap might not. I ran into this situation several years ago when called upon by a neighboring farmer, Harry Wilson, to come and get rid of the beaver which were eating all of the trees around his pond. Harry had spent a lot of money damming up a large draw on his property to water his livestock and to serve as a recreation area for his family and friends.

However, a few beaver moved into the area and began eating every bush in sight. With that task out of the way, they turned to the larger trees, and Harry became concerned.

I went over to look at the situation. The pond was a good-sized body of water, along one corner of which was a sheer limestone rock bluff plunging straight down into the water. In front of the bluff were tops of old trees which had been flooded over when the dam was

(Left and below) Kent Dederick uses a trap setting device to set a Victor Conibear No. 330 body-gripping trap. The scissor-like tool offers plenty of leverage to compress the stout springs. Note that one spring is already compressed and held in place by a safety latch. Once the second spring is compressed it, too, will be secured with the use of the safety latch to prevent injury to the trapper until the trap is actually positioned. Then, the safety latch will be swung out of the way so that the trap will operate.

How to Set a Body-Gripping Trap

1. (Left) First, position the springs, as shown here on the No. 330 Victor Conibear.

2. (Below) Using both hands on one spring, stress it by squeezing its extreme ends together, as shown here.

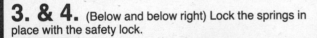

3. & 4. (Below and below right) Lock the springs in place with the safety lock.

(Continued page 20)

(Continued from page 19)

5. Here is the trap with both springs retained by the safety locks. When setting the Conibear, do it so that gravity holds the safety locks in place. If you turn the trap over, the locks could swing out of the way, unknown to you.

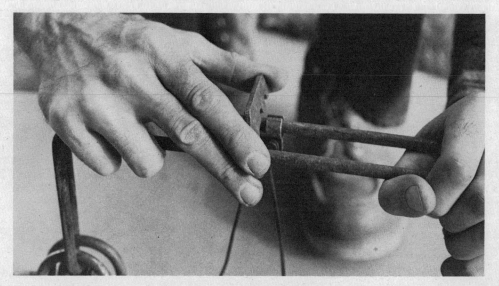

6. & 7. (Above and left) Squeezing the jaws of the trap together, engage the latch in the trigger notch.

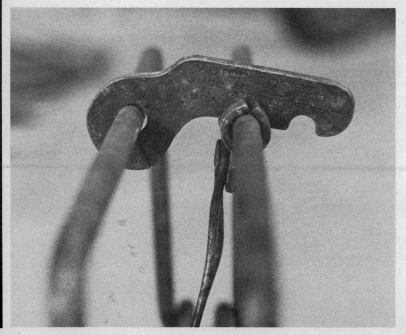

8. Here is the Victor Conibear with safety locks disengaged.

Jim Nolan is using another type of device to compress the springs of a Victor Number 330 Conibear. A foot is placed on the lower end of the setting device to hold it in position while the opposite end is pulled upward to compress the trap springs.

A very large beaver with its head in Victor Number 330 Conibear trap. A beaver this size could not pass completely through the opening of the Conibear trap. However, as one can see here, the trap still worked very effectively. (Photo courtesy Kent Dederick)

built, and among them I noticed some freshly cut limbs. It looked like a feed bed. The top of the bluff was perhaps 10 feet above water level and, while I stood eyeballing the freshly cut saplings, I heard a splash at the base of the bluff. Looking quickly I saw a beaver disappear into the face of the solid rock cliff.

At least I thought it was solid rock. Leaning out and looking into the face of the bluff, I noticed a crevice about 10 or 12 inches wide. It appeared the beaver were going in and out of this crevice — possibly they had a bank den farther back in the rock. This seemed like a natural place for a trap because of the continuous beaver activity.

My first thought was that I didn't know exactly how I was going to set my trap. I didn't have a boat, and there was no way I could reach the crevice on foot. The water was extremely deep in front of and on either side of the

The author is shown here with the results of matching the trap size to the intended quarry. When the traps are selected properly, they can produce a higher percentage of catches with fewer misses.

Preferred Trap Sizes

Furbearer	Foot-hold Trap	Body-Gripping Trap
Badger	3, 4	
Beaver	3, 4	330
Bobcat	3, 4	
Coyote	3, 4	
Fox	2, 3	
Marten	1, 1½	120, 220
Mink	1, 1½	
Muskrat	1, 1½	110, 120
Opossum	1½	
Raccoon	1½, 2	
Skunk	1, 1½	
Weasel	0, 1	

Regardless what brand of trap you buy, the trap-size numbering system is standardized in the industry. The smaller the number, the smaller the trap size.

crevice for perhaps 5 or 10 yards.

Further scouting revealed a couple places the beaver used to enter the water, and here I placed foot-hold traps at the water's edge. However, the best sign was still at that crevice and I couldn't get it off my mind. Finally, I had an idea that I had never tried before nor had I ever heard of it being used. I pulled a No. 330 Conibear out of my trapping equipment and jammed a roasting ear on the trigger. Then I found a long stout pole and a long length of baling wire. The wire was doubled and attached to one end of the long pole, then the pole rotated to wind the wire around that end. The Conibear's chain was then attached to the free end of the baling wire.

I carefully set the Conibear and, after raising it off the ground, released the safety locks. I slowly and carefully extended the pole out over the water and lowered the

trap until the roasting ear trigger was perhaps 18 inches below the surface of the water and dangling over the fresh cut saplings. I secured the long pole by placing it in the crotch of a tree and wiring it securely so there was no way that it was going anywhere.

I could hardly wait to check the trap the next day to see if the unusual set would work. That night the temperature plummeted and, when I pulled my pickup in to Harry's barnyard, I could see ice on the surface of the pond.

The first thing I did was check the foot-hold traps near the water's edge. I could clearly see the traps under the thin, clear ice. Nothing. Then, I came to the Conibear set and saw that the baling wire was stretched tight. Through the ice, I could see that I had made a catch the first night! I broke the ice where the wire entered the water and pulled out my prize, with no small

It takes a well made trap to hold the lunges of stronger predators such as this big male bobcat.

amount of effort. It was a sizable flat-tail and I was thrilled with my catch in the unusual set.

I reset the Conibear with another roasting ear, and lowered it back into the water. To say the least, Harry was quite pleased when I showed him the prize, caught the first night. To make a long story short, that particular set turned out to be a real producer, and in no more than 2 weeks the farmer's beaver problem was solved and to my knowledge, they have never returned.

The Cost of Getting Started

Trapping does not have to be an expensive sport. For the hobby trapper, or the young trapper just starting out, very little investment is required. When I began trapping as a young lad, my father bought perhaps a dozen various-sized muskrat and raccoon traps at a farm sale for 75 cents. I'll admit that this was an exception. However, even if new traps are bought, the size needed to catch muskrat, for example, they might cost $36 for a dozen. Of course, as trap size increases, so does the per-trap cost. For example, a dozen coyote-size traps would cost about $80.

After my father bought those initial traps, I was able to find everything else I needed around the house. For trapping muskrats and raccoons, I used baling wire to attach the traps to trees. Back then I never even dug trap beds, I simply covered the traps with leaves and other natural debris.

Various baits can generally be obtained around the house for many of the furbearers, and stretchers can easily be made from scrap lumber. Actually, all a person has to have in order to have a good time is just a few traps. It's really a lot of fun to use one's imagination in coming up with all the other supplies.

The professional trapper, on the other hand, can spend a considerable amount of money. I have more than $1,000 invested in traps and related trapping equipment and my outfit is not nearly as extensive as that of other trappers. Again, the best way to get started is to get a dozen traps and just go have some fun. You'll learn a lot and it'll be more enjoyable than you ever thought possible.

chapter 3
TRAP COVERINGS

FREQUENTLY, when trapping on dry land, it's necessary to dig a trap bed in order to seclude the trap below the ground. Generally, soil is sifted over the trap to prevent sizable stones and sticks from jamming the jaws. However, a trap covering is needed to prevent this sifted earth from eventually finding its way underneath the trap pan. A trap covering will assure the trapper of plenty of air space underneath the trap pan so that the treadle, when stepped on by an animal, will depress easily.

A trap covering is generally a paper or fabric material which is cut to size to fit over the trap pan and extend underneath the trap jaws when the trap is set. In most instances a trap cover is cut in a square or rectangle with a slot cut along one edge for the trap dog or trigger. The cover material then can extend under the jaw on that side of the trap. With the cover in place, dirt can be sifted directly onto the trap.

One of the first coverings most beginning trappers use, particularly in timbered areas, is large leaves carefully laid over the trap so that nothing will jam the jaws. Instead of leaves, it could be grass or moss. The only problem with these trap coverings is that if the leaves, grass or moss aren't subsequently covered with earth, the

wind will blow them off, exposing the steel jaws. This is generally what happened during my early trapping days when traps were placed on top of the ground.

Then, a fellow trapper told me about trap covers made from paper and described how to properly lay the traps out. It all made sense to me, and I felt it was a major breakthrough in my trapping career. I could hardly wait to rush home, grab a couple of coyote traps, go down to the pasture and try out the new technique which would allow me to bed the traps beneath the ground surface. I improvised the trap coverings from brown paper bags right where I was making the set. To my delight, I found that it worked quite well. I covered the trap with soil which had been thoroughly broken up and sifted through my hands. I didn't have a trap sifter during those gradeschool years nor was I savvy yet to the fact that coyotes are extremely wary of human scent.

The next day, when I visited the set, I found that the soil had settled around the trap pan, making the trap very visible even though it was still bedded beneath the surface.

I felt at that time that moisture in the soil was causing the paper to become soggy and consequently sink inside the jaws around the trap pan. So my next step was to use waxed paper. Some butchers use waxed paper supplied in tissue-like dispenser boxes where one sheet at a time can be pulled out. What's more, these boxes can be purchased in a sheet size that is ideal for setting No. 4 double-spring traps. All that's required is to tear a slit in one edge for the trap dog and treadle.

However, even with waxed paper, the sagging was still a distinct problem. I found that even though a heavier waxed paper would prevent the sagging problem around the trap pan on a dry night, a rain would insure my sinking trap cover problem all over again. I still have a carton of waxed paper in my trapping gear and have found a number of other trapping uses for it though I now believe that it is not an ideal trap covering material.

There are several problems associated with any sort of paper whether it be waxed or unwaxed. For example, many of these papers are quite porous and prone to absorbing various home or vehicle odors. I'm talking about foreign odors which alert the land dwelling fur-bearers, such as fox and coyote, that something is awry.

Secondly, paper has a tendency to crinkle underfoot when an animal steps on the pan, particularly waxed paper. It is common to wad up waxed paper in order to give it more flexibility and to avoid the noise problem. However, by crumpling it up, the trapper risks imparting more scent to it. Even if he somehow doesn't impart human scent to it, the crumpled waxed paper is no longer as stiff as it once was and has a greater tendency to sag. Also, any moisture resistance that the waxed paper might have had is decreased once it is crumpled. Furthermore, paper, particularly waxed paper, being as slick as it is, allows the covering soil to be easily swept off in a strong wind. Also waxed paper, being light col-ored, really stands out if the least bit shows. I have discovered that waxed paper is useful for some specialized snow-trapping but overall, any of the paper coverings are poor substitutes for a good trap cover.

After trying the various papers, I then tried canvas as a trap covering material. Again, I felt like I had made a breakthrough in my trapping technique. Canvas is much more durable than paper and doesn't have a tendency to sag and tear when it gets wet. It is porous, however, and does have a tendency to absorb and retain foreign odors. This problem can be solved, as it is with traps, by boiling the canvas to eliminate these odors. Canvas does work fairly well although white canvas shows up quite clearly if the soil is blown off by the wind. However, soil isn't as prone to blow off the rough canvas as it is to blow off the slick waxed paper. The other advantage to canvas is that it is quiet and makes no noise when an animal steps on the pan.

To tone down or eliminate the whiteness of canvas, boil the covers right along with the traps — dye and all. I generally use a walnut hull, logwood crystal, and/or creosote bush mixture in the solution to impart a black dye to the traps and covers. I also put a bit of juniper sap or sage into the mix to impart what is hopefully a natural odor.

Overall though, I am still not satisfied with canvas trap coverings. After boiling, each one has to be individually unfolded and laid out to dry — otherwise it dries into a wrinkled up mess, making it difficult to use in the field. Secondly, though canvas doesn't tear once it's moist, it still has a tendency to sag around the trap pan if it has been washed and ends up in a set that may be exposed to rain. Even if the animal isn't frightened away by the unnatural looking sagging cover, the trap pan may be blocked by the soil sagging around its edges.

An animal must depress the round treadle in the center of the trap, shown here, in order for the trap to be triggered. A soft, flexible covering, such as weathered canvas, prevents a trap from triggering unless the animal's foot is directly in the center of the treadle or pan. On the other hand, some trappers prefer to have the trap go off whenever a foot is placed anywhere inside the trap jaws. In order to do this, it's a simple matter to use a stiffer trap cover, such as aluminum screen.

Canvas is also prone to picking up foreign odors from the trapping vehicle even though it has been boiled before trap setting begins. I learned this lesson when trapping for coyotes. Several years ago, I began running a trapline almost exclusively for coyotes. The first week of the season I did quite well, averaging nearly four catches per day. With a lot of coyotes in the area and relatively few people, the area hadn't been trapped extensively, and it appeared that I was nailing nearly every canine that passed by one of my sets — with a few exceptions. Then after a week or so of trapping the exception became the rule. To my dismay, I found that coyotes were beginning to dig some of my traps out of the ground.

At first it had me puzzled. I couldn't figure out why coyotes were beginning to dig my traps when they hadn't earlier. Obviously, when an animal digs around the edges of a trap, rather than getting caught, there is something in the trap that it is emitting an odor — something that is tipping the animal off.

Fortunately, I was keeping detailed records about each trap — when it was placed, numbers and types of catches from the set, the type of trap that was used, the scent that was used, the type of set, etc. In short, I was keeping detailed notes on just about every aspect of my trapping, hoping that a season or two of such detailed notes might produce more knowledge about which scents, sets, traps, etc., were the best producers.

Late one night, I was going through the trapping notes in the pickup camper and realized that only the traps which had been recently reset were the ones currently being dug out. None of the traps that had been set at the first of season were being dug up, and some of them were still nailing coyotes occasionally. There was something about the traps (that had been set after a week's trapping) that was different from the traps originally set.

Thinking back, I mentally analyzed my trapping technique. I was trapping out of a four-wheel-drive Bronco and kept all my traps, stakes, grapnels and trap covers inside an open-topped wooden box in the back of the Bronco. I didn't want to waste daylight by skinning animals on the line, so trapped animals were quickly dispatched and placed inside the vehicle but outside of the trap box. It was my thinking that since no blood was coming in direct contact with the trapping paraphernalia there would be no problem.

Obviously I had been mistaken for I was now positive that somehow the traps in the trap box were being contaminated as I traveled my line. Was it the scent of the dead animals? Was it the scent of myself or gasoline around the vehicle? I don't smoke nor were there any smokers inside my vehicle during the period.

Due to the nature of some of the dig-outs I felt that the canvas trap covers were more likely the problem than the traps themselves. Since I didn't have my trap-boiling equipment in the field with me, I decided to boil just the canvas trap covers in a cooking pot on top of the stove in the camper. I did this, then laboriously dug out and reset all my traps, replacing the canvas trap covers with freshly boiled ones.

My catching success improved dramatically. From that point on, I kept the canvas covers boiled regularly and carried only those with me that I felt I would need for resetting traps for a single day. The extra covers were kept outside the pickup camper until I was ready to use them. This was no doubt an important factor in keeping my coyote catching success high during the rest of the season.

As long as canvas trap covers are kept clean and they're camouflage dyed, they do a fair job as a trap covering material. They usually work better when they're new and stiff than when they've been washed and boiled a few times — they don't sag around the pan.

Another reason for dyeing a canvas trap cover has to do with what happens after the animal is caught. Most trappers know that animals such as coyotes and foxes have a habit of traveling Jeep trails in backcountry. There is no better spot to place a trap than right along the side of a road in good coyote country, where state laws and/or private land owners allow the practice. The traps can be attached to a grapnel rather than a stake so that when an animal is caught, it runs off into the brush where bypassing motorists will not see it. However, it seems that eight times out of ten the trap cover will be found lying right in the middle of the road. It seems that a trapped animal generally jerks the trap out of the bed and heads for the middle of the road where the trap cover is left behind.

A white trap cover lying in the middle of the road hardly goes unnoticed by a bypassing motorist. It is so unnatural and out of place, particularly in the woods or brush, that the motorist might stop. Then there's a chance he'll hear br'er coyote a few yards away in the brush jerking on the trap chain and raising havoc at the sight and scent of an approaching human.

No doubt the motorist traveling a Jeep trail will have a centerfire rifle and, thinking he's doing the right thing, will blast the coyote. Since he is an outdoorsman, he'll probably be kind enough to leave the coyote in the trap though its pelt may require ½-hour of sewing to close the large bullet hole.

It must also be said that some passing motorists will spot that white-canvas cover, locate your catch, and take both trap and coyote. If the person is *looking* for traps, a single, highly visible trap cover, found along the road, could give away an entire trapline. In short, it pays to dye the white canvas.

A few years ago I was trapping in the high desert mountains of southeastern Arizona. There was a switchback in a canyon road where I noticed a few grey fox droppings near a small bush. I stopped, got out of my Bronco, and made a grey fox set near the bush and drove away hoping to have a fox at the set in a day or two. I was trapping, with permission, hence I was allowed to trap along the road.

The next day, on the eve of javelina season, I drove up to the set with friend Jim Nolan and saw the trap cover lying in one of the tire tracks. We got out of the vehicle and began following the grapnel marks. Instead of taking the downhill side of the mountain road, as I suspected, the trapped animal went up the bank and latched onto a tree. There was torn up earth and scratching or gnaw marks around the base of the tree. From all the evidence, I knew I had trapped a bobcat, not a grey fox. However, there was no trap nor were there any grapnel marks leading away from the tree. A closer examination revealed a small puddle of blood such as one might expect from dispatching a trapped animal with a .22-caliber rimfire. A closer examination also revealed distinct but unfamiliar boot prints.

Jim and I memorized the pattern of the distinct footprints and decided to go visiting the parked pickups of javelina hunters. We didn't have far to go — about 2 miles down the trail we spotted a pickup camper parked off the road. Jim and I pulled up alongside it, got out and examined the footprints. Sure enough, there in the dusty soil were distinct tracks which undoubtedly were the same as those found near the trap site. No one was around the pickup so we waited for a bit. No one returned. We went looking. Shortly, we spotted three hunters across a small canyon, and motioned them over. I asked them if the truck was theirs. It was. I then asked if they had removed a trap and animal down the road. Before they had a chance to answer, I mentioned that the boot tracks matched. With a lot of stammering

The author is shown here positioning aluminum screen for a trap cover. It prevents rocks, dirt, and other debris from rolling underneath the treadle which could prevent the treadle from depressing when an animal steps upon it.

(Above) The aluminum screen trap covering, shown here, is in place on a trap in its "bed." If an animal steps anywhere on the screen, the trap will trigger.

(Left) Sometimes the "tails" of the trap covering have a tendency to stick up, particularly when aluminum screen is used. It's a simple matter to weight them with dirt prior to covering the trap. This weight on the "tails" also serves to support the screen and prevent it from bulging upward inside the trap jaws.

27

and stuttering there was an explanation about finding the animal and intending to turn it in along with the trap at the ranch house. Shortly, my trapped bobcat was pulled out of the truck.

It was about 9 o'clock in the morning and the hunters had shot the bobcat and removed it from the trap early that morning. Instead of placing it in the shade underneath the truck, the hunters had thrown the bobcat and trap inside the pickup camper. In the desert mountains the temperatures were destined to soar to the 70-degree mark that day and, had we not gone after our bobcat, there's no doubt that it would have spoiled.

We didn't really believe the story about their intentions, but we had the bobcat. I advised the hunters that it was against the law to disturb anyone's trap or trapped animal in the state of Arizona and that I figured that they just weren't aware of the law. We left it at that and continued trapping.

It was after that season when I discovered what I believe to be the best trap covering material I have found to date. Clifford Gilliam, an expert bobcat trapper, introduced me to the use of aluminum screen several years ago. Aluminum window screen has many advantages. First, it can be cut to any size desired though it has a stiffness that far surpasses any canvas or paper covering material. Aluminum screen can be placed in position, and if it's of the proper size, the most severe pelting during a rainstorm won't cause it to sag.

It is stiff enough that, if an animal places its foot anywhere inside the trap jaws it is going to trigger the trap. Clifford, after making a bobcat set, lines the outside of the trap jaws with tiny stones which a bobcat will not step on. If a cat places its foot inside the ring of rocks, there's no way that the jaws are going to miss or throw its foot out because the cat stepped on the jaws rather than the pan. I have used the same aluminum trap-covering material, for coyotes, with complete success.

Aluminum screen is rough enough that wind does not have a tendency to blow soil off it. If it does, the screen shows up clearly though not as much as the shiny waxed paper does.

Aluminum screen is also quiet, unlike some paper materials. What's more, though I have had all sorts of trap-covering materials blown out of the ground by exceedingly strong winds, I have not yet had an aluminum window screen trap cover blown off.

I remember several years ago when I was trapping in an area of high plains country when high winds blew away a good portion of my canvas trap covers. In some cases the covers were found 15 to 20 yards downwind, leaving the traps fully exposed. I have never had this problem with aluminum trap covers. Because of the rigidity, once an aluminum screen cover is secured over the pan and under the jaws, the wind doesn't seem to blow it off like it does paper or canvas.

Very moist dirt can even be sifted with a lot of force over traps covered with the aluminum screen and it won't sag — this is something that cannot be said of either paper or canvas. However, unlike canvas and paper, very fine sand will sift through the aluminum screen cover, exposing parts of the trap. This is a slight disadvantage, though most soil isn't that fine. One of the most important aspects of using aluminum trap covers is that they aren't as prone to absorbing and retaining foreign odors as canvas is. Remember the instances mentioned earlier where only the canvas covers (not the rest of my trapping gear) became contaminated. I believe that the aluminum trap covering material — like other metallic trapping gear — is not as apt to retain foreign odors like canvas does. Also, rodents such as pack rats aren't as likely to dig out and chew aluminum as they are canvas.

If the covering material is cut to the proper dimensions, the trap will lie flat. There will be no humping of the material over the trap, yet the "tails" or cover corners will extend underneath the trap jaws to be held in place once earth is sifted upon the trap. Earth on the corners keeps them weighted down, thus preventing the aluminum screen from sagging around the pan inside the jaws.

There are instances, even in land trapping, where trap covers may *not* be the best method of covering a trap. There are experienced red fox trappers who, instead of using an artificial trap cover, prefer to use nothing more than chopped grass or leaves. The grass, if it isn't chopped too finely, can be poked all around the trap jaws, inside and out, but not underneath the pan. The grass offers a type of supporting material around the pan when a very thin sifting of dirt is placed on top of the trap. Using grass also helps to prevent freeze-up when trapping in cold weather. If a light mist or rain falls and then freezes and a trap is covered with canvas, the canvas will absorb the water, freeze and form a hardened crust over the pan which will not give when an animal steps on it. However, when using the chopped grass as mentioned earlier, this problem does not exist. A grass-covered trap will frequently work very well even after a light freeze.

It is important, however, that the grass be dry when it's placed in position. Otherwise, like canvas or paper, it will sink in around the pan and jaws thus exposing the trap. In some instances, the grass is not used in conjunction with sifted dirt. Chopped grass alone is sometimes the best way to make a set look natural when setting in a grassy meadow or pasture as is often the case in red fox trapping. A covering of dirt, even if it's topped by a sprinkling of chopped grass just does not appear as natural as if the grass is inserted down around the trap so that it appears to be growing out of the ground. The use of any trap covering material and topping of camouflage is limited only by the imagination of the trapper in trying to make the set appear as natural as possible. This is where the fine tuning of the trapper's skills come into play.

The trapper does not have to use an artificial covering material. (Above) Here, Roy Daniels prepares to use dry grass as an effective replacement for a trap cover. (Top left) The dry grass is pulled up and folded in half, then (bottom left) chopped into short lengths with the use of a hachet or pocket knife. (Below) The chopped grass is then placed underneath the trap, around the pan, and over the jaws until it finally appears like this. This makes for an effective trap covering, particularly in a grassy area.

Underwater Foot-Hold Trap Coverings

The trapper pursuing land animals is not the only one who may need trap-covering material. There are some instances where it is desirable to cover traps even though they're below the surface of the water.

Trap odors are not critical when a trap is placed underwater. It's not usually important to conceal an un-

Though this trap is placed below the surface of the water it is readily visible to anyone walking along the creek bank. It would have been much better had the trap been camouflaged with a few water soaked leaves. It's best to place one large leaf over the trap pan so that it just fits inside the trap jaws. A light covering of leaf material can then be placed over the springs. However, a trapper must beware not to get too many slippery, water-soaked leaves over the trap jaws. These can not only clog them, but can serve as a slippery surface to allow a furbearer to pull its foot out of the trap jaws.

derwater trap either. Most animals which live in or around the water are so used to an uneven bottom, rocks, or even human trash, that they aren't wary of a fully-exposed trap that is placed a few inches below the surface of the water. There are water trappers who believe that any trap placed under water does not have to be camouflaged in any manner. There are other trappers who think differently and say that there are animals which will detect such a fully exposed trap. Some trappers want to conceal traps, not from furbearers, but from trap thieves. A trap that is fully exposed, even below the water's surface, is quite obvious to someone walking along the bank. What it all boils down to is the fact that, in some instances, there are good reasons for covering an underwater trap.

Generally, in most underwater trapping, the trap springs can be somewhat concealed by the silt on the bottom of the stream or river. Also, a trapper can generally find a water-logged leaf which can be placed over the trap pan to aid in camouflaging it. Place a little bit of bottom silt on top of the leaf and the leaf is held in place, adding further camouflage. In addition to this, there's no reason why an aluminum screen cover cannot be used underwater just as it is on land. Instead of sifting dirt on top of the trap, bottom silt can be sifted over the aluminum screen to make the trap almost invisible to either man or animal. If you do use a natural type of underwater trap covering such as leaves, it is important to make sure that it is fully water-logged and won't drift away in the current.

There are some heavy leaves such as those which have fallen from a sycamore that can jam a trap's jaws, or be so slick that an animal can pull out more easily. Keep this in mind when covering any trap with leaf litter. A waterlogged leaf, if it's not rotten, is quite tough, and the weight of the leaf (or leaves) can also serve to slow down a trap's action. All it takes is a bit of common sense and judgment to prevent these potential problems.

chapter 4

TRAP SECURING DEVICES

ONCE YOU'VE worked really hard to outwit an animal, and have trapped it, you'll need some means of holding or at least restraining it until you arrive. There are basically four different types of trap securing devices that are used by land trappers: *stakes, drags* or *clogs, grapnels,* and *natural attachments.* A stake is a long pin driven into the ground to which you attach the trap. A drag or clog is nothing more than a weight attached to the trap to cause resistance and tire a trapped animal out so that it won't go far. A grapnel, a hook type device sometimes called an "anchor," is generally attached to the trap by a long chain. The hook, by catching on natural elements such as rocks, brush, etc., momentarily detains the animal until it hooks up more firmly. Natural attachments, as the name implies, are simply trees, logs, rocks, etc., to which a trap may be secured.

Methods of securing traps are frequently taken for granted. However, if a trapper puts a bit of thought into these devices and his trap chain, it can make the chore of setting traps easier and quicker.

The type of trap-securing device used by the trapper is dependent, for the most part, upon the amount of vegetation in the area. For example, when trapping in open country where for miles there are no trees or brush, which is often the case in the open West, a stake is the natural and many times only solution. An animal the size of a coyote can drag a trap and grapnel for several miles if there is nothing for the grapnel to hook onto.

Stakes

For the most part, stakes are made of either wood or metal. For land trapping, hardwood has been the common stake material used in the East while metal is probably more popular in the rockier West. The main thing to remember when making a stake is to make it plenty long. How long depends upon a number of factors including the size of the animal and trap, whether the ground is frozen, the consistency and composition of the soil, etc.

A 1 × 2-inch piece of seasoned hardwood (such as oak flooring) can make a very good stake for trapping red fox in open fields. However, there's a bit more to it than simply getting a length of hardwood, pointing one end, and attaching a trap chain to the top by nails.

For one thing, when br'er fox is trapped it'll have plenty of time to chew the top of the wooden stake off and free itself unless you do something to prevent it. One means is to fasten a piece of sheet metal to the top of the stake and bend it down both sides. Then drill holes through both metal and wood for a couple of through bolts. This serves as a cap over the top of the stake and prevents the animal from chewing on the wood. Using bolts also prevents the animal from pulling any staple or nail out of the wood. Furthermore, the metal cap helps prevent the stake from splitting when it's being driven into the ground.

Metal stakes have advantages over wooden ones in that they're easier to drive into rocky or frozen soil. What's more, with metal stakes you don't have the problem of stake splitting or breaking that you do with wooden ones. It's also easier to make a swiveling device around the top of a metal stake than around a hard wood stake. Whenever an animal is trapped, it immediately begins to lunge to try and free itself. It's important that the chain be allowed to swivel around the stake rather than to wrap around it and kink up tight. An animal that wraps the trap chain around the stake is more likely to twist free.

Metal stakes are frequently made of rebar material which is relatively inexpensive and readily obtained. The rebar is generally cut into desired lengths, which are then pointed on one end, and knobbed or flattened on the opposite end. The rebar can be cut into sections either with a hacksaw, a cutting torch, or large scissor-like bolt cutters. For cutting relatively soft rebar, the bolt cutters, frequently used on construction sites, are probably the quickest and easiest to use. If you're using a tougher steel, a cutting torch or hacksaw would be the best method of cutting.

There are several ways that a stake can be pointed. Some people simply cut the rebar at an angle and this serves as a point of sorts. Others use a forge to heat the stake end red hot, and then pound it with a sledge to form a point. For a person who has become skilled in the use of a hammer, it's a very fast method. Some trappers, rather than using a forge, heat the end of the stake with a torch to achieve the same effect. Another method of pointing a metal stake is to shape out the point with a grinder or grinding wheel.

When I decided to assemble a large trapping outfit several years ago, I chose the emery wheel grinding method. Before I finished pointing nearly 100 stakes, I

(Below) Slim Gilliam welds a knob onto the stake just above the point. This makes the stake pull out of the earth much harder. This trick has prevented many a lunging coyote from pulling a trap stake.

(Above) The end of this stake was pointed by heating it with a torch and pounding it with a hammer on an anvil.

(Below) This stake consists of cold rolled steel which has had the end heated to a cherry red and then pounded flat. A washer is slipped onto the stake, small enough to prevent it from slipping off the top. Then, the trap chain is attached to a lap link which makes an excellent swiveling device, preventing the chain from kinking.

had consumed an entire grinding wheel and a lot of time and effort. I've since watched another trapper use a hammer and forge and this appears to be one of the most efficient methods.

Stake length varies, depending on the animal being trapped. For coyote trapping, I have used stakes from as short as 10 or 12 inches in very tough clay and gravel, to stakes nearly 3 feet long in sandy loam soil. The most useful length is about 20 inches.

There are several methods of capping the top of the steel stake. I simply weld a 1-inch hex nut on top of the stake which prevents the trap chain ring from sliding off yet allows the ring to swivel on the stake.

Another excellent trapper, Jim Nolan, prefers to use a torch when making his stakes. When it comes to forming the top end, Nolan clamps the stake in a vice, and using the torch to heat the top red hot, he then whacks the top a few strokes to put a mushroom cap at the top of the stake, somewhat like a big nail head. The next step is to slip a large flat washer onto the stake with a center hole small enough to prevent the washer from slipping off the "knob." The washer provides the surface necessary for the chain ring to swivel smoothly around the stake.

Half-inch rebar is generally used to hold animals the size of coyotes. Three eighths-inch rebar is fine for foxes. Cold rolled bar stock can also be used and this is what Nolan uses to make the stakes mentioned earlier.

Slim Gilliam uses ½-inch square bar stock. The bar stock is heated in a forge and then the ends are twisted in opposite directions so that a type of "threaded" stake results. Slim made about 50 of these stakes for me and I've found them to work ideally. After the bar is heated and twisted, it's pointed at one end, and a nut is then welded to the top. Once the stakes have been driven into the ground it's almost impossible to pull them out. However, applying a wrench and turning the top nut makes pulling them very easy. I carry a large Crescent wrench to screw the stakes out of the ground. In fact, this is the best trap stake I've seen yet. By using stakes of the proper length—sufficiently long so that it takes some effort to drive them with a 6-pound hammer—it's almost impossible for a trap thief to pull them.

Don't underestimate the ability of an animal to pull out a conventional stake, even quite a long one, if the soil is not firm. Also, if you don't have the proper type of trap chain attachment around the top of the stake it is possible for an animal to "pump" the stake out of the ground, particularly if you have a short chain on the trap. By "pumping" I refer to the practice of an animal standing over the stake and alternately raising and lowering its foot in an upward-jerking manner. The ring that's generally used around the stake slides down next to the ground when pressure is released from the chain. Then, when upward pressure is reapplied, the ring grips the stake to pull it upward and the process is repeated. The stake eventually becomes loosened and starts to move out of the ground. Perhaps it's only pulled ½-inch at a time, but even if the stake is 3 feet long, a persistent "pumper" can eventually pull it out. The animals that will pump a stake are relatively few, though in a few seasons of trapping, it's not uncommon to encounter a half dozen or so.

I was once trapping coyotes, running an 80-mile figure-eight trapline over low rolling sagebrush hills with juniper trees interspersed here and there. I decided to make a set a short distance from the road in a large open area of short grass. Due to the lack of vegetation I decided to stake the trap rather than put a grapnel on the chain. The soil was not particularly loose, nor was it particularly rocky though it did have some gravel in it. I pulled a 2-foot stake out of my gear, bedded the trap, and drove the stake down through the ring in the trap chain. When everything was complete, I left the set with high hopes, as I always do.

I returned the next morning, and when I drove up to the set I knew that I had caught something for the ground was ripped up where the trap had been. There was no trap or animal in sight. My first thought was that a trap thief had been there earlier. However, I was trapping in an area where I hadn't seen another person in 2 weeks and the dusty jeep trail revealed no sign of automobile tracks other than my own. When I walked over to where the trap had been, I was surprised to find the 2-foot stake lying on top of the ground about 8 feet from where it originally had been driven. The soil was dusty, and I could see no sign of human footprints.

Examining the area more closely, I found the canvas trap cover about 15 feet from the site in a northeasterly direction. I examined the ground around the trap cover closely and found that the animal had somehow pulled the stake and was dragging the trap, leaving a mark in the dusty soil. I could see for perhaps ¼-mile in the general direction that the drag mark led. As far as I could see, there was no sign of life. I went back to my Bronco, pulled out my 22-250 rifle and then proceeded to follow the drag mark on foot to see if I could find the animal or at least my No. 4 double spring trap.

Actually it was quite an education following the drag marks. Early in the trailing I determined that the animal was, indeed, a coyote. At several points along that trail I found a distinct track in the soil. After ¼-mile or so, the open country became interspersed with juniper trees and other small clumps of brush.

The trail in the dust revealed that the coyote had gone to the first thick patch of brush, its instinct apparently telling it to try and rake the object off with the brush. It didn't work. The coyote then emerged from the other side and went several hundred yards across the dusty soil and into another patch of brush.

On and on I followed, over one low hill after another. Finally, about ½-mile away I spotted the coyote. Unfortunately, it had seen me too, and was really making time with the No. 4 trap securely on its foot. I had been

The trapper is best advised never to use a trap attachment such as baling wire for trapping large, strong predators like this coyote. Repeated lunges can cause a wire attachment to break.

running the trapline for several weeks, and as any full-timer knows, trapping has a tendency to eliminate the flab from the body in short order and strengthen the muscles. My trap setting and walking was to pay off.

I put it in high gear trying to gain ground on the coyote. As long as the coyote kept to the open country, I wasn't able to close the distance. But fortunately, it kept running into the thick patches of brush and becoming entangled momentarily. Though the small patches of brush were perhaps only 5 or 6 feet in diameter, they delayed its progress for a few seconds each time and allowed me to gain a few yards on it.

After nearly a ½-mile chase, I was becoming winded though I had closed to within perhaps 300 yards of the coyote. Knowing that this was well within range for the .22-250, I plopped down on my rear end, put my elbows on my knees, and tried to settle the crosshair on the moving target. Due to my pounding heart, and heaving chest, my rifle seemed to be moving more than the coyote. I decided that I'd have to get closer.

By this time, the coyote was apparently getting desperate and trying harder to get away. I ran another 100 yards without gaining an inch. Then, it ran into another clump of brush and became tangled, a little longer than usual — long enough for me to gain another 100 yards.

Then, it burst out of the brush. I decided to try a shot — I didn't know how much longer I could keep up the pace, and I was afraid it might outrun me. I plopped down on my rump, and with all the will I could muster, managed to hold my breath and stop my heaving chest long enough to jerk the trigger. I missed. I worked the rifle's bolt to chamber another round, held the crosshair on the animal's nose as nearly as I could and squeezed again. I saw hair or dust fly from the coyote. A satisfying "whomp" returned, indicating a solid hit.

I chambered another round and didn't take my eyes off the coyote's position while I made my way over to it. It turned out to be a well-furred male. The No. 4 double spring was latched onto its front foot above the pad.

The trap wasn't damaged in the least and the 52-grain Speer hollow point bullet had not exited, leaving only a 22-caliber bullet hole in the pelt.

I later received $55 for the coyote's pelt and chalked the stake-pulling incident off as a fluke for it seemed that the possibility of another animal pulling a 2-foot stake out of the ground was slim indeed. No more than a month later, it happened again. The second time I wasn't so lucky. The animal was again a coyote, trapped in barren country. Other than a few small canyons here and there, there wasn't so much as a woody bush in that short-grass country. The coyote had been trapped in the bottom of a small canyon alongside a cow trail. Again, the stake was lying on top of the ground with no sign of a human being having visited the area since I was last there. I was able to follow the trap's drag mark in the dusty soil for perhaps 200 yards before the coyote entered a rocky area where I could not follow the trail.

I searched in increasingly large circles, concentrating on the direction the coyote had been going, and finally found where the trail emerged from the other side. I was able to follow the trail for perhaps another ¼-mile before I could no longer make it out. I spent perhaps 2 or 3 hours trying to pick up the trail again but to no avail. I lost not only the trap, but the coyote as well.

After those two incidents, I analyzed what the problem might be. I finally traced it to "stake pumping." The end rings on the trap chain where the stakes pass through were too small. I've since seen a remedy for this problem applied by trapper Clifford Gilliam. Clifford gets pipe large enough for his steel stakes to slip in,

34

but small enough that the pipe won't slip off the re-straining nut or bulge at the top of the stake. The pipe is then cut into 2-inch lengths. A hole is drilled in one side and a trap chain swivel is attached to it. The stake passes through the pipe and the pipe allows the chain to swivel around the stake, yet the section of pipe is long enough that it won't grip the stake in a ratchet-type pumping manner as it does with smaller rings. Instead, the pipe slips upward to the top of the stake.

When it comes to driving the steel stakes I use a 6-pound hammer. I like the stake to be long enough so that it drives hard the last couple of inches. If I initially select a shorter stake, and it pounds in too easily, I generally pull it and use a longer one. In some instances, there is nothing but topsoil for several feet and a stake pounds into it quite easily, no matter how long it is. In such a case I'll generally put in a 26-inch steel stake and let it go at that.

Drags and Clogs

A good many trappers use short stakes, knowing they'll sometimes be pulled. But these same trappers attach a drag or clog to the trap chain which serves to detain the animal by wearing it out. As mentioned earlier, a drag or clog is nothing more than a weight which serves to sap the animal's strength as it drags it over the ground.

Some clogs consist of nothing more than a tree branch. Its diameter and length is dependent upon the size of animal being trapped. For an animal such as a coyote or bobcat it should be about 3 inches in diameter.

For the wilderness trapper, the tree limb clog is excellent as it can be readily obtained at the trapping site with a hatchet. This way the trapper doesn't have to carry stakes or grapnels with him; all that's necessary is a short piece of wire to attach the trap chain to the limb.

The use of a small tree limb as a drag has other advantages. Actually, when using a 3- or 4-foot limb with the trap chain attached in the middle, the limb works somewhat like a grapnel for it will become temporarily entangled among brush and rocks.

Some trappers prefer to use evergreen branches, complete with needles, for drags. A branch frequently doesn't leave much of a drag mark though most animals seldom get far if a proper-sized one is attached to the trap. In the case of the evergreens, the needles will generally leave a trail where they fall off as the trapped animal drags it along. It's not as difficult to follow a trapped coyote or bobcat across the forest floor when it's leaving a trail of juniper needles behind.

A rock is also commonly used for a drag and, like a tree limb, can be obtained at the trapping site without having to carry it around. However, if you've ever tried to attach a trap chain to a rock you might think again about the "convenience" of using a rock as a drag. Actually, the rock has to be one with slab sides or edges

An excellent clog for coyote-sized animals can be made out of a beverage can filled with lead with a chain attached. This can be snapped onto a trap chain, the heavy weight slowing down the animal's progress while leaving a distinct drag mark in the soil, much like a grapnel.

because a rounded stone is next to impossible to contain within a wire wrapping. An angular rock, however, can be wrapped with wire and the wire attached to the trap chain so that the animal dragging it won't pull the wire off the rock. Be careful when wrapping wire around a rock drag for it is actually quite difficult to make the wire secure so that the animal won't be able to pull it off. Don't twist the wire too tight around a rock with pliers; this can weaken the wire.

For the trapper who is moving on four wheels, as opposed to two feet, a heavy, artificial drag is no doubt the most convenient of all. For example: A large soup can may be filled with concrete and, before the concrete hardens, a wire loop can be inserted to later serve as a trap chain attachment.

A more compact, more efficient weight can be made in much the same manner with a lead-filled beverage can. Just melt the lead and pour it in. Be sure there's *no* liquid in that can, *before* you pour in the molten lead.

Lead for making drags can be obtained from wheel-weights, linotype, cable sheathing, etc., and is sometimes available from a junkyard for a nominal fee. Lead melts at a relatively low temperature and can be melted in a bullet alloy furnace, a plumber's lead melting setup, or simply in a cast iron pot on top of the stove. I have used all of these systems and all of them work well. Be sure to have adequate ventilation when melting lead for it releases toxic fumes. Be sure to wear safety goggles when working with molten lead and don't accidentally spill any water into the molten alloy — you'll end up with an explosion.

Because lead has the advantage of being quite dense and heavy per volume, it doesn't take a lot of it to slow up or stop a trapped animal. A lead weight the size of a beer can can work quite well for an animal the size of a coyote. Not only is there the effect of the weight slowing the trapped animal down, but the small heavy can has a tendency to dig into the ground and catch on any small tufts of grass, rocks, etc. It's unlikely that any trapped coyote will get far with several pounds of lead attached to the trap.

It must be said that a small lead weight is also easier to conceal than a larger clog, and it is important for any clog (such as a rock or beer can full of lead) to be sufficiently heavy to restrain the animal you're trying to trap. With a clog such as a limb, weight is not a factor. That limb simply serves as a type of grapnel that will, in brushy country, slow an animal's progress.

The use of a drag or clog can be desirable in some trapping situations over staking a trap solid because an animal that is solidly staked has the opportunity to lunge and jerk against the solid resistance of the stake. This can increase the chances of it jerking out, particularly if the trap doesn't offer a good foot hold. Furthermore, an animal which is solidly staked, in open terrain, such as a coyote or a fox, sometimes appears to be more frantic than one which is restrained in a trap that has been set in heavy brush. An animal that has the ability to move a grapnel or drag into the brush is less likely to fight the trap as severely as an animal staked in the open. Any animal that runs into the brush after being in a trap generally spends much of its time chewing on and fighting the brush rather than the trap.

Another advantage of the drag or clog is that it allows the animal to get into the brush where it's not as likely to be seen by other people passing by. An animal with a grapnel or drag attached generally runs to the nearest brush, becomes entangled, and will generally remain in place until the trapper arrives. (Usually, the trapped animal is not more than 30 yards away from the set, frequently much less). Nevertheless be it a drag or clog, the device, assuming it's properly constructed, will usually provide the trapper with an easily-followed trail.

A trap that is solidly staked does, however, have the advantage of keeping an animal anchored until the trapper arrives — there is no having to look for it. The trapper who is trying to run all the traps he can in a day's time doesn't want to spend time looking around for trapped animals. For this reason, stakes have a certain advantage over grapnels and drags.

Dogs

Some trappers, particularly those who are partial to using drags or grapnels, have a dog to accompany them on the trapline. A dog can be a definite asset, particularly if it's familiar with what's happening on a trapline and has a good nose. A dog with a keen sense of smell can trail any animal if a stake is pulled, a clog comes off a trap chain or, if for some other reason, the animal escapes with the trap. A good dog can see to it that the fur makes it to the stretcher — fur which otherwise would have been lost.

One of the first things a trapper must do, if he does decide to take a dog along on the trapline, is to train it to keep it from getting trapped. I recently had the opportunity to run a trapline with Clifford Gilliam who has an Airedale for a trapping dog. "Pup" knows precisely what a set is and, though he doesn't seem to fear the sets, he's educated enough to know not to get into them.

Clifford said that when Pup was growing up he kept small, cushion-jawed traps set in the yard where the dog was. Naturally, the traps were baited with the same scent that Clifford used on his trapline. The first thing Pup did was to get into a trap whereupon Clifford released the dog, unharmed. Shortly, the dog got into another trap. That was all it took — from that point on Pup wouldn't go near a set.

Pup is now about 7 years old and knows what a set is

Slim Gilliam makes grapnels, clogs and stakes with the use of a hammer and forge. Here, Slim has already built a fire in the bottom of the forge with the use of kindling to ignite the coke. He is turning the crank to blow air into the bottom of the forge to cause the coke to glow red hot.

and seems to be as eager as Clifford when it comes to checking the traps. The dog walks up to a set, stands just a few feet away, and stares at it for a few seconds. I don't know whether he's eyeballing the trap or trying to catch the fresh scent of an animal that can be tracked down. At any rate, whenever an animal is caught, Pup ends up ahead of us and has the drag followed up by the time we get to the trap site. Clifford related several instances wherein the dog located a trapped furbearer that would have otherwise been lost.

Grapnels

Grapnels are generally either of a two- or three-prong design with each particular type of grapnel having its own advocates. Probably the most popular and compact grapnel design is the two-prong affair which is frequently used in fox, coyote, wolf and bobcat trapping. This type of grapnel consists of a shank with two hooks on either side. For a coyote grapnel, the hooks may measure 3 or 4 inches from the point of the hook to the shank, while the shank itself may be perhaps 8- or 9-inches long. Grapnels are generally buried beneath the surface of the ground and usually underneath the trap. A two-prong grapnel has the advantage of being easier to bury underneath a trap than the three-prong variety because the two-pronger lies flat underneath the trap bed. A three-prong grapnel, according to some, always has one prong sticking up in the air which must somehow be concealed. However, proponents of the three-prong grapnel say that it leaves a better trail and hooks up in brush more quickly than the two-prong variety.

I have used two-prong grapnels with complete success and, as long as they're made properly, there is no problem when it comes to following the trail, nor is there any problem with a well-constructed grapnel hooking up on vegetation be it a two- or three-prong affair.

Though grapnels are generally constructed of metal, and are commercially available, most trappers make their own. Making a grapnel is not difficult and most serious trappers have their own preferred grapnel styles. In the case of a two-prong grapnel, the two hooks are generally turned in opposite directions. In other words, if the grapnel is lying flat on the ground, one hook tip would be turned up and one would be turned down. When the grapnel is lying in this position, the turned-down hook will dig into the earth when the grapnel is pulled along the ground by its shank or trap chain. If the grapnel becomes "flopped," the opposite tip will dig in.

The manner in which the tips are turned, the distance between the tip and the shank, and the sharpness of the tips are all important. If a grapnel has sharp, pointed tips which are pointed in the proper direction, (up and away, slightly angled from each other) an animal will hook up quite well, even in nothing more than soil. It's all in how the grapnel is made. I have seen grapnels supplied by commercial firms which are made out of soft, rolled steel with points that have been made by cutting the steel at an angle. In my opinion they are poor substitutes for a well constructed grapnel.

Making a Good Grapnel

When I began assembling a complete trapping outfit for full-time trapping, I made two-prong coyote grapnels out of ⅜-inch rebar. It wasn't until I was finished making over 50 of them that a couple of other experienced trappers informed me that the ⅜-inch rebar would not be big enough — that there wouldn't be enough weight for the grapnels to work properly. You needed ½-inch rebar for a grapnel to work well.

With so many grapnels already made, I had little choice but to use them. To my delight, I found that the ⅜-inch grapnels worked very well. It is now my feeling that if a grapnel is properly constructed, a lot of weight

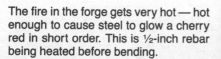
The fire in the forge gets very hot — hot enough to cause steel to glow a cherry red in short order. This is ½-inch rebar being heated before bending.

isn't necessary.

I purchased that ⅜-inch rebar from the local lumber company which was having a sale I couldn't pass up. When it was delivered, I used bolt cutters to cut it into 17-inch sections, each section serving as one half of the grapnel.

The next step was to take each of the sections and grind a very sharp point on one end. As with the trap stakes, I used an emery wheel for grinding the points on the grapnels. However, if I had it to do over again, I would heat them in a forge and pound the ends to a point with a hammer which is a much faster and more convenient method.

Next, I consulted with a neighbor, Ralph Simpson, on the best way to assemble the grapnels. Ralph, though not a trapper, is a fine welder and mechanic with a lot of good ideas. He suggested a novel way of making the bend for the hook of the grapnel — and made a jig for doing it. Ralph clamped about a 3½-inch diameter pipe in a vise and then took a link of chain from an old set of truck tire chains, cutting one of the links in half. This U-shaped piece of metal was then welded onto the side of the pipe so that the point of the rebar section could be inserted into the loop and the rebar simply bent around the pipe to form a perfectly shaped hook in the rebar.

Two of those hooked sections were then put on a concrete floor, side by side, and the shanks joined by welding them together at three places. The next step was to take another chain link, clamp it in a vise, and hacksaw one side of it in two. Vise grips were then used to twist the link, making an open gap for inserting the end of a 4-foot length of stout chain. The link was then twisted back in place and the heavy link was welded to the tip of the straight portion of the grapnel shank with the gap in the cut link welded closed in the process. Now, the 4-foot chain was permanently attached to the grapnel.

The next step was to use the vise to twist the two hook points in opposite directions. The vise jaws were opened just enough so that the ⅜-inch rebar could be slipped between them. Using the shank for leverage, it was simple to bend the hooks so that one pointed up and the other down.

Next, a spring-snap device was attached to the free end of the trap chain so that the grapnel could quickly and easily be snapped on or off the trap chain, as needed. Using the spring-snap attachment, on the trap chain, allows you to quickly opt for either stake or grapnel in the field.

As soon as I made the first grapnel, I went outside the workshop and dragged it across the ground to see how it would work — it appeared that it was going to be effective, and it was. However, if I had it to do over again, I would make the shanks of the grapnels shorter. I later found, even with the large trap bed required with a No. 4 double-spring trap, the shank of the grapnel just mentioned was too long. A shorter shank would have made the grapnel easier to bury under the trap with little or no sacrifice in performance. It's now my opinion that two, 12-inch sections of rebar would be best when it comes to making a grapnel.

I later watched friend Slim Gilliam make a grapnel at his forge. Slim heated the steel and proceeded to beat one end of the rebar into a point. On the anvil, he then shaped a bend in that end for the hook. He followed the same procedures for the opposite end. With the use of the forge, Slim makes his grapnels from a single long piece of rebar, rather than two. This approach can also save the welding steps mentioned above. To do it, Slim heated the midpoint of the simple section of rebar and bent the center of the piece sharply around a large chain link already in place.

There are several things to remember when using a grapnel: First, make the length of chain between the grapnel and the trap sufficiently long, allowing the grapnel to trail some reasonable distance behind the

Here, it can be seen how the rebar is bent into a "U" shape, using the anvil as a type of template and the hammer to shape it.

(Left) Here Slim is using a hammer to pound a point on the rebar prior to shaping the opposite hook of the grapnel. Note that one end of the grapnel hook is already shaped.

(Below) After the points and hooks are pounded onto the ends of the rebar, the steel is heated in the mid-section so that a loop can be bent into the rebar, as shown here.

(Below) This illustrates how a well-shaped grapnel plows into the earth, leaving a distinct drag mark. When a trapped animal leaves the set, it leaves a distinct drag mark, as shown here. This makes it easy for the trapper to follow it up later. A grapnel has an advantage in that it prevents the animal from getting a solid jerk on the trap before the trap springs have a chance to maintain a good hold on the animal's foot.

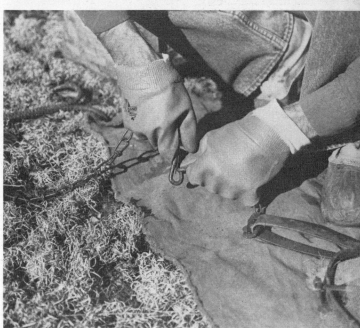

Snap-on trap grapnel attachments are convenient though the trapper needs to remember to snap the grapnel into the trap chain as shown here. If this step is forgotten, the animal will be free to run away with the trap.

(Left) This grey fox ran into the nearest thick brush where the trap's grapnel hooked up. As can be seen, the trap has a good hold on the grey fox's foot. When an animal becomes entangled in such heavy brush, devices such as swivels can prevent them from twisting out.

trapped animal. How long? Three feet would be absolute minimum for most furbearers. Four feet is generally recommended for coyote trapping while 5 or 6 feet is even better, i.e., the larger the animal, the longer the chain.

Secondly, beware the possibility of the grapnel becoming entangled by a rapidly departing animal. If the point of the grapnel engages one of the links in the trap chain there's no way the grapnel is going to hook onto brush or otherwise become entangled simply because the hooks are being dragged in a reverse manner and won't be able to hook onto anything. Keep this in mind when bedding a trap and positioning the chain around the grapnel. Generally, it's best to bury the grapnel, place dirt on the top of it, then lay the trap chain on top of that, followed by more dirt on top of the trap chain, then the trap.

Swivels and Chains

It doesn't matter whether it's a drag, stake, or grapnel, swivels in the trap chain are an excellent idea. In fact, with a staked trap, I feel that they're almost mandatory. It's generally best to have three swivels in every trap chain — one right at the stake or other attachment, one near the trap, and one in the center of the chain. These three swivels will prevent a trap chain from becoming twisted and kinked upon itself and around other objects. In otherwords, the animal won't be able to bind the trap down tight and pull itself free of the jaws.

There are all sorts of different swivels that can be put on a trap chain — unfortunately they vary in quality. I have seen some trappers replace the factory trap swivel with a better one and include two other high quality ball-bearing swivels in the trap chain as well. No doubt, swivels that are designed to be free turning and rust re-

(Below) Grapnels do not always hold an animal on the ground and a trapper should beware when trailing up trapped animals. It's not uncommon for a trapped bobcat to slap or lunge at an unsuspecting trapper. This grey fox was able to climb approximately 12 feet up this pine tree with a number four trap, a grapnel and about eight feet of chain. The author is shown here preparing to dispatch the animal. It can sometimes be difficult to find such animals.

(Right) All trap chains and trap attachments should be checked before the season to make sure they're in good working order. This trapper has attached a heavy duty swivel and special twist link chain to his trap. Make certain that the swivel turns freely where it's attached to the trap.

(Left) A swivel in the middle of the trap chain is an excellent idea to prevent kinking.

The end of the trap chain attached to the grapnel has a third swivel. Though these swivels are expensive, this professional trapper deemed it well worth it to have three swivels. He's also fitted the trap with twist link chain which goes into a hole and lies very flat, without kinking. This grapnel was made from cold rolled steel and shaped by heating with a torch and pounding with a hammer rather than being shaped on a forge.

sistant are a decided asset, but they are expensive and time consuming to install.

As for myself, I have always depended upon the trap swivel normally supplied with the trap and find that as long as one other swivel is placed in the chain, the setup is complete. There's no doubt that the type of chain supplied with most traps will kink upon itself, but there are other types of chains that are superior when it comes to preventing a gob of chain from wrapping around a trap stake or other object.

Expert trapper, Jim Nolan, goes first class in equipment and purchases expensive twist-link chain in addition to three high quality ball-bearing swivels for each of his traps. In addition, his selection of trap is the high quality Victor 3N. Nolan is a professional trapper and wants to go first class all the way — no doubt it'll pay off in the long run. However, when I began assembling trapline equipment, I was lucky to be able to scrape up enough cash to purchase traps, much less additional equipment.

The twist link chain that Nolan uses is superb — it will go into the bottom of a hole like water flowing into a glass. It makes trap bedding immensely easier as there's no problem with the chain links kinking up and projecting above the surface of the soil (or causing a poor bedding surface under the trap). The twist-link chain goes in easily, and comes out of the bed easily— once an animal is caught—without kinking; that's something that can't be said for most types of trap chain.

Anything that a trapper can do to make things easier and faster on the trapline is definitely to his advantage. I use a system copied from trapper Slim Gilliam that beats anything I have seen. Basically, the system allows a trapper to attach either a stake or drag to any trap as the need in the field dictates.

Here in the West there are large tracts of available trapping country that consist either of wide open flat grassland where most traps can be staked or of thick, brushy growth where grapnels work ideally. Frequently I'll be trapping in country which I have never been in before and have no idea what to anticipate in terms of the number of stakes vs. the number of grapnels that I'll want to use. With the Gilliam-designed setup, anyone can use either at will. The system, mentioned briefly earlier in this chapter, basically involves having a small ring at the end of a short trap chain. This ring is designed so that the steel stakes slip through it yet it won't come off the nut at the top. Furthermore, the ring should swivel freely around the stake. This is all that's necessary for staking a trap solidly. The grapnel itself has a long chain permanently attached and with a snap

wraps around the stake.

When using a grapnel with the snap-lock, you must remember to secure the grapnel's snap ring on the trap chain. (It's very easy to forget to do this.) Also, when purchasing any snap ring for such a system, be sure to keep in mind that you don't want a snap ring that will allow the trap chain ring to slip out. Also keep this in mind when laying the trap chain and snap into the trap bed.

Securing Water Traps

Basically, what we've covered so far involves land trapping. The trapper who is pursuing water-dwelling furbearers has a different set of problems with their own unique solutions when it comes to trap attachment.

The person who sets traps under water has a whole different set of trap attachment circumstances than the trapper who goes after land-dwelling furbearers. Most

Make sure that all traps, trap chains, etc., are in excellent working order. It does not pay to have inferior equipment because all it takes is the miss of a cat such as this and it can cost the trapper several hundred dollars.

lock on the free end of the grapnel chain. This snap can be locked into the ring at the end of the short trap chain in a second, if desired. I use one of the hook snaps with a flat piece of spring steel closing the point of the hook. These can be readily obtained at any hardware store.

Today, many traps come equipped with short 7½ or 8-inch chains where they once had chains as long as 16 or 17 inches. According to current trap-company literature, the short chains prevent trapped, staked animals from running and jerking their legs free of the trap. I also suspect that the current use of short chains saves the trap companies a fair amount of money. It is true that an animal caught in a trap that's equipped with a short chain can't get as much of a run while in the trap. However, the shorter chains are also conducive to "stake pumping" as mentioned earlier. An animal that is attached to a stake by a long chain won't be able to pump the stake out of the ground unless the chain first

trappers who trap in or near the water with foot-hold traps attempt to make drowning sets. This is an excellent idea for it reduces the number of animals that might otherwise escape. It's also said to be more humane.

There are some water-dwelling furbearers that can be difficult to hold securely unless the animals are, indeed, drowned or some other provision is made to prevent them from getting out of a trap. One way to make a drowning type of a set is to simply stake the trap out in deep water. A long chain or wire is used to extend the trap attachment to shallow water where the trap is generally set. An animal normally heads for deep water when it's caught in a trap. It is, no doubt, instinctive for a water-dwelling animal to try to escape from potential danger by diving to deep water. In nature, this is an escape tactic used by animals trying to avoid the jaws of a predator. It's not, however, an effective escape tactic for an animal caught in a drowning set. The weight of the trap alone can keep a smaller animal, such as a muskrat, down. Of course, drowning quickly takes place.

Driving a second stake but 8 or 10 inches away from the trap attachment stake makes for a sure-fire drowning system. When you put that second stake in place, be sure the top of the second stake is angled slightly away from the attachment stake. An animal such as a muskrat, when trapped, will struggle and attempt to swim to deeper water. In the struggle, the muskrat will usually manage to wrap the chain around both stakes. The trap chain is not generally long to begin with, and once a muskrat struggles and wraps the chain around those stakes, the amount of remaining, untangled chain isn't enough to allow the animal to get back to land or lift its head above water. This type of staking works very well, and aids in humanely dispatching the animal.

The water doesn't have to be very deep to drown an animal. For several years I trapped muskrats and raccoon along a small creek which could easily be waded with hip boots. In many places, the water was only 2 or 3 inches deep, although I generally prefer a foot of water to quickly drown a muskrat.

I was using, primarily, No. 1½ single-spring traps, and, most of them were not of the stop-loss type nor were they of the double-jawed variety. The traps had the large 2-inch diameter rings, just as they come from the factory. I would simply cut or break a stout dry stick small enough to slip through this large ring. I generally tried to find a stick with a branch coming off it that would prevent the trap ring from slipping off the top once the base of the stick was firmly set in the creek bottom. It doesn't take a lot to hold a muskrat, but I was careful to push the stakes in very deeply and securely, just in case I caught a raccoon.

The traps would generally be placed in relatively shallow water at a den entrance or feed bed, and staked where the bank dropped off steeply into the water. Then a second stick, mentioned earlier, was shoved into the bottom about 6 or 8 inches from the first. Since the water was not deep the animals were easily retrieved, most drowned.

When a trapper is going after sizable animals that he wants to hold in deep water, a heavy clog, used where the bottom of the creek or pond drops off rather sharply into deep water, can be a decided advantage. Such a clog is preferably used where there is little underwater trash and the bottom is simply mud-packed. Otherwise, the animal could wrap the trap chain around an underwater object and then it would be difficult for the trapper to retrieve.

To use such a device, the trap chain is attached to a clog weighing several pounds. (The amount of weight depending upon the size of the target animal.) If necessary, a built-up shelf can be constructed for the clog on the bottom of the stream, underwater, and within trap-chain reach of the trap bed. When the animal is trapped, and starts to struggle, it will pull the clog off the shelf. The clog will then start sliding down, into deep water. This type of setup is sure to hold an animal under water until it drowns, and it works quite well for such animals as raccoon which have a tendency to wring and gnaw out of a trap.

When using such a setup, it's a good idea to have a long trap retrieving pole complete with a hook at one end. You simply reach under the water with this device, feel around on the bottom and hook the trap chain, pulling the trap and animal out. The body of water you're working with this method should be small enough so that you can retrieve the animal easily. If you're working a larger, deeper body of water, the trap should be attached to a long wire, the other end of which is staked on the bank, above the waterline.

There are other, more elaborate methods of drowning an animal, some of which work with certainty though they require a bit more rigging. A favorite of beaver trappers is the use of a slide-lock device on a taut wire. To rig the set, get a long piece of No. 9 to No. 12

This is the Victor slide lock. The lock will slide down the wire toward deeper water (left), but it locks against the wire when an animal such as a beaver attempts to pull it the opposite direction (right). This makes for an effective drowning device.

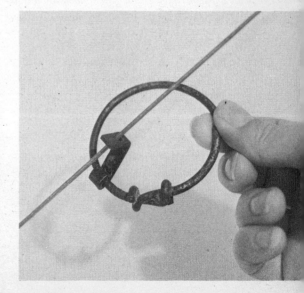

If a trapper does not own a Victor slide-lock, he can make one out of a beer can opener. It operates basically the same as the commercial lock does.

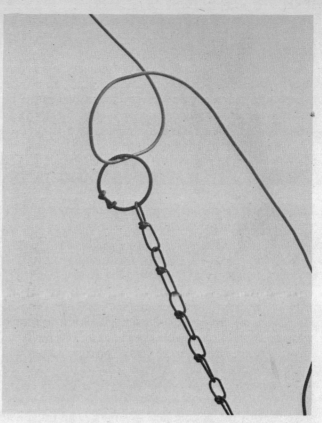

The drowning effectiveness of looped No. 9 wire staked to the bank can be seen here. The trap chain ring drops to the loop readily when the trapped animal dives to deep water. However, the ring will not slide back up the wire.

wire, and place a slide-lock on it. (A slide lock is designed to move in only one direction on a taut wire.) In recent years, Victor Trap Company has been supplying slide locks on its larger traps. These locks consist of nothing more than a piece of flat strap bent at a 90-degree angle, complete with a hole drilled in each end. The trap is attached to one hole with the drowning wire passing through the other. Make sure the slide lock is positioned to go the proper direction — toward deep water. (With the Victor lock, the leg of the L-shaped strap, which is attached to the trap, is the portion of the slide that should be pointing toward deep water.)

Next, drive a stake near the water's edge, then tie one end of the wire to the stake, connecting the other end to a long stake driven into the bottom of the pond in deep water. Stretch the wire fairly taut. If you're unable to place the second stake in deep water, a heavy weight can be substituted by attaching it to one end of the drowning wire and then throwing it into a deep-water area. A burlap bag partially filled with rocks happens to work well for this purpose.

Though a trapper can make his own slide locks, I prefer the use of the old beer opener or "church key." These devices, which were once given away free for the asking (and which now cost only a few cents), are an excellent investment for the beaver trapper. Just slide the wire through the hole in the bottle-opening end so that the lock will slide in the proper direction, toward deep water. The sharp edge serves to clamp the drowning wire when pulled one way.

Another way to make a drowning setup is to form a series of loops in some heavy No. 9 drowning wire which has been staked on the bank as well as in deep water. The wire is passed through the trap chain. No slide lock is necessary. A trapped animal will generally make its way to the bottom while the trap chain slides around the loops on the way down. However, the chain won't clear the loops when the animal tries to get to shallower water. Use a stiff wire when making such a drowning set so that the loops stay firmly formed, and don't kink up, preventing the trap chain from traveling down the wire.

It is important for a trapper to keep an open mind and use his imagination regarding the situation and materials at hand to devise whatever type of natural trap attachment that is most convenient and quick to construct. The trapper with a bit of wire, a hatchet, and a few good sized staples can devise all sorts of convenient means for anchoring traps. Heavy staples can be used to attach a trap chain to a log or fence post while wire can be used to attach the trap to almost anything. The hatchet serves for cutting stakes.

chapter 5

DYEING AND WAXING TRAPS

IF YOU'VE purchased new traps, or even if you've bought used traps from someone else, they're not ready to be set as-is. It is my feeling that any trapper can benefit his trapline by dyeing and waxing traps, no matter whether they are to be used under water or on land. Dyeing a trap is simply staining it, usually a dark black color with some type of vegetable matter. The dye, in effect, camouflages the trap so that it is more concealable than a shiny new trap. Dyeing a trap, much like blueing a rifle or shotgun barrel, also helps to prevent rust.

After dyeing, the trap is generally waxed. A molten wax coating is applied to the trap which aids in preventing rust. This is not only important to the trapper who is trapping water-dwelling furbearers, but also to the land trapper who must worry about the moisture in the earth and the exposure of his traps to rain. For winter weather trapping, calcium chloride antifreeze is often used to prevent trap freeze-up. This agent can cause severe trap rusting unless the traps are thoroughly waxed.

Perhaps more importantly, wax makes a trap very fast because it acts as a lubricant for stiff springs and other moving parts of the trap. A wax coating may also aid in preventing the trap from freezing down as solidly as it might without the coating. One of the most important aspects to trap waxing, however, is to seal in steel and rust odors so that scent-wary furbearers won't be able to detect a set. For all these reasons, it's best to dye and wax traps if you want the most effective trapline operation possible. Actually, dyeing and waxing is not difficult, but the process doesn't really start with the dyeing or waxing itself. There are a couple of preliminary steps.

The first step is to thoroughly inspect all traps that are to be used on the trapline. Make sure that each one is in good working order. Then set each trap individually, checking the pan height. When set, the trap pan or triggering device should be level with the jaws. If the pan lies above jaw level, the trap is liable to spring prematurely before the animal's foot is well down within the jaws. This can cause a miss or perhaps a toe catch. On the other hand, if the pan lies too low, it's possible that the pan cannot be depressed enough to allow the trap to spring. While setting each trap, also check it over carefully for signs of severe rust or pitting, particularly in the chain area. Any trap chains that are severely pitted should be discarded and replaced. Also, be sure to feel for trap spring strength. Trap springs that feel weak

This ingenious trap boiling device was designed by Slim Gilliam. It consists of a metal container for holding the trap boiling solution. It is raised high enough to build a fire underneath and there's a stove-pipe chimney to get rid of the smoke.

Dyeing and waxing traps is definitely an outdoor job due to the size of the equipment and the chemicals used. This trapper has his traps ready to boil in the 55-gallon drum, under which he's lighting the fire. (Photo courtesy Mark Horwath)

should be replaced with new ones. New springs can be obtained from trapping supply houses for nearly any popular trap. As an alternative to replacing springs entirely, auxiliary springs can be purchased to "boost" existing springs to like-new strength. Also, each trap should be thoroughly cleaned with a wire brush to remove all dirt, grit, and rust. There's no question about the fact that a coating of rust not only weakens a trap but slows its operation. Removing the rust tends to make the trap operate faster.

Once the traps have all been inspected, repaired, adjusted and thoroughly brushed, the next step is to boil them to remove any oils or foreign odors. Boiling traps is an outside operation. This way you make certain not

to impart any household odors to your traps. Furthermore boiling traps is a big, messy operation.

An ideal container for a large quantity of traps is a 55-gallon drum with one end cut out. I generally build a circular, block type platform underneath the drum to elevate it a foot or more off the ground but leave an opening where wood can be added to build a fire. Remember not to fill the drum completely for the water level will rise when the traps are immersed. If you don't have a setup for using a 55-gallon drum, a clean washtub (available from most hardware stores) is also a good container for boiling traps. Basically what you need is a very large container to hold as many traps as possible. Regardless of what that "used" container once held, it is a good idea to boil a can or two of Sani-Flush or lye in the water-filled drum, and then flush it out thoroughly before putting in any traps. The lye has a tendency to thoroughly clean metal of any foreign materials. Just boil the water 30 minutes to an hour, then dump the water out, hose the drum out and refill it after making certain that the sides are *absolutely clean*.

New traps always come with a light film of oil to prevent rusting. This oil must be removed for it does have a scent and will tend to alert scent-wary animals. To remove it, boil the traps until the oil comes to the surface of the water — then pour the oil off. Before boiling the traps, place a part of the trap chain or a nail between the jaws so that the boiling water will clean every surface of the trap. Do this when dyeing and waxing later, as well.

For used or rusty traps, boil them in a solution of lye water. For trap boiling, I generally put two or three cans of Sani-Flush into a 55-gallon drum which is filled approximately three-quarters full. I use a heavy wire or metal milk carton basket that fits inside the drum. The traps are stacked in the basket, and then the basket of traps is immersed in the drum. A long heavy wire attached to the basket is looped over the sides of the drum. I can stack two of these baskets one on top of the other inside the drum so that the traps can be easily removed from the solution. I like to boil the traps in the lye solution 30 minutes to an hour before removing them. The lye water has a tendency to remove all foreign materials including rust so that traps come out of the lye water very clean. Lye is excellent for removing any blood, animal hair, etc., that was not removed with the wire brush. It also serves to remove any foreign odors from the trap. The traps are then pulled from the lye solution. I generally dump them on the ground in a clean grassy area and rinse them off *thoroughly* with a garden hose.

The next step is to let the traps sit long enough to acquire a thin film of rust. This thin film does no damage whatever and serves as a base to "take" the dye later. If you rinse the traps daily with the garden hose it may

Trap dye usually comes in powdered form.

(Left) A number of metal milk cases can be stacked in a 55-gallon drum for processing traps. Rather than elevating the drum, this trapper has dug a below-ground fire pit and lined it with concrete blocks. One end is left open for adding firewood. (Photo courtesy Mark Horwath)

serve to speed the rusting process. For new traps it may take a couple of weeks. Of course, the rusting process is, to some degree, affected by the area you live in, i.e., the temperature and the amount of humidity normally present.

If you're in a rush, new traps can be rusted almost immediately by immersing them in a muriatic acid solution which can be obtained from nearly any block or masonry supply plant. I have done this several times and find the muriatic acid works quite well. After dipping traps in the acid and allowing them to rust (perhaps 24 hours) I rinse them thoroughly with the garden hose. Because muriatic acid quickly forms a gas and evaporates completely in the air, no objectional odor remains — the

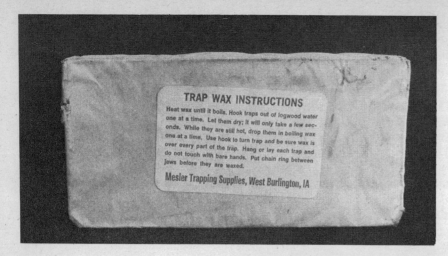

A bar of trap wax from Mesler Trapping Supplies.

Once the traps have been boiled they're hung by their chains to cool, dry. Note that they're handled only with gloved hands to prevent human contamination. (Photo courtesy Mark Horwath)

rinsing off with the garden hose is simply a precautionary measure.

Once the traps have acquired a coating of rust, they're ready for dyeing. Again, the 55-gallon drum is the best container for the purpose — it should be emptied of the lye water and *thoroughly* rinsed out. Or, if you so choose, you can use a separate drum for the dyeing so that both drums can be left set up and used throughout the trapping season as necessary. Indeed, the process does need to be repeated each time a trap catches an animal, or becomes contaminated in some other manner.

For dyeing, fill the drum three-quarters full of clear water and insert a prepared trap dye as recommended on the package. Trap dye can be obtained from any trapping supply house and usually 1-pound of dye is recommended for each 4 to 5 gallons of water. A trap dye is generally a dry cake-like black substance made of logwood extract. It's generally referred to as logwood crys-

tals. I have also used other materials which are found in my local area. When I used to trap in the Midwest, I used a walnut hull mixture to accomplish the same process. Here in the dry Southwest, creosote bush works to some degree. In addition, I prefer to add just a bit of sage, juniper, or other evergreen material to impart a scent to the dye water. It doesn't take a lot of this for you don't want to concentrate the odor — just add enough to impart a slight hint of natural smell to the dye and trap. If you use too much pine or juniper gum, the solution will impart a gummy substance to the traps which probably doesn't do much for their speed.

Once the dye has dissolved, the traps are placed back into the milk carton container baskets and immersed in the drums. The dye water is brought to a boil and then allowed to simmer. Don't let the fire to get too hot— just enough to keep it simmering. Traps should simmer preferably for an hour or more. If you can leave them overnight in the dye, it's even better. The next morning, bring the water to a boil again and then lift the traps out. Now, they can be hung up to dry. Remember, not to touch the traps with your bare hands once you begin the boiling process. I generally handle the traps with the same rubber gloves that I'll be using to set them with later. Still, I don't handle the traps any more than necessary and usually use a rod with a hook on the end to pluck the rings out and hang them up. Once the traps have cooled and dried, they're ready for waxing.

Prepared trap waxes can be purchased at any trapping supply house although Pero wax, which can be purchased at the grocery store, does just fine. There is a great argument constantly waged among trappers over the use of beeswax as one of the components in trap wax. Some say it's the best wax to use. Others say it imparts a slight honey odor to the trap wax, causing some animals to dig traps out. I've bought and used prepared trap waxes and have used the Pero wax from the grocery store and I cannot detect any great difference between them. However, I have never used, and therefore cannot comment on, a wax with a strong beeswax mixture in it.

Make certain that traps are absolutely dry before putting them in the wax mixture for water added to hot wax can create a reaction that amounts to the wax violently bubbling and popping. Also remember that wax is *extremely* flammable.

There are trappers who prefer to wax traps by placing the wax right on top of the dye water. It is quicker this way although I prefer to keep the wax as pure as possible and free from the odors of the dye. Instead, I wax the traps two or three at a time in a bucket. First, a *clean* bucket is filled about half full with water and then a good quantity of wax chunks are placed into the pail. The water in the bucket is then brought to a boil which will melt the wax. I like a thick film of wax on top of the water — 2 inches isn't too much. The traps should still have the chain links or nails between the jaws. Now, take the traps one or two at a time and immerse them in the water and molten wax mixture. The traps should remain in the hot liquid for a minute or so to allow the trap metal to come up to the same temperature as the molten wax. Then, the traps are hooked with a rod, as mentioned earlier, and pulled up through the molten wax film very slowly. There should be an almost invisible thin coating applied to every metal surface on each trap. Actually, you can hardly see the coating. A properly waxed trap should just look wet. If the wax is thick enough to see, you probably didn't leave the traps in the solution long enough for them to come up to the proper temperature. This causes the wax to clump on the trap and when hardened, these wax clumps will flake off during transportation. If traps are properly waxed, they will be very fast yet there will be no great amount of wax on them to slow their action. Immediately upon pulling the traps through the wax, and while they're still hot, they should be shaken and freed of the excess wax ma-

A properly dyed and waxed trap resulted in the catch of this Dakota red fox. A properly waxed trap can help keep the trap from becoming inoperable through freezing. (Photo courtesy of Tal Lockwood.)

terial.

Once the traps have been waxed, they can be hung out in the open air to cool, and the wax allowed to harden. However, be certain not to hang your traps out where any foreign odors can come in contact with them. The open air isn't always free of foreign odors. For example, supposing your neighbor has been dressing chickens upwind next door; if he decides to burn chicken feathers that day, the smoke will come in contact with your traps. Automobile exhaust fumes can be another contaminating source. Just keep these things in mind when hanging traps.

Also, when conducting dyeing and waxing operations around the house, it's a good idea to prevent advertising the fact any way you can. It's bad enough to lose one or two traps to trap thieves on the trapline, but it's really unfortunate when, a short time before trapping season is to open, a trap thief takes every trap you have right out of your backyard!

Once the traps have been thoroughly cooled, they can be stored in a clean wooden box somewhere out of the elements. It's best if they aren't stored in a musty basement or shed along with the farm machinery where odors of grease or gasoline come in contact with them. I generally store my traps packed with evergreen branches or creosote bushes to impart a natural scent on them. Be sure to also place traps where someone else won't be handling them. Someone may unknowingly nullify all your efforts in eliminating foreign odors from the steel by picking them up or handling them.

chapter 6
MISCELLANEOUS TRAPPING EQUIPMENT

GOOD EQUIPMENT is one of the best investments any trapper can make, and the trapper who doesn't have good equipment is handicapping himself. The equipment needed by the trapper for going after land animals is different than that needed by the trapper for pursuing water animals.

Land Trapping Equipment

Boots

The trapper's boots are important, for both the land trapper and water trapper, and deserve some amount of thought before being purchased for wear on the trapline.

When trapping the scent-wary animals such as fox and coyote, a trapper's boots are the only things that come in direct contact with the earth to leave any scent, that is if the trapper is very careful not to brush against taller bushes or weeds. Some trappers don't give scent enough consideration, particularly scent while walking to a set. I think it is vital to trapping success to leave as little scent as possible wherever the trapper is on his line. It is true that a trapper's scent will dissipate in a few days and even the scent-wary animals probably won't notice it. But why not make catches the first

night? In addition, the trapper risks leaving human scent behind when checking his established sets to make certain everything is as it should be. To help reduce the possibilities of leaving scent, I believe that rubber-soled boots are the best bet. However, boots must also be comfortable and rubber can be one of the least comfortable materials to wear, particularly when it's warm and dry.

For trapping in the drier portions of the West, I prefer the L.L. Bean boots that have the rubber soles extending 1½ inches up the side and leather uppers. I bought mine large enough for me to wear an extra pair of wool socks for when I do my winter trapping. Such boots work well not only in dry but also wet weather. Rubber, unlike leather, canvas or other materials, doesn't seem to hold a scent. Also, it doesn't seem to allow human scent to pass through the soles like other boots do. Of course, if a foreign odor is on the outside of the boots, it must be removed. Rubber can easily be cleaned with a mild detergent and water.

The most scent-proof boots in the world will still leave scent if they aren't kept clean and odor free. My trapping boots are never brought inside the house, nor are they worn in town. Once I have scrubbed them vigorously with a mild detergent and warm water, I rinse them thoroughly in clear water and put them inside an open wooden box with juniper and sage branches. The box is stored in an open shed. When I'm ready to go trapping, I put the box, containing boots, evergreen branches and all, into the vehicle. I also have a rubber mat which is cleaned and stored in the same way. When I'm running an automobile trapline and am within a mile or two of where I'm stringing steel, I'll get out of the vehicle, go around to the back of the truck and put my boots on. I'm careful not to contaminate the soles of the boots by touching them. I then put my "every day" boots on the floor of the passenger side of the truck where they won't contaminate my traps or other trapping equipment in the back. Handling the rubber floor mat very carefully and by the underside, I place it on the floor of the driver's side before getting in the truck with my "scent free" boots. The mat provides an uncontaminated area for my feet while driving from one set to the next. I also give the foot pedals inside the vehicle a good scrubbing before going trapping. Of course, there is no way to keep all foreign odors off, but anything you can do to decrease their presence is no doubt a step in the right direction.

Some trappers, particularly in the East, who trap for both land- and water-dwelling furbearers simultaneously, prefer to use hip boots. There are advantages in wearing hip boots for land trapping. For one thing, they come up so much higher on the legs that the trapper isn't as likely to leave scent if he brushes up against bushes and weeds. Furthermore, the rubber knee covering helps prevent scent contamination if the trapper has to kneel at the trap site. I don't wear hip boots, so when I'm setting traps, I simply squat down on my feet and don't allow my knees to touch the ground.

Gloves

The feet aren't the only portions of the body which come into contact with the surroundings and must be shielded against leaving scent. The land trapper's gloves are perhaps even more important because they come in direct contact with the trap when it is set and placed in the trap bed. I prefer to use rubber gloves and wash them daily during trapping season with a mild detergent.

Once the gloves have been washed and thoroughly rinsed, I wear them outside and grab handfuls of evergreen branches, right on the trees. While squeezing the branches tightly, I pull them through my hands to cover the hand surface of the gloves with a pine scent. Juniper, or creosote bush works well in the West. Other local evergreens in other sections of the country will work just as well.

I prefer the rubber-coated cotton gloves which also serve to keep my hands warm in cold weather; other trappers use the plain, uncoated cotton gloves. These trappers generally have several pairs and wash and change them regularly. In addition to washing, some trappers sprinkle urine of the species being trapped onto their gloves in an attempt to mask or cover up any human scent.

All this talk about how to prevent leaving human scent behind, is mostly theoretical. We don't have an acute smelling ability that can detect foreign odors like that of the coyote or fox. All we can do is use our brain and hopefully be a little more effective in not leaving human scent. Even though we cannot smell our own scent, we do know that human scent left at a set can alert animals.

As a result I make certain that nothing at a trap site is touched by my gloved hands. The only exceptions are the trap, trap cover, and stake which must be handled in order to put them in place. The dirt which is excavated for the trap bed is shoveled out with a small trowel and into the trap sifter; it is not handled directly.

Digging and Scratching Tools

Besides boots and gloves, the land trapper needs good digging tools because nearly all of his traps will be placed below ground surface. A small gardener's hand trowel is excellent for digging a trap bed in softer soils

This illustrates the use of a homemade trap-setting device designed by Slim Gilliam. Once the springs are depressed and the trap is set, the trap setting device is scissored open, and the trap is removed.

or for making dirt holes. Here in the West, much of the soil is quite tough and rocky so, in addition to the hand trowel, I also use a brick hammer. It is effective for chopping hard earth or for digging rocks out of the trap bed without dulling the trowel.

Incidently, I file the edges of the hand trowel regularly to keep them sharp and to keep the digging quick and easy. I use the brick hammer much like one would use a pick. However, it is more convenient to use than a spike-like pick because of the wide blade on one end which can be used in a shoveling or raking motion during the hammering to aid in the excavation. I have never found need for a long-handled digging tool.

In addition to the digging tools, some trappers also use a scratching tool to simulate coyote, fox or bobcat scratches. These trappers feel that scratches, left near the trap site where a gland lure or urine is used, adds a natural touch to the set. I don't regularly leave scratches at sets because I haven't found them to be a definite advantage. If you want to give it a try, a scratcher can be made from a gardener's claw. You may want to bend the prongs of the claw closer together to more closely simulate a coyote or fox foot.

In recent years, another type of tool has been introduced that leaves a simulated, false footprint of a fox or coyote near the trap site. This too lends an air of naturalness to the set. I haven't used them though they may have some merit.

Trap-Setting Cloth

The trapper going after land animals will need some type of trap-setting cloth. I use a piece of heavy canvas

A scratching tool can be used to imitate the scratches of canines such as foxes or coyotes to lend an air of authenticity to a set.

which measures 35 x 46 inches. I find this size to be convenient for not only standing upon but for placing my trap basket and all my tools upon. Some trappers use smaller trap-setting cloths though I prefer to have one large enough for all my tools so they do not come in direct contact with the ground.

Like the boots and gloves, it's important to keep the

(Left and above) A trap setting cloth placed next to the intended trap-setting site prevents human scent from contaminating the area. The button sewn onto one side of the cloth allows the trapper to always lay the same side on the ground each time. The dirt sifter holds the excavated dirt from the trap bed and is used to sift dirt back over the trap once it is set.

trap-setting cloth clean by washing or boiling it regularly in a mild detergent and thoroughly rinsing it in clear water. It's a good idea to have several so that an uncontaminated one is available at all times. I perhaps go to extremes in my care and caution toward not leaving scent, for I boil my trap setting cloths just as I boil my traps — even in the same dye water. Rather than having a white canvas trap-setting cloth, mine is logwood crystal black — just like the traps.

I have sewn buttons to each corner on one side of the cloth. When preparing to make a set, I always make sure that the buttons are up when laying the cloth on the ground. This way, the same side always comes in contact with my feet and tools. The canvas is also zig-zag stitched around its perimeter to prevent it from unraveling.

The trap-setting cloth is used not only to stand upon, but also used to place the dirt sifter and excavated earth upon while making a set. Once the set is made the cloth can be used to pick up all excess dirt and rocks and fling them far from the set. Then, the folded trap-setting cloth can be used to brush out the now-mashed-down area where the trapper squatted while making the set. Some trappers prefer to use a whisk broom or a nearby tree branch for this purpose but the trap-setting cloth is convenient and always available. A small whisk broom is still a good idea for touching up details around the trap itself.

Dirt Sifter

A dirt sifter is an absolute necessity for the land trapper. Actually it is nothing more than a coarse screen in a wooden frame through which all the trap covering dirt is sifted. This is insurance against a sizable stick or stone getting caught between the jaws to jam the trap and prevent the jaws from closing completely.

I prefer ¼-inch wire mesh screen for sifting dirt. The exposed screen inside my particular sifter measures 8½ x 14 inches which I find to be a convenient size. I like to have the sifter large enough in diameter that it covers the set completely, and a No. 4 double spring set is good sized. Other trappers use smaller sifters so they can control where the sifted material falls more precisely. However, the choice is simply a matter of personal preference.

A sifter is easy to construct from 1 x 2 wooden strips and screen mesh. I made my sifter from firring strips and steel mesh. I started with a piece of ¼-inch mesh measuring about 11 x 16 inches and then cut eight wooden strips. The strips are cut so that when they're laid flat the ends overlap. The overlapping ends add strength to the design. Two square fir strip frames are then constructed and with the screen sandwiched in between are nailed or screwed together.

Actually, a dirt sifter can take quite a beating and should be strong enough to withstand the abuse. A trapper in a hurry sometimes has a tendency to shake the sifter vigorously, with sizable rocks in it, in an effort to get the job finished; thus the need for strength.

My sifter does not have much depth to it; however, I know of other trappers who prefer to build up the sides of their sifters to a height of as much as 4 inches. This way the sifter will hold more dirt or sand.

Hammer

The land trapper needs some sort of hammer for driving stakes. I prefer to use a 6-pound sledge hammer to give plenty of force for driving steel stakes. Much of my land trapping is for coyotes, and I want a heavy hammer that will put a stake down far enough that it won't pull out. However, for the trapper who covers a lot of ground on foot, such a heavy hammer might be a decided disadvantage; it does add considerable weight to the trap basket.

Wire

I almost never use wire when running a trapline for predators. An animal the size of a coyote is best trapped without the potential weakness of any wire. All my trap attachments are by chain and are hooked either to a grapnel or to a stake directly without an intervening wire. If wire is used to hold coyotes, the trapper will pay for it in lost animals. However, wire can work well for other furbearers and for other trapping purposes. The raccoon or marten trapper can use it to attach a trap to a limb drag or the limb of a tree. How the trapper uses the wire will determine the wire size and the amount used. If it is used for holding an animal, it should be inspected regularly for breaks or rust and should be replaced each season with new wire. I recommend using annealed wire which is not as stiff and is much more flexible so that the trapper can do with it as he pleases.

Miscellaneous Land Trapping Equipment

Each trapping situation, depending upon the animal sought, does require different equipment and a lot of common sense must be applied to this aspect. For example, a coyote trapper probably wouldn't have much use for a small hatchet but the marten trapper certainly would.

Staples can be of benefit to the trapper when fastening traps to leaning poles for marten — or even attaching traps. I have known bobcat trappers who attach their traps to the bases of trees using very large staples. I don't recommend the practice for it appears that sooner or later a cat is going to pull a staple out, and with the current price of bobcat pelts running upward of $200, I wouldn't want to lose one after trapping it.

Pliers are an asset on any trapline, and it's not a bad idea to carry two pairs in case one is lost. For the land trapper, they can be useful in reshaping trap pans or trap dogs as well as for cutting wire.

A *catch stick* is needed for releasing non-target animals. Mine consists basically of a hollow pole or tube about 5 feet long with a steel cable running through the length of the tube, looping and then attached at one end of the pipe. The rest of the cable slides freely within the tube to enlarge or decrease the size of the loop. The steel loop can be placed over an animal's head, the loop drawn up tight from the far end of the pole, and the pole used to hold the animal away from the trapper while the trapper releases the trap from the animal's foot. Once the trap is off, the loop can be loosened and the animal freed unharmed and without danger to the trapper.

I also carry a Crescent wrench for turning stakes out of the ground as mentioned in an earlier chapter.

Trap Basket

The trapper will also need something to carry his equipment in, and the traditional trap basket is a tough-to-beat solution. My trap basket is the woven wooden style, although if I were going to purchase one today, it would be one of the fiberglass designs. They are more durable and yet aren't as apt to absorb moisture or scent.

I also have seen some homemade trap baskets which look fine. One was made from nothing more than a canvas bag which was lined with a trash can. Metal plates were used for reinforcement in the top and bottom of the trash can where the canvas web shoulder straps were attached. For the trapper in a rush, a plastic trash basket placed inside a conventional backpack sack can do the job.

Handgun

A .22-caliber handgun is probably the best means for dispatching the catch. A holstered revolver or semi-automatic worn on the belt can work fine as long as you're able to place your shots where you want. Don't carry a handgun that must be babied because a trapping gun is out every day in all kinds of weather. It usually takes a beating.

That's about all that a land trapper needs to carry into the field with the possible exceptions of a skinning gambrel, knife, sharpening tools, etc., if he intends to do the skinning on the line. He'll also need a good supply of the various types and sizes of traps that he'll be using. Of course, those traps should be dyed, waxed and ready to go. There should be some provision for keeping contaminated traps separated from the clean ones you're transporting in the vehicle.

Once a trap is sprung and catches one of the scent-

(Right) Jim Nolan is shown here with a "catch stick" which is nothing more than a pole with a loop at one end that can be slipped tightly around an animal's neck, holding it away from the trapper while it is being released unharmed. Catch sticks are used for non-target animals and are required by law in some states. This is a commercial variety which has a twist lock in the end opposite the cable loop, allowing the loop to be locked into position. By placing one foot on the end of the pole, his hands are then free for releasing the trap from the animal's foot.

This is one example of a homemade catch stick consisting of a cable passing through a hollow pipe and tied at one end. The user simply pulls the loop tight by pulling the cable out the other end.

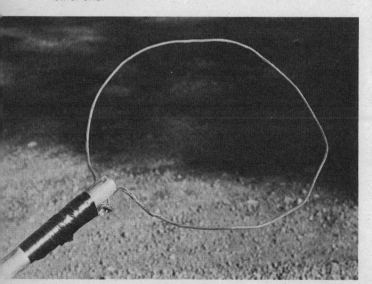

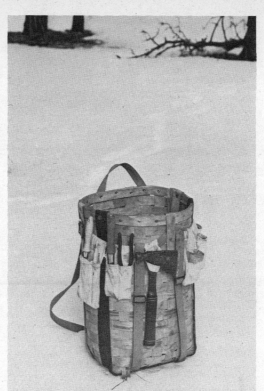

This trapper has devised a looped and pocketed belt which fits around the outside of his trap basket for holding various trapping tools.

The trap basket, shown here on Clifford Gilliam, is practically synonymous with trapping. Also, his holster gun, a .22 rimfire, has proven effective for dispatching any fiesty furbearer, such as this bobcat.

(Right) This ingenious trapper made a trap basket out of a plastic waste container. The plastic trash can slips inside a canvas bag designed to fit around the waste container.

(Left) The plastic trash container is reinforced by a metal strap, as shown here. This takes the strain of the shoulder straps on the outside of the waste container. This inexpensive trap basket works very well.

wary animals, it should not be used again but rather replaced with a clean one. The contaminated trap should be re-boiled before being used again. Though this is not critical for all animals — just scent-wary ones such as coyote and fox — the trapper of mink and raccoon might benefit from following the same practice.

Again, the equipment needed is a personal thing and most of what I have mentioned above is what a person would carry in his automobile when working his trap line. The wilderness trapper, on the other hand, could dispense with quite a few of the above items. One who travels many miles on foot with all of his equipment on his back would no doubt want to dispense with whatever he could.

Water Trapping Equipment

The man who is water trapping is generally either traveling by boat or on foot. The type of equipment needed by each trapper will differ depending upon which way he's traveling.

Boots

There are a good many water trappers who trap the smaller creeks and streams and in this instance a good pair of hip boots or chest waders will allow the trapper to navigate most of these tributaries. The depth of the water will dictate whether hip boots or chest waders are more appropriate. For the trapper who has worked in both, there's no doubt that hip boots are much easier to get around in. Chest waders can be cumbersome for the uninitiated, but for the person wanting to wade deeper water, they may be indispensible.

The person who is trapping water animals doesn't have the problems in eliminating scent that a land trapper does. Generally, the water trapper wades the streams — at least near the sets so that there's no problem of leaving scent to alert the more wary water dwelling furbearers.

Rubber Gloves

Rubber gloves are a decided asset to the person going after water animals. I prefer to wear the gloves with long gauntlets that come completely up to the armpits and allow the trapper to reach into a couple feet of water without getting wet. Because trapping is a wintertime sport, the temperatures can get cold anywhere in North America, and keeping dry means keeping warm and preventing hypothermia. I have seen serious trappers remove their coats and work in a T-shirt, plunging their arms into ice covered waters way up past their elbows, but I don't recommend the average person do this. If I were to do it, my hands would become cold in a matter of seconds and I wouldn't be able to set my trap. As far as I'm concerned, rubber gloves are a must when trapping water animals. They certainly make trapping more pleasant.

Wire

The water trapper, probably more than the land trapper, needs wire. The soft annealed type is, again, the easiest to work with. A single strand of 16-gauge annealed wire will hold muskrats. However, if you're trapping animals such as mink or 'coon, be sure you double strand the wire. Since the wire will be used in quantity it's a good idea to have plenty of it; the trapper should not skimp here. Also never attempt to use last season's wire. It will become rusted over the summer, and tightening it again by twisting will tend to weaken it. There's no need to take chances with old rusted wire; just get rid of it and use new wire when setting traps.

Jim Nolan illustrates the use of a trap-setting tool which compresses the springs of a No. 330 Conibear trap.

Pliers

The trapper after water-dwelling furbearers will also need a good set of pliers for cutting and twisting wire. Two pair are better. In fact, it's a good idea to have the pliers attached to either the trap basket or the trapper's belt by some type of cord or chain to prevent losing them. If you're out trapping and lose a set of pliers, it can mean that you'll have to go back to town if you don't have another set along.

Hammer

A small hammer or, more preferably, a hatchet with a hammer head, is necessary for a water trapline. The hammer head on the hatchet can be used to pound stakes into a muddy bottom, or to drive staples into a platform that will hold a trap in place, or staple a trap chain to a pole. The hatchet can also be used to cut stakes, drags or bait bundles for animals such as beaver.

Retrieving Hook

One tool the water trapper needs that the land trapper doesn't is a retrieving hook, which is nothing more than a hook attached to a long handle. A hoe handle works ideally and a simple hook complete with screw threads for mounting to the handle can be purchased at nearly any hardware store. The hook is primarily used for retrieving drowned animals that have gone into deep water. The hook can also be useful for retrieving traps during high water periods. A trapper working from a boat can also use it to latch onto a tree branch and pull the boat precisely into a setting site. For the beaver and muskrat trapper, a retrieving hook can be used to probe the bottom and determine depth or possibly den entrances, and for the muskrat or beaver trapper walking on ice the hook may save his life if the ice gives way. If the trapper hangs onto the long pole in that situation, the ends may straddle the hole so the trapper can pull himself up by it. Or, if he is close enough to the bank, the trapper can hook onto a sapling to pull himself out. It will suffice to say that experienced trappers won't travel over ice without a long pole at their side.

Ice Cutter

The water trapper who is trapping in the winter will also need some means of cutting holes in the ice. A lot of trappers use nothing more than a hand axe and, indeed, this works quite well. Others, however, use an ice spud or ice chisel. An ice spud is a chisel-shaped tool that's attached to the end of a long pole. The tool is used in a jabbing or up-and-down thrusting motion to break holes in the ice. Some have a hook on one end, and a chisel on the other to serve a dual purpose.

Miscellaneous Water Trapping Equipment

Like the land trapper, the water trapper will need some form of carrying all this equipment. The trap bas-ket works as well for the water trapper as it does for the land trapper. Again, a woven wood or fiberglass pack basket is the best choice though homemade ones can serve the purpose. Unlike the land trapper, the water trapper needs a digging tool with a longer handle. The small spade-like tools with 24-inch handles or so work ideally for this purpose as the long handle allows the trapper to rearrange the bottom of a pond or creek, or to dig deep holes into the side of the bank at water level for pocket sets. The long-handled digging tool makes it much easier for the trapper to accomplish this task without getting wet.

The water trapper may be working an area where he can't always set his trap basket down in order to get something out. For this reason, it's a good idea to have some sort of waist belt with tool loops and pockets or, the same type of belt around the top of the trap basket.

Unlike the man who has to check his water sets on foot, the trapper who is working his line from a boat will be confronted with a different gear-storage problem. On the "plus" side is the fact that a trapper who is using a boat has a little more latitude about the amount of equipment he can carry since he won't have to pack it on his back. In many respects, it's a lot better than navigating a stream by foot. Why? You aren't confined to packing a few traps on your back and having to return to the vehicle when those run out.

The trapper who is traveling by boat can take a large quantity of traps, and it's a good idea to have several types at hand — body-gripping traps, small foot-hold traps for muskrat or mink, larger traps for raccoon, very large traps for beaver, etc. You might even want to carry a few Stop-Loss traps or snares in the bunch.

Whatever traps you decide to use, it's a good idea to put each type into separate compartments or baskets in the boat. This way, a trap can quickly and easily be pulled out of the batch, and be ready for setting even before you pull into the trap-setting site with your boat. Here again, the trap retrieving hook can be an advantage when it comes to reaching and grabbing a trap at the bow of the boat when you are sitting toward the stern. As long as the traps are separated by type and aren't tangled together, it's not difficult to hook a single trap and pull it out of a batch resting in a box or basket. Fruit crates or steel milk carton containers can work very well when it comes to transporting traps in a boat. However, it's a good idea to make sure that the containers you use will slip inside each other when they're emptied — it saves space.

Aside from the above-mentioned equipment, the water trapper, depending upon what he is after, may also have need for burlap bags which he fills with rocks to make a drowning set. A heavy type of wire for making a sliding drowner for beaver and some sort of a slide-lock setup may also be needed. Lastly, don't forget the appropriate bait and lure ingredients which we will cover in Chapter 7.

chapter 7
BAITS AND LURES

ONCE THE trapper has gathered all the traps and other equipment associated with maintaining a trapline, he still needs some means of attracting the animal to the trap. In some instances, simply placing the trap exactly where the animal will step is all that's required. Indeed, the very best sets are already located where an animal normally travels, a "blind" set often being the most effective for trapping wary animals.

For the most part, however, trapping success can be enhanced by using a lure or bait. These attractors not only entice the animal to the set, but cause it to investigate the area where the lure is placed and, consequently, spend more time at the set. The result for the trapper is an increased chance of making a catch.

There are all sorts of commercial trapping lures available to the trapper which are, for the most part, quite good. A trapping-gear supply house is probably the best place for the beginning trapper to obtain his lure. However, it is still important for the trapper to know why lures work and what type of lure is most effective for use on a particular set.

One of the most basic types of lures used for winter trapping is a "food-type" of lure or bait. As the name implies, this type appeals to the basic hunger instincts of the target animal. It may consist of simply a natural food item of the furbearer, or it may be a combination of ingredients (in paste form) devised to make it even more appealing. The scent of such a lure might make the animal think that there is something nearby to eat, or that some other animal has visited the area and eaten something.

The dirt-hole set, commonly used for fox and coyote trapping, is one situation that calls for a food-type lure, wherein a small chunk of meat is placed down in a small hole. Frequently, a liquid or paste-type of food scent is placed into or near the hole along with the meat. Usually a little fox or coyote urine is added to the set to make a bypassing fox or coyote think that another of its kind has perhaps buried something in the hole and left it. The bypasser is, hopefully, fooled into thinking that there might be something in the hole worth investigating. Raccoon and muskrats are also frequently lured to a food scent placed along their travel ways.

Another type of lure, a gland scent, commonly made from the glands of an animal, attracts animals of the same species. In fact, with canines, this is one very basic way of communicating and marking territories. To passing canines the sign of another animal will generally prompt them to stop and use their noses to inspect the area, possibly urinating upon the spot with the greatest concentration of scent.

A gland scent might be used at a "flat set" where the trap is placed next to a likely urinating bush along a cow trail. The gland lure is placed upon the small weed, bush or rocks in hopes that a bypassing coyote or fox will stop and urinate on it.

Another situation calling for the use of a gland type scent is a beaver "scent pack" along a stream. During the mating season beaver build scent packs of mud and then scent them with their glands. The scent packs usually have a strong smell, prompting any bypassing beaver to stop and investigate. If you can't find any of these scent packs, it's a simple matter to make your own and top it off with beaver scent or castoreum.*

There is yet another type of gland lure. Those of you who have pets know how effective a female dog in heat is at attracting other neighborhood dogs. It's the same in the wild. When glands are taken from a female animal in heat, the lure is generally referred to as a "matrix." Though matrix lures work at all times of the trapping season, they generally produce the best results during the mating season. Consequently, knowing the thinking behind a matrix lure can increase its effectiveness.

A "call" type of lure can be made of various ingredients, some of them artificial or perhaps some of them made from musk materials—they are designed to attract animals from some distance. However, don't depend upon a call lure, exclusively, to bring furbearers in to your sets. Animals don't roam around the countryside looking for a trapper's lure, they're interested in food, water, or each other. A good trapper doesn't depend wholly upon a lure to call an animal from a great distance. Rather, the selected lure should be used as an enticement to make a set appear more natural to the furbearer. It's important to keep this in mind when placing any lure at the trap site.

One of the strongest attractors to many animals is, simply the smell of another animal of the same species. Furthermore, a gland lure, properly used, is one of the least likely types of scents to arouse suspicion from the more wary furbearers. For this reason it's one of the very best scents a trapper can select. Gland lures are available commercially but many trappers prefer to make their own from animals caught in their locale. It's not difficult for an experienced trapper to obtain his own glands and make his own lures, and, there's something about catching an animal with a lure of your own making that adds a lot of excitement to the sport of trapping.

*Castoreum or castor is a reddish-brown substance having a strong smell and nauseous bitter taste. It is obtained from two sacs in the inquinal region of the beaver.

Some commercial scents have the strong smell of skunk in them. This trap, intended to catch a fox, was baited with a commercial scent that had a strong skunk essence and attracted the non-target skunk.

The scent glands of mink, weasel, beaver, muskrat and skunk are all located in basically the same place—at the base of the tail. These animals have two scent or musk glands which are quite noticeable during certain times of the year. The canines, on the other hand, have a number of glands and organs frequently sought after by experienced trappers. Here're some of them: a gland located at the base of the ear, the pads of the hind feet, the reproductive organs, the anal glands (including a length of the large intestine with some fur around the outside of the anal opening), the bladder and the gall from the liver.

Insofar as canines are concerned, the trapper can remove the above glands and grind them up with a meat grinder or blender. (Please, *not* the grinder or blender used by your wife.) Once the glands have been blended or ground, you should add a "binder" or base which will serve to hold and carry the scent. Glycerine, propylene glycol, mineral oil, alcohol or urine, are some of the commonly used liquid bases. Not all bases are liquid. Some are made of animal fat, such as lard, or even vegetable shortening. A good base is free from unnatural odors and should not be the dominant odor in any scent formula. However, it should hold the desired odor of the ingredients and should serve to keep the ingredients from freezing. Some excellent lures are composed of nothing more than glands and a base. For example, canine glands, ground as above and mixed with an ample quantity of urine will provide a scented paste that serves as a very good lure. It can be used at temperatures to 0 degrees, generally without freezing. At colder tempertures, an antifreeze base such as glycerine

This large male bobcat was trapped with nothing more than the use of urine taken from a female bobcat in heat. This lure has proven deadly on the large male cats.

oil can be added.

Such a gland lure can be enchanced by other ingredients such as *asafoetida* which is derived from parsley roots and serves to arouse passion in the canines. Another passion ingredient for fox, wolf, and coyote is *lovage*—it has the same effect. Lovage is an aromatic herb of the carrot family.

The beaver castor, mentioned earlier, is a very important lure ingredient in a wide number of trapping lures and has applications for trapping practically everything from muskrats or raccoon to fox, mink, coyotes and bobcats. However, there are usually other ingredients mixed with the beaver castor, depending upon the target animal. For example, muskrats might be attracted by *fennel* or *carrot oil*. For the raccoon it could be sun-rendered fish oil. For the fox it's perhaps asafoetida or civet oil.

Lure making is quite a science and a complex process. Besides the various types of lures, the would-be lure maker needs to be familiar with such items as preservatives and fixatives. A preservative does just what the name implies—preserves—and is like a base. Examples of preservatives are, high-proof vodka, glycerine, mineral oil, etc. Good examples of meat preservatives are sodium benzoate, zinc valerate or even 20 Mule Team Borax. A fixative is used to stabilize the strength of a lure's odor. Examples of fixatives are *orris* and *cumin*.

The application of a proper lure for the proper species can result in an excellent day's catch, as shown here. The author caught these predators in a single day with 15 traps while trapping in Arizona.

(Orris is a plant derivative that has been used as a fixative in cosmetics for centuries.)

Not only are animal glands useful for making your own scents, but they have some value to commercial lure makers. The trapper interested in marketing glands would be wise to contact lure makers and see if he can pick up a few extra dollars from his furbearers.

Food scent is probably easier to concoct than a gland type of scent, and the novice trapper runs less risk of frightening an animal away due to an improper formulation. For example, a food scent may consist of nothing more than tainted meat, as a fall fox attractor. It is generally made from the meat of a prey species of the fox. The meat can be cut into chunks no larger than a walnut, and placed into a sealed glass jar. It is then buried in the shade on the north side of a building for 2 or 3 weeks whereupon it will acquire a strong odor, though it won't be rotten. Then, a preservative such as one of those mentioned earlier, can be added to the meat to hold this stage of decomposition. Again, the meat has a very strong odor and carrying quality that serves to attract animals from a distance; yet, it isn't so rotten that it is offensive to them. A food scent is one of the best types of lures for raccoon trapping and can easily be concocted from a mixture of peanut butter and honey with a little anise added for a call ingredient.

Lure formulation is a science, and a knowledge of all

This bobcat was taken with the use of a gland scent made from the glands of other trapped bobcats. In the author's opinion, nothing can beat natural scents for lures.

Commercial lure making is big business. This trapping supply store offers a wide selection of various scents to the trapper. Due to the ready availability of all kinds of commercial scents, the trapper really doesn't have to make his own unless he wants to. No matter how they are obtained, they greatly increase success.

Skunk essence is one of the most sought-after ingredients for trapping lures because it has a carrying quality second to none. To remove the glands which are located at the base of a skunk's tail, the initial cut is made around the glands at the base of the anus.

Once the gland is exposed, it can be gently pulled out of the skunk and the tissue around it cut away with a sharp knife to free it.

the uses for the many possible ingredients would require a book in itself. The quantity of an ingredient is important, and it may vary depending upon the other ingredients in the formulation. Also, ingredients may react with other ingredients to produce an adverse effect. Most trappers would be wise to stick to matrix lures, food lures or even simple gland lures compounded with a base; and, the trapper should be very conservative about adding "extra stuff" at random—it may do more harm than good.

Furbearers aren't always attracted to a set by their sense of smell. Animals living in the wild generally have all their senses well developed; lures that appeal to the sense of sight can be another very important attractor for some types of furbearers, particularly predators.

For example, bobcats may be readily attracted to a set by the sight of a tuft of rabbit fur dangling on a string. Cotton, feathers, or even Christmas tree ornaments can have the same effect. Grey fox may be similarly attracted. A few feathers scattered around the set can be a very effective attractor for bobcats. However, the trapper must be cautious when using such sight attractors for he's also liable to entice non-target species such as raptors—hawks, eagles, etc.—which will come to the feathers or cotton tufts much like a bobcat will.

One way to prevent a bird from getting into a set is to hang the sight attractor underneath the dense overhanging branches of an evergreen tree. Animals on the ground can easily see it while birds flying overhead cannot.

Sound has even been used as an attractor to some extent. According to a report from the U.S. Fish and Wildlife Service, a study revealed that a ticking alarm clock, placed in a plastic bag and lightly covered with soil, is an irresistible attractor to a coyote. However, I'm not sure about the longevity of alarm clocks when buried under the ground. Furthermore, I'm not sure how practical it would be to have to return to the set, take the clock out and rewind it every 24 hours. However, if a trapper keeps an open mind, it's surprising how much useful information can be gleaned and noted for future use.

This chapter wouldn't be complete without mentioning some of the basic lure formulations that have proven successful, for me, over the past 20 years. The following recipes all have one thing in common—they work!

Lure Formulas

Opossum

Cut a fish into small pieces and place them in a glass jar. Leave the cover loose and place the jar in the sun, permitting the fish to decompose (usually one or two

All that remains is to cut the gland free with the sharp knife. Be certain not to cut into the scent-containing glands, releasing the valuable essence.

Once the glands are freed, they're placed in a glass jar until they're ready to be used. Then the essence can be squeezed out of the glands by pointing the "nozzles" in the proper direction and squeezing the essence out by thumb pressure on the gland itself.

weeks). Pour the oil off to use as a lure.

Raccoon

Mix 2 ounces of fish oil, 2 ounces of honey, 20 drops of oil of rhodium and 40 drops of oil of anise. Shake the mixture well and let it stand outside in a loosely covered jar for 10 days to 2 weeks, then add 1 teaspoon of sodium benzoate and mix well.

Skunk

Use several drops of pure skunk essence near the set.

Muskrat

Mix 2 ounces of ground, spring muskrat glands with 40 drops of oil of rhodium and 20 drops of oil of anise.

Bobcat

Obtain a bobcat liver and the last 6 inches of a bobcat's large intestine, with fecal matter, and anal glands. Cut up the liver and place it in a jar for 2 months and let it rot. Grind the intestines and anal glands. Grind 2 beaver castors in a separate container. Mix 1 quart of rotted liver, ½-cup ground anal glands, 12 drops anise, 12 drops oil of valerian, the 2 ground beaver castors, and enough bobcat urine to make a paste. Add ½-teaspoon of zinc valerate and mix well.

Beaver

Use a paste made from ground beaver castor (75%) and glycerine oil (25%).

Fox

Mix 6 ounces of ground fox anal glands, 1½ ounces of glycerine oil, 30 drops tinctured asafoetida, 3 ounces beaver castoreum, 30 drops tinctured skunk essence, and ½-pint fox urine. Let it age, outside, in a loosely covered jar for 6 weeks.

Mink

Mix the musk glands from two mink with 1-ounce of fish oil, and 1-ounce of glycerine. Shake well and let it stand for a week, covered, then add a preservative.

Coyote

Obtain gall bladder, ear glands, anal glands, hind foot pads, sex and reproductive organs and final 6 inches of the large intestines, with fecal matter, from several coyotes. Grind all of this up, place it in a jar with a loosely fitting cap, and place it in the shade and let it stand for 6 weeks. Add 4 tablespoons of glycerine per pint and enough coyote urine to make a paste. Add ¾-teaspoon of sodium benzoate per pint and mix well.

chapter 8
MARKING TRAP LOCATIONS

IF THE trapper is working country that is familiar to him—country he's grown up in or hunted frequently—and if he's running no more than a couple dozen traps, he can generally remember where each trap has been set. He doesn't have to make a logbook detailing the location of each trap nor does he have to mark each set location. However, I still recommend maintaining a trapping logbook because of the trapping knowledge that can be gleaned from the use of carefully kept records.

I use a pocket-size spiral notebook. In it, I usually diagram set locations, note the type of set, the type and size of the trap, whether it was staked or attached to a grapnel or drag, the scent used and the type of bait used, if any. I then make daily notations regarding the trap—whether it was undisturbed, visited and not sprung, sprung, or made a catch. If a catch was made, I make a note regarding which foot the furbearer had in the trap and what kind of a hold the trap had on the animal.

Even if you can remember where the trap was placed, you can't always remember what type of scent was last used at the set. When it comes time to re-scent the set, I refer to the logbook and use the same type of scent that I first used. This way, I know exactly what types of

scents and baits are working best. If I didn't keep records and simply randomly re-scented, I would have no way of knowing which scent was doing the pulling.

After a season or two of keeping such careful records, the notebook really spells out the success or failure of the types of locations, scents, traps, trap placement, bait, etc., that have been used. In a short time, a logbook can streamline the trapper's operation and make a very refined trapper out of him.

Besides making a diagram of trap location, it is sometimes helpful to put notations in as well. For example, a description of a trap location might read something like this: "25 yards north of large rock," or "base of big dead tree, 100 yards west of road." This might seem like a lot of effort at first, though most of the notations are made when the trapline is first established. Once these initial notations are made, the record keeping is minor. If you're like me, you'll spend more time using the information in the book, even while running the trapline, than you will in making notations.

It's really exciting, after the traps have been initially set, to check them out the next morning. The logbook then becomes a guidebook, describing what type of set is coming up next on the line. It's quite a thrill to see if

Anyone who goes walking cross-country with a basket on his back is readily identifiable as a trapper. By following this man and remaining secluded, a trap thief could learn all the trap locations on the trapline. Fortunately, this wilderness trapper will not have this problem but trappers in more populated areas may wish to disguise such obvious signs of trapping.

(Right) One way to avoid the problems associated with trap thieves is to place traps where they're not easily reached. Here, Kent Dederick crosses a log on a beaver creek to check a beaver set underneath a brushpile on the opposite side. The only access to the trap site is the one that Dederick is taking here.

the trap caught the animal you were after. In short, the logbook can add an exhilarating dimension to the sport of trapping.

If you're a serious trapper, you may have more than 100 sets in the ground, and the more you make, the easier it is to forget the location of a set. In most states, the law requires that traps be checked once every 24 hours. Even if it were not the law, I would do it anyway, for several reasons. First of all, if you've made a good set in a good location, you're likely to have a furbearer in it the first night. If you don't bag that animal the next morning, the trap won't be available to catch a second animal the next night. Hence, the trapper who doesn't check his traps every day is losing fur. Secondly, even if you don't make a catch, something might disturb the set. The wind might blow the covering off, a pack rat might dig around the edge of the set, exposing a portion of the trap, etc. Thirdly, the checking of traps and the removal of trapped animals every 24 hours is the responsible, humane approach to trapping.

When you do get a lot of traps out, it may be necessary to mark the location of the traps at or very near the trapping site. It's a common practice among trappers to place a "flag" or strip of brightly colored ribbon near the set, or if not near the set, alongside the road to mark a set location off in the brush. There's no question that such markings will quickly reveal where every set is as you drive down the road. The only problem is they're a clear advertisement to trap thieves as well.

Trap thieves are, indeed, a problem, though I have not had the problems with them that some trappers have. In fact, I've only had a trap taken every now and then. In many cases, a change in trapping practices will prevent losing an entire trapline to trap thieves. In marking trap locations then, it is beneficial to mark a site in a way that means something to the knowing trapper but will otherwise go unnoticed by the casual observer.

The wise trapper is careful not to reveal his method of marking traps to anyone. I have my own favorite method which will not be revealed, not even in this book. However, let me give you some examples of various types of trap markings that could very well go unnoticed by most casual observers or even trap thieves. For example, a blaze on a tree alongside the road is easily spotted if you know approximately where it is and what you're looking for. What's more, you know what the blaze means, but no one else does. The end of a sizable limb sticking out into the road might be another indicator. A dried cow chip stood on edge alongside the road is yet another example.

When marking traps, and when using such systems, I

An excellent way to take either grey foxes or bobcats is by closing up the sides of the trap site to direct the furbearer into the trap. However, this type of a set location is also obvious to a trap thief. This is something to keep in mind when setting traps.

This is another obvious set location. One familiar with trapping techniques can readily discern where this trap is positioned as indicated by the stepping sticks and brushed-in sides to direct a furbearing predator's movements.

prefer to not let the markers reveal where the traps are. For example, rather than placing a marker immediately opposite the location site of the trap, it might be wise to place the markers 200 yards ahead of where the trap is in the brush. It might even be a good idea to put a few "false" similar markers alongside the road just to throw a trap thief off.

Another method of determining where your set locations are is simply to check locations that look good. If you see a place that looks like you *should* have made a set there because it's a good set location, then very possibly that's where the missing trap is. There are some trappers who use this system exclusively. If they find there's no trap there, then they'll set one.

If I'm trapping land bordering a public road, I always try to place my traps where they can't be seen from the road. Remember, though you may not be able to see the *set* from the road, a trapped animal makes it much more visible. In such a situation you lose not only the trap to trap thieves, but the animal as well.

It's usually possible to set the trap over a small knoll, or somewhere else out of sight from the road. Doing so may require a short walk to check the trap, but this is no doubt a more worthwhile alternative to losing it. Also, don't overlook the use of binoculars to check a distant trap. It's probably best not to walk right up to each set location every day anyway, particularly when you're after scent-wary predators. I check traps from a distance with a good pair of binoculars every day but walk right up to the set every 3 days just to make sure that the set is still natural in appearance. This is something that can't be determined from a distance, even with the best binoculars. Long-distance inspection also works well for traps that have been staked solidly. On the other hand, any trap with a grapnel or a drag attached must be checked by walking or driving right up to the set in order to determine whether or not the trap has been hoisted from its bed.

Checking traps early in the morning, right after daylight, is another way to avoid trap thieves. Remember, it's the trap that holds an animal that's noticed. It likely won't be spotted in the dark, but will be after the sun comes up.

In general, I try to avoid advertising what I'm doing. For example, I try to keep my trapping paraphernalia out of sight in my vehicle; and, when I prepare to make a set, I try to pull the trap basket out when no other cars are passing by the road. If I hear one coming, I'll simply wait until it passes, then pull out the equipment and take off into the woods.

If you pull off the road and park in the same place day after day, it quickly arouses interest from a trap thief, particularly if you're in a national forest where there's

Though the trap site may not be noticeable when it is set, it can become very obvious when it catches a furbearer.

If a trapper takes care to seclude his traps as this one is doing here, there's much less likelihood of traps being stolen. Though this trap is positioned near a jeep trail, it will not be noticed by any bypassing motorists. A grapnel is attached to the trap so that if a furbearer is caught, it will run into the brush where it will not be noticed.

no good reason for the same vehicle tracks to be pulling off day after day. It almost advertises "trapper."

Your footprints leading into a set can also reveal the set's location. All of these things should be taken into consideration if you're trying to avoid trap theft. If trap thieves are a suspected problem in your area, you may wish to make only those types of sets which aren't readily recognizable. For instance, when it comes to fox, a flat set is not recognizable to anyone except the trapper who knows it's there. A dirt hole set, or a cubby, on the other hand, is immediately recognizable to the trap thief who knows what this type of set looks like.

Any time the exact trap location is readily discernible, you run the risk of a visit by a trap thief. Trappers who are after water-dwelling furbearers sometimes place traps right next to the water's edge just a couple of inches under the surface and with no covering whatever. Throwing bottom silt or waterlogged leaves on top of the trap could help camouflage it a lot. Freshly cut stakes are also readily visible when they're sticking above the water. It sometimes pays to smear mud on the white-looking end of a freshly cut stake. This will camouflage it quite well.

In some cases where trap thieves are a severe problem even a trap basket may not be a good idea. It might make more sense to carry the trapping paraphernalia in some other type of container such as a bucket. Everyone recognizes a trap basket and what it is, but someone walking through a field with a bucket is a different story altogether.

It is bad enough when a trap thief makes off with a trapper's trap, grapnel, chain, etc., but when that trap holds a valuable furbearer such as this bobcat, the loss to the trapper is multiplied many times over.

Generally it's best not to even reveal the fact that you're trapping to the average fellow that you run into. There are going to be people who know that you're trapping but don't you reveal *where* you're trapping. Though the person you are talking to may not be a trap thief, he may mention the fact to someone else in casual conversation, not really thinking about it. Before you know it, the word gets around. Not only will others *know* that you're trapping, but *where* you're trapping and, perhaps, even *what* you may be catching. The interesting part of it all is that it originated from the trapper himself.

The various states have laws regarding the theft of a trapped animal, a trap or even the disturbance of a set by a person other than the man who made the set. Another trapper rarely steals a furbearer or a trap. A *serious* trapper certainly wouldn't. However, various regions have different "customs" regarding finding a trapped furbearer. What might be considered the proper thing to do in one area, is frowned upon in another region.

For example, it is the custom among some midwestern trappers, when finding someone else's trapped fur-bearer, to dispatch the animal without damaging the pelt, and then leave the animal near the trap. The reasoning behind this is sound—the bypassing trapper is dispatching the animal quickly, in a humane manner. Secondly, he's eliminating the possibility of that animal escaping between the time that he leaves it and when the man who owns the set arrives. However, this practice is frowned upon in the West where golden and bald eagles are plentiful. Eagles will ruin the pelt of a furbearer in no time once they find that the animal doesn't have any fight in it. For this reason, in the West it's definitely *not* acceptable to dispatch the animal that another person has trapped. Rather, it's better to rely on the fact that the trapper will be coming along soon, and he'll take care of his catch as he normally would if you hadn't happened along.

"Customs" aside, the best thing any trapper can do is to simply obey the laws of the state he is trapping in. Beyond this, the trapper *must* develop a marking system that's effective and inconspicuous if he wants to continue to find his traps and the valuable fur they contain. In short, one of the prime goals of trapping amounts to stopping trap and fur theft, *before* it starts.

chapter 9

THE TRAPPING VEHICLE

PROBABLY the most important part of any trapper's outfit is his vehicle. The vehicle, no matter what it is, must get the trapper around his trapline in all types of weather. This could be over extremely rough terrain, in very deep snow, or boggy mud. Since the law in many states requires that traps be checked every 24 hours, it will take a dependable vehicle to traverse rough terrain, in all kinds of weather, day in and day out. The vehicle for the land trapper may be an automobile or truck, motorcycle or mule. For the water trapper it will be some type of boat or hip boots.

I do a lot of trapping in the West over jeep trails through extremely rugged terrain. Frequently it snows, and frequently the roads wash out in the low spots. There's always mud and big rocks to give trouble. Running lines that require the four-wheel-drive all the way is extremely telling on some vehicles. Some traplines may not require the use of a four-wheel-drive all the time, though it can sure add a lot of confidence to the trapper in certain types of weather. The vehicle should have plenty of clearance underneath and/or a short wheel base to aid in navigating difficult terrain.

The vehicle should be equipped with all-weather mud and snow tires and possibly a winch just in case you get stuck and there isn't anyone else around to pull you out and it is too far to walk to town. A spare tire, tool kit, jumper cables and good tow chain go without saying.

If necessity calls, nearly any automobile can be used for trapping with a little preparation and observance of its limitations. If you are trapping scent-wary animals, there must be some place in or on the trapping vehicle to carry a large selection of traps and transport them in a manner that will keep the traps from becoming contaminated with scent. The vehicle must also have a separate place for transporting the trapped animals or fresh pelts. In addition, there must be a third separate area for transporting lure and bait ingredients in a manner that will avoid any contamination of the traps.

Perhaps the most important part of the trapping vehicle is having a separate wooden trapping box or other container where the traps, stakes and grapnels can be kept isolated from everything else in the vehicle. When I owned one of the older, smaller Bronco four-wheel-drives, I built a wooden trap box that nestled neatly between the wheel wells in the back. I later bought a four-wheel-drive mini-pickup and found that the box also fit nicely inside the back of the truck bed. If you're trapping from an open-backed pickup, it will be necessary

(Left) A good four-wheel-drive vehicle such as this older Bronco is an excellent investment for the trapper. Its small size and short wheel base permit it to traverse many areas that conventional two-wheel drive vehicles cannot. Several coyotes were taken at this set where a cow trail crosses a sandy wash.

This four-wheel drive Toyota is also an excellent trapping vehicle. Note the metal baskets attached to the front bumper to hold traps and other paraphernalia.

to build a box that can be locked to secure the traps and other equipment. The open-backed pickup is perhaps the best type of vehicle for trapping due to the open-air design of the back; traps and trapping equipment are probably less likely to become contaminated. With the enclosed Bronco mentioned earlier, any foreign odors such as pipe, cigarette or cigar smoke inside the cab will naturally be transmitted to the traps. I am not a smoker nor has anyone who smokes ridden with me on my trapline. Otherwise, having traps inside the Bronco would have been a problem. For the trapper using a conventional automobile, it might be best to build a rack on top of the car for carrying the traps. This can be easily constructed and a car top carrier can be used as a platform base. The trapped animals and lures could be placed in the trunk.

The trapper who navigates large marshes or creeks should have a very stable boat so that traps can be set right over the gunwales, without having to get out. The boat should also be large enough to easily transport all the trapping paraphernalia. An outboard motor is indispensible and a 5-horsepower unit will have all the power you'll need. That motor should also start easily considering the number of starts and stops made during the course of a trapping day.

A motorcycle can be an asset on some traplines. When trapping an animal such as a bobcat, which tends to travel according to the lay of the land, getting away from the road can increase a trapper's success. In areas where they're allowed, such as on private land, a motorcycle will get a trapper back into the woods faster and farther than can his own legs. Some trappers place large metal milk carton baskets on the front and back of the cycle for holding plenty of traps and other related gear. Friend Slim Gilliam, uses a three-wheel ATC for carrying all sorts of trapping gear back into areas that cannot be reached by a conventional vehicle.

Other trappers may prefer to use the methods of our forebears and travel by horse or mule. However, if you're not familiar with packing a horse or mule with trapping equipment, it could be more of a headache than it's worth. Even when you're not using the beast, you have to care for it. However, a horse or mule does have an advantage, particularly in cattle country where furbearers have become accustomed to the sight and scent of livestock and their tracks. With the use of a horse, one can ride right up to a trap and check to see whether it's been sprung, whether its cover has been blown off, etc., without leaving scent or telltale human tracks. In fact, with a little practice, the horseback trapper can step off his horse right onto the trap-setting cloth without having to set foot on bare ground. This does take a bit of doing, particularly when it comes to getting back on the horse, but it can be done. Also, traps can be re-scented periodically without getting off the horse. However, trying to put the carcass of a freshly killed predator on the horse may turn into a rodeo unless you have a horse that is accustomed to it.

A horse may also serve to get you into areas which may be impassable for a vehicle. For this reason, 4-footed transportation may be useful not only for running a line daily, but for pulling traps, if necessary, when roads become snowed in or washed out.

In regions where heavy snowfall occurs, trappers have taken to snowmobiles and, these can be an excellent means of getting into the backcountry when the snows arrive. Also, snow trappers have found that some furbearers will follow the ready-made trails left by the track of the snow machine.

Whenever you're traveling in snow-covered wilderness areas, it's a good idea to travel with a buddy who is, preferably, riding his own snow machine. In addition, always take matches, snowshoes, food, a warm sleeping bag and anything else you might need for survival, just in case. If you must travel alone, which is never recommended, always tell someone when you leave, where you are going and when you plan to return.

The type of vehicle that you use for trapping is generally dependent upon the type of trapping that you intend to do and the means you have available. With a little common sense, nearly any vehicle can be modified to make it efficient for your trapline travels.

A trapping box to store all your gear in is one of the most important parts of the trapping vehicle. Your trapping equipment is less likely to pick up human or foreign odors. This trapper has lined the bottom with juniper cuttings to impart a natural scent to his traps.

chapter 10
SCOUTING FOR FURBEARERS

ONE OF THE most important things any trapper can do before laying out a trapline is to find where the furbearers are. Perhaps that sounds a bit elementary, but I don't think most first-time trappers in particular, scout an intended trapping territory as thoroughly as they could. Instead, many trappers depend upon finding sign during the season while they're setting traps. The fact is, the trapping season is too short to be spending valuable trapping time looking for sign that could have been found long before the season began.

I'm talking about the trapper who is really serious about catching a lot of fur. For the part-timer, or trapper just wanting some healthful recreation, scouting isn't all that necessary, but it is fun. Scouting for furbearers and finding sign is one of the most exciting aspects of trapping. Best of all, this sort of recreation begins long before the trapping season and, if done most effectively, will continue all year long. The more time that a trapper spends in his intended trapping territory, the more effective he's going to be when it comes to taking furbearers once the season opens.

First of all, scouting does not mean that the trapper is only looking for a place to make a set, but more to find denning areas or game trails. And, if scouting is con-

ducted in a given area over a period of many months, the trapper can pretty much determine what the animals are doing at various times of the year. Ideally, scouting for furbearers in a particular territory should begin the winter before the actual trapping begins so that the trapper will know what the animals are going to be doing during the time of year he intends to trap them. Furthermore, the amount and quality of sign that is revealed in the snow cannot be equaled. There's just no substitute for scouting.

Before going into the field, however, the trapper needs to know something about the animals he intends to trap. If a trapper doesn't have this information, he may glean it from other trappers, or from books, which are a goldmine of information on animal habits, habitat, preferred food, etc. This is all valuable information that may tell the trapper not only where to begin looking for sign, but what to look for. Only after a trapper is armed with this information is he ready to think about scouting.

The trapper is wise to take notes while scouting, particularly once he gets into an area that he knows has a lot of sign. By doing a thorough job, the trapper can actually outline his placement of traps over the entire

(Right) An experienced trapper can tell by looking at a given section of country whether it is likely to have the desired furbearers in good numbers. After spotting good country from a distance, it can be scouted for sign more closely on foot. This type of country is excellent coyote, grey fox, and bobcat habitat.

(Below) Excellent bobcat habitat. Notice the rim in the background which is generally traveled by the feline predators in their search for rodents. This trapper is scouting extra country while running his line in order to find better, more productive sets.

Sometimes, a trapper must be in good physical condition to traverse rugged terrain in his search for certain furbearers. This trapper is looking for bobcat sign along the rimrock. This is good bobcat country.

trapline before the season begins. Depending upon the species, the skill of the trapper, and the intensity of trapping, an area will generally be trapped for a period of only 2 or 3 weeks before the trapline should be moved. For this reason, just because a trapper finds one area that contains a lot of fur, he shouldn't be satisfied. Rather he should scout and pre-season plan perhaps five or six different traplines.

Planning several traplines has saved the season for many a trapper, who found an excellent looking area, sign-wise, but was discouraged to find other trappers already working it once the season opened. As long as he has several alternatives, the trapper can move, with no time delay, for he knows where several other excellent furbearing areas are.

When it comes to scouting any unfamiliar, but potentially productive trapping country, there's probably nothing more valuable than a good topographical map of the area, detailing the location of all the water holes, trails, power lines, etc. However, a topo map generally covers a relatively small section of real estate. This is okay for the trapper going after water animals, but the coyote trapper may need a map depicting a larger hunk of territory. The U.S. Forest Service puts out excellent

In time, bobcat droppings become bleached to an almost pure white and can be much more easily spotted.

A trapper who knows where to look can generally find bobcat sign such as this. Like housecats, bobcats frequently leave scratches and droppings in an area that is convenient and easy to scratch. Juniper duff is an excellent place to find these signs.

These bobcat droppings were found where a bobcat attempted to cover them with debris on the forest floor. Sometimes bobcats are successful in covering their droppings, and sometimes they are not.

maps covering the National Forests of the West and detailing not only the roads, but the water holes, major mountains and canyons as well. By using one of the Forest Service maps in combination with a topographical map, a trapper can be well prepared before going afield.

By knowing the basic habits of the animals, the trapper already knows what type of habitat is likely to contain the target species. These habitat types are noted in part on the maps — not only in regard to terrain, but water, and in some cases, vegetation. In one instance, I obtained a vegetation map for a particular area from a museum. A graduate student had gone to the trouble of constructing a detailed map of all vegetation types in the area. That map helped me quickly determine likely feeding areas, and even spots for den trees.

Maps are useful not only in detailing where the animals might be but can illustrate where public as well as private lands are. If you happen to find a good trapping area on private land, you will then want to go to the owner and ask permission to trap. In much of the West where public land is wide open to trapping and gets all the trapping pressure, one can find, by looking at maps, private land which may be locked to public access. By getting permission to trap such land, the trapper has an ideal setup. He will be assured of having no competition from other trappers because he's behind locked gates, and there won't be any "casual bypassers" to lift traps.

Once you've armed yourself with a good supply of maps, get out there and do a lot of searching. Scout the outside corners of fencerows for coyote and fox sign, and you might even spend a little time in the area at night to listen for howls. A fire engine siren cranked up at night is sure to arouse the howls of coyotes, and instantly tell you whether or not the area is potenitally productive.

If you're after animals such as foxes and bobcats, which don't necessarily follow the artificial terrain features but travel according to the lay of the land or the cover, you'll have to get out and do a good amount of walking. For instance, bobcat scratches are often found near the top lip of a canyon. You won't see this sign from the road. Generally, bobcats scratch under juniper trees in the West or in other convenient scratching areas. Their bleached-out droppings can be easily spotted near scratches.

Grey foxes generally leave droppings on rocks in brushy country. Once you've spotted a few grey fox droppings it won't be difficult to spot lots of them if there are many grey foxes in the area.

The more time you spend on foot and the more ground you cover before season, the more effective your trapline is going to be once the season begins. The footwork will reveal where the animals are traveling, where they're spending the most time, and where to make your sets.

Pre-season scouting allows the trapper to outline a trapline that will be efficient in terms of distance traveled. For example, it's easy to lay out a long trapline which has a lot of "empty" spaces with relatively few furbearers. However, by a lot of pre-season scouting, one can generally plan a trapline that eliminates or reduces those "empty" spaces. It's a matter of making the line go where the furbearers are, even if it means taking some rough roads or traveling cross-country for a distance.

The western trapper may see a lot of sign by slowly driving seldom-traveled jeep trails. The trapper farther east may not have the benefit of jeep trails and country wide open for trapping. Generally, however, he'll have a pretty good idea about potential trapping areas around his home just by judging the terrain and studying the habits of the animals that he's after. By doing so, the trapper will know what sort of terrain and vegetation is peculiar to the furbearer he is after. Furthermore, the area around a trapper's home will be more familiar and provide plenty of opportunity to frequently judge the relative numbers of animals through sightings or reported sightings by neighbors.

The trapper in the East generally has the problem of having to ask permission to trap because most of the land is privately owned. Furthermore, the size of those privately owned pieces of land generally become smaller the further east you go. Consequently, the serious trapper may have to obtain permission from quite a few landowners in order to simply put out an effective trapline. However, this is all part of the game and again, by so doing, the trapper may be eliminating competition from other trappers. Once a landowner has given permission to trap his land he generally prohibits others from doing so.

Since there aren't as many jeep trails in the East, it's absolutely necessary to spend time on foot. Also, sign can be a little more difficult to spot in the East where it rains more frequently. Those rains may promote lush vegetation, but they also wash away sign. However, once the trapper knows where an animal is likely to leave sign, he can quickly ascertain whether a given area has the animals in good numbers. This is another reason for scouting during winter snowfall. Tracks readily show up in the snow if there are many furbearers around.

In any given country there are natural terrain features which act as "squeezers" that concentrate animal movements and, subsequently, serve as good spots to check for sign. In some instances, the "squeezer" could be a large draw which forces most of the animals in that area to travel around its head or perimeter where traveling is easier. Another example of a "squeezer" is a wide creek that has a narrow point with a log laying across the stream and serving as a bridge for a good number of raccoons, bobcats and other furbearers. The outside corners of fencerows, mentioned earlier, is an-

Brushy draws form a type of "squeezer" to concentrate animal movements. Furbearers will generally take the path of least resistance and cross the draw at its head rather than trying to cross the ditch. Also, brushy "points" which extend into open areas also make for excellent set locations. This is an excellent bobcat set location which the author spotted from a distance of several hundred yards. There is a packrat's nest in a brushpile at the bottom of the shallow draw next to the big tree. The author placed a bobcat set at the base of the tree (below left) and a coyote set at the point of the draw. In 3 day's time, these two sets accounted for three bobcats and one coyote.

A large male bobcat nabbed on the first day at the "squeezer" set location.

Trapper Kent Dederick is shown here approaching a beaver hut (left). Contrary to what some people believe, inhabited beaver huts are not always located in the water. (Below) He spreads branches aside to peer into the hut to see whether it was inhabited. Indeed, beavers were living inside this partially constructed hut. In many states it is against the law to molest animals in dens or huts such as this. Be sure to check local laws regarding this practice.

(Left) Dederick is shown here examining beaver gnawings. Close examination can establish the relative size of the beaver based upon the size of the tooth marks on the trunk and the height of the gnawings from the ground.

(Right) The place that you will be scouting for furbearers is dependent upon the furbearer that you intend to take. Here, Kent Dederick examines the mud along a lake inlet where beaver have been dragging trees into the water.

The scouting trapper will immediately recognize this beaver dam on a small creek as an active beaver colony and a possible place for set locations.

Here is a very small beaver dam, actually many yards below the main beaver dam above. On many streams beavers will have several dams constructed. There's generally one large body of water where beavers will be living and working, from either huts or, in the case of this creek, bank dens.

other type of "squeezer." Foxes or coyotes will generally travel along a fencerow and then around the outside corner where they'll frequently have a scenting post. Open gates, pond dams and cow trails also concentrate furbearer movements.

Such areas should be scouted for sign as they generally make excellent setting locations. When you're scouting for furbearers watch for all types of sign, not just tracks and droppings, but scratches, burrows, den trees, any signs of feeding, etc. Of course, the sign you look for will depend upon the specific furbearer you're after.

You may be trapping small creeks or streams which run through farmland. In such areas the creeks will undoubtedly be crossed, periodically, by roads and bridges. Concrete bridge abutments along creeks are excellent places to scout for the sign of furbearers that live in or near water. One can simply park his vehicle near the bridge, get out, and walk down under it to scout for tracks along the water's edge. This is an excel-

lent place to scout for raccoon and mink. Mink will frequent the grassy areas around those bridge abutments, possibly looking for cottontail rabbits, mice or other rodents.

A good mink trapper once told me that he could scout a bridge and quickly determine whether or not mink were inhabiting the area. However, you're not really doing your job if you only scout around bridges. It's frequently only a mile or two up or downstream to the next bridge, and if you have a partner who can drop you off at one bridge and pick you up at the next, your walk may be very revealing as to the activities of furbearers along the creek. (Be sure to take your hip boots!)

Muskrat dens can be seen in the bank; beaver cuttings are readily noticeable; mink tracks can be spotted on mud bars; the tracks of a raccoon and its food droppings can be seen at the water's edge. In short, the trapper quickly gets a feel for the relative numbers of each type of furbearer that is using the area. Not only will

Kent Dederick is shown here probing for a beaver runway to a bank den. Sometimes such den entrances cannot be seen—they must be felt. One of the best ways to scout for beaver "runs" is to simply put on the chest waders, get in the water, and feel for them with your feet. Note the thin ice on the water.

Here is an area where beaver have been dragging their cuttings down the steep bank along the water's edge. Such a site makes an excellent set location for snares located along the "slide."

This beaver den entrance at the small inlet of water on the opposite side of the creek can be covered with either a Conibear trap or a foot-hold-type trap.

you spot sign, you'll also determine potential areas for sets.

Once the trapper ascertains that there are a good number of furbearers in the area, it may pay to go back and map out each set location. Information about a particular concentration of muskrat dens, feed beds, natural investigation holes for mink or 'coon, etc., should be jotted down in the notebook. In fact, a trapper may wish to construct artificial cubbies or pre-make other types of sets which will pay off in time saved later when the opening of trapping season arrives.

A scouting trapper who is traveling by boat can accomplish much the same thing on a lake or marsh. By spending several days in pre-season scouting a given stretch of river or marsh, you can also learn to anticipate the water level. It can be helpful to know how much a stream or marsh will fluctuate after a heavy rainstorm, or even under normal rainfall or dry conditions. In coastal areas the tides must be studied and anticipated. This information could be a factor in determining the types of sets you'll need to make in order to avoid problems associated with changing tides. Walking a creek or cross-country over a future trapline also offers the trapper some idea as to how long it will take to

Here's a beaver slide leading down the steep bank down into water. Note the beaver-chewed trees up on the bank.

Beavers have been working along this muddy bank and dragging cuttings into the water. Again, these are excellent set locations for snaring beaver.

cover his chosen line once the season opens. What's more, he's developing muscles that will be used later on when its time to check the traps. When the season does open, running the line will be more of a pleasure and less of an effort.

Pre-season scouting can become as time-consuming and thorough as the trapper wishes to make it. There are some trappers who, once they have established a trapline, will pre-make each individual set. For example, fox trappers often dig dirt holes and bait them several weeks prior to the season. In short, the trapper is conditioning the local fox population. Then, when the season opens, all that's necessary is to place a trap in front of the hole and begin harvesting the "trained" animals.

The bobcat and marten trapper can also get a jump on things through the pre-season building of cubbies and leaning-pole sets. Just like the fox example used above, bobcats and martens will become used to the presence of those cubbies and leaning-pole sets well before the season starts. A leaning-pole set, if it's constructed in the proper place, may see steady use by pine marten long before the season begins. A hollow log, rolled into the right place, will become a familiar run to

Beaver droppings, unlike the droppings from other animals found along the creekbank, can readily be discerned due to the sawdust in them.

This intermittent stream offers excellent set locations. Predatory furbearers such as coyotes and bobcats travel along the edge of the stream, possibly on top of the bank at the upper left of the photo. Other furbearers such as raccoons and mink travel right next to the water's edge. Raccoons travel in the shallow water while animals such as foxes and bobcats seek out rabbits and other rodents in the thick brush shown in the lower portion of the photo

mink. Then, when the season opens, all you have to do is place the trap.

Mink generally have certain routes of travel and sometimes definite paths, particularly when it comes to dense marsh grass between ponds. Pre-season scouting reveals where these are so that natural travel routes can be immediately covered once trapping season opens. This way, you will be able to set a higher number of traps on the very first day of the season.

Remember, it's the first of the season that generally produces the most fur and anything you can do to get effective fur-producing traps out the very first night, the better off you are. Later in the season the animals will become fewer because of the foul weather and the fact that other trappers will be successfully working the areas. In short, the animals will become more wary due to the increased trapping pressure. For these reasons, the successful trapper is the man who gets a head start and knows what he's going to do *before* the season starts.

There's no limit to the detail that pre-season scouting might involve. For example, good beaver and muskrat trappers make it a point to learn every beaver and muskrat runway along the line before the season. Each bank den can be noted or even marked with a stick. (The runways and dens are found by probing any likely-looking denning spots along the bank with a long pole. When the pole easily slips through the surface of the bank, you've found your den.)

By getting a head start, you'll generally end up working a particular area for a shorter period of time. This means that you're more efficient at removing the available furbearers and can pull your traps and move to a

Coyote droppings found on the forest floor are a surefire indication that a coyote has been here and very possibly will return.

second or third trapping area before someone else moves in later. The longer the trapping season runs, the greater the chance that someone has already trapped a likely area.

The last few pages have been directed primarily at the serious trapper. For the person doing it on a recreational basis, such factors can be important though not imperative. It may be a disappointment if you're a recreational trapper and find that someone else moved into your intended trapping area before you did. But, for the full-time professional, it can mean a slim Christmas.

Don't overlook the landowners themselves as valuable sources of information regarding the presence and habits of furbearers. There are few people who know the land better than the farmers who spend all year on it. They're there all the time, and notice when a fox

This is another example of beaver droppings; sawdust very noticeable. Sometimes, this type of sign can be found even when beaver cuttings, slides, etc., are not readily visible.

This beaver hut has been packed with mud. Though it is located along the edge of the water, rather than in it, trenches dug under the hut lead into the inlet. These are the places to position traps.

crosses the back pasture when they're doing chores in winter. They will also know if muskrats have been digging into their farm-pond dam, possibly draining it. Believe me, a farmer will know if a raccoon gets into the henhouse and cleans the eggs out of the nests. They can also hardly ignore the fact that a mink got into the brooder house last spring and killed 40 young chickens. For these reasons, and more, farmers are usually pleased to see a trapper stop by. For the same reasons, the average farmer is usually eager to supply information as to the location of furbearers on his property.

The trapper is wise to help a farmer any way that he can. One form of assistance is to eliminate problem animals — even if it means trapping an animal which is not necessarily desirable to the trapper. It may require taking extra time to run half a dozen traps at an isolated pond, even though there are relatively few 'rats in it. Such efforts will be more than repaid to the trapper, in terms of hospitality, the next time he wants to trap that farmer's land. In the end, the trapper's job of scouting isn't just a matter of finding furbearers. The wise trapper is the man who befriends the landowner and is willing to promote his hobby in a positive manner. In short, "courtesy" and "diplomacy" are two of the trappers best tools when it comes scouting out new trapping locations.

chapter 11
LARGE FURBEARERS

COYOTE

TRAP SIZE: No. 3 or 4
BAIT: Gland lure
PRIME: December
STRETCHER: No. 6
TRACK:

THE COYOTE *(Canis latrans)* is a member of the dog family and in many ways resembles a small German shepherd. Coyotes vary considerably in size, with adults usually measuring 40 to 53 inches from nose tip to tail tip and weighing 15 to 50 pounds. One New Mexico sampling of 829 coyotes indicated an average weight of 24.4 pounds for males, 22.2 pounds for females. I once weighed 77 northern Arizona coyotes taken during the first half of November; their weight ranged from 17 to 34 pounds with the average about 21 pounds. I'm certain that I have taken coyotes weighing in the neighborhood of 50 pounds though I have never put any on a scale that ran that high. The heaviest coyote among Fish and Wildlife Service records is a male killed near Afton, Wyoming, on November 19, 1937 — it tipped the scales at 74¾ pounds! This coyote had been killing sheep, was very fat, and measured 63 inches from the tip of the nose to the tip of the tail.

Coyotes range in color from browns to greys to whites — depending partially upon the latitude, the local habitat, and the individual gene pool.

The coyote, though it somewhat resembles a small German shepherd, has a more pointed nose, and ears that never fold over or droop. Male coyotes have a bushier tail than do the females with the male dog frequently appearing larger overall. When a pair is running together, as is often the case during mating season, the trained eye can determine at a glance which one is the male and which one is the female.

Nineteen subspecies of coyotes have been defined, most of them found in North America. The coyote is indigenous to the western United States, Canada, and Mexico. All evidence indicates that the coyotes' range has been increasing in this century, particularly since World War II. This is amazing when you consider the fact that *Canis* has been and is being constantly poisoned, trapped, dug from dens, gunned from planes, coursed with dogs and shot on sight. The coyote's status has been elevated among trappers in recent years, due in part to high pelt prices which have renewed the interest in trapping this furbearer. Even though the trapping of coyotes has been intensive and widespread, it has had little or no effect on coyote populations.

Until recently, many states offered bounties for killing coyotes; as late as the latter '60s I collected a $2 bounty (paid by the county) for eastern Kansas coyote ears. Some 30 miles away, across the state line in Missouri, coyote scalps brought $15; as a result a lot of Kansas coyote ears illegally ended up in Missouri. This is only one of the problems associated with bounties. On the whole, bounties have proved to be expensive with negligible long-term effects on coyote populations.

It must also be mentioned that the coyotes' range extends into Central America, and its numbers have increased dramatically in the northeastern United States.

Reportedly, it frequently interbreeds with dogs in the Northeast to form an even larger subspecies.

One reason that coyotes are expanding their range is that they have the ability to adapt readily to man's spreading urban development. This is in contrast to the wolf which has been forced into the more remote northern regions by encroaching civilization.

Another reason the coyote is expanding its range and increasing its numbers, despite intensive predator and fur-hunting pressure, is that the animal is so prolific. Female coyotes often breed at the age of 1 year and generally have from 2 to 10 pups with an average litter running around 5 or 6. However, as many as 19 pups have been recorded in a single litter.

Studies indicate that coyotes multiply at a rate relative to the available food supply. If food is abundant, litters are larger. If coyote populations are high and rodent populations, or any other food is limited, litter size decreases.

The breeding season varies with latitude but is generally during February and March with the young being born in April and May after a 63-day gestation period. Coyotes generally whelp in a den consisting of a modified abandoned badger burrow, but they have been known to give birth in many other locations such as in a ravine, under tree roots, in a brush patch, etc. Prior to having her young, a female coyote will sometimes prepare a number of denning sites. Then, after the pups are born, if one den is disturbed or visited by man, she will move the pups to one of the other dens. It is not unusual for two families to occupy a single den. To wit, a young female bearing her first litter will sometimes occupy the same den as her mother.

Coyotes frequently retain the same mate for several years — the male generally breeding with only one female. In some instances, though, a single male will mate with two females, both of which will occupy the same den. When the pups are young, the male coyote plays a major role in hunting for food. The bitch, of course, nurses her pups. However, when her milk begins to dry up, she will then take to hunting. She will gorge herself on food and then return to the den, disgorging the partially-digested food for the pups to feed on. If the bitch is killed and the pups are too young to wean, they die. However, if they are old enough, the male will care for them until they are able to make it on their own. When the pups are 8- to 10-weeks old the coyote den is abandoned, the family traveling about in search of food.

Coyotes are not selective regarding their diet. This, no doubt, is a major factor in their adaptability to a variety of climatic types and geographic conditions. They apparently prefer to eat meat whether it be beef, lamb, pork, poultry, game birds, deer, elk, antelope, rabbit, ground squirrel, or prairie dog. They also eat insects, worms, fish, frogs, fruit, grass, sticks, berries, carrion

Coyotes are very scent-wise and wary and are thought by unknowing trappers to be very difficult to trap. However, the wise trapper who is careful to take all precautions to avoid leaving scent at the trap setting site will find that coyotes are very susceptible to proper trapping techniques.

— almost anything that can sustain them. In a 6-year sampling of 30,000 coyote stomachs, the U.S. Fish and Wildlife Service found that, in most cases, rabbits comprised the bulk of the coyotes' diet, with rodents, carrion and livestock also turning up in high percentages.

The coyote is an efficient killer. A few years ago I watched a coyote patrol a grassy meadow during late September. It was hunting field mice, and in three attempts at mouse catching, it never missed. Though a mouse would appear to be a relatively small tidbit for an animal the size of a coyote, the coyote, due to the efficiency of its predation, can apparently fill itself readily on such small morsels. A stomach examination of one Oregon coyote taken during September revealed 20 meadow mice and one song sparrow. In another instance, 30 pocket mice and one kangaroo rat were removed from the stomach of a California coyote taken during November.

Once, I watched a coyote chase and catch a cottontail rabbit in Arizona during the dry, dusty summer season. *Canis* surprised the rabbit in open country, and the quick cottontail rapidly gained a lead before the pred-

This coyote was trapped at a scent post set along a cow trail. Few coyotes can resist a scent post set.

ator got into gear. *Canis* closed the gap fast, hit the rabbit, and tumbled end over end in a cloud of dust. When the air cleared, the coyote emerged with the rabbit in its mouth.

Coyotes are extremely fond of young deer and antelope. Given this, it's not surprising that recent studies reveal coyotes as the primary limiting factor to antelope fawn survival rates in many areas. But it's not only the young of these animals that the coyote preys upon. They have also been known to take down healthy, full-grown deer and antelope. There is at least one documented instance of several coyotes working in unison to kill a cow elk in deep snow.

The coyote is equally efficient at killing domestic livestock such as sheep and poultry. This latter diet has resulted in intensive coyote trapping from time to time, even though its fur has traditionally been worth very little in relation to other furbearing animals. As mentioned earlier, fur prices of long-haired animals have soared in recent years, and the coyote is now being trapped for more positive reasons.

Scouting for Sign

Droppings are perhaps the most frequently seen sign of the coyote and can even be readily seen by the observant traveler motoring down roads or highways at high rates of speed. In fact, I have found that this is one of the best ways to scout for coyotes in my area. I simply

A well-furred coyote is a prize. The trapper who takes these predators really has to know his stuff.

If the trapping country is brushy, a grapnel can be used to the trapper's advantage. When the trapped coyote hooks up on brush such as this, it spends all of its time chewing on and fighting on the bushes, rather than the trap.

scout and drive, particularly over the seldom-traveled, four-wheel trails common here in the West. If there are a lot of coyotes in the area, there will be a lot of droppings. Coyotes not only leave their droppings in jeep trails, but in cow trails as well, for they, too, travel those convenient pathways.

There are certain points along those routes where coyotes are more likely to leave droppings than others. One example is where a road or trail crosses a ridge that is flat on top. If the country is flat, droppings are likely to be found near the intersections of roads or cow trails. In a dry year when water is scarce, droppings will often be found in proximity (1-mile or less) to a water hole. In some cases droppings will be found around water holes in great number while few will be found elsewhere.

It's a good idea, in scouting for coyote sign, to walk the perimeter of water holes and look closely for coyote tracks in the soft mud. Tracks may also be seen in the dust of cow trails and along the edges of dirt roads. Coyotes seem to be particularly fond of hanging around herds of cattle, and if livestock is plentiful, coyote tracks in cow trails are continually being obliterated by passing cattle. This can be an advantage to the observant trapper because he then has an ongoing record of how many coyotes are *currently* in the area simply by looking for coyote tracks on well-used cow trails. If coyote tracks are found on those well-used trails day after day, the trapper can be certain that coyotes are in the area.

An observant trapper can also learn to distinguish dog tracks from coyote tracks. The tracks of the *Canis* are not as round as a dog's. In general, a coyote print is more ovate, its toes closer together — not splayed as a dog's toes generally are. The toenails in a coyote track appear separate from the rest of the track and are generally pointed forward or inward — not outward as a dog's frequently are.

If the trapper is scouting an area that has had a lot of rainfall, it's a bit more difficult to spot coyote sign for a couple of reasons: first, rain washes away both tracks and droppings; secondly, a lot of rain promotes the growth of grasses and other vegetation that make it more difficult to spot coyote sign, particularly tracks. Also, because there's more water available in such a region, coyote tracks aren't as likely to be concentrated around any single water hole.

In the farmlands of the Midwest, coyote travels are frequently influenced by fencerows. Look for coyote droppings around the outside corners of long fencerows, particularly in pastures. Coyotes also tend to travel along the edges of a field. For example, when a farmer plants wheat there are several feet between the last row of wheat and the ground cover next to the fencerow. This leaves a natural pathway for a coyote to trav-

The author examines a coyote dropping. The hole in the background at first appeared to be a coyote den, but closer examination revealed that it was a burrowing owls' den, and coyote(s) had apparently excavated and eaten the owls.

el; and, it should be checked for tracks and droppings.

Denning sites are yet another form of coyote sign. Coyote dens are more easily found just after the pups have been whelped. The presence of abandoned dens aren't, however, of much value immediately before trapping season as the occupants may have left those dens several months before. But, if you find *active* dens in the early spring, it's likely that the coyotes won't be far away next fall. Besides tracks and droppings, coyotes leave scratches in the soil similar to the scratches that a dog might make. Scratched areas will be found in close proximity to the droppings.

Another method of scouting for coyotes is with the use of sound. As odd as the following sounds, all you have to do is get into coyote country at night, and turn on a siren — the coyotes will respond with a lot of howling. By moving through potential coyote country and sounding the siren every mile or two you can get a rough estimate as to the number of coyotes present.

Another method of determining local predator populations is by looking at a copy of "Indices of Predator Abundance in the Western United States" published by the U.S. Fish and Wildlife Service. This federal agency has been taking a coyote "census" of sorts in the 17 western states since 1972. The information contained in this sizable publication is interesting and valuable, particularly for the trapper who is willing to travel in order to get into the best coyote trapping areas.

Coyotes can be found nearly anywhere, but, low brush country that harbors a good rodent or small game population is an excellent place to start looking. I have hunted and trapped coyotes in dense forest, open plains, farmlands, etc., all with excellent success. The trapper's best method for determining local coyote population density is to simply get out and scout for sign.

Coyotes do move from one spot to another — apparently staying in one area for a few days and then moving on to another not far away. For this reason, I find it's particularly advantageous to scout for coyote sign and monitor their movements for a couple of weeks prior to trapping season. Believe me, it's to the trapper's advantage to know where the coyotes are when trapping season opens.

Because coyotes travel, it's beneficial to run long trap lines. If a trapper runs only a few traps in a limited area, he may have a good catch for a few days; however, the coyotes in that area may move out and nothing will be caught until the coyotes return. A few years ago I ran a 60-mile, figure-eight trapline in very open, barren, flat country. One reason that I trapped so much country was that there were not a lot of coyotes per square mile, nor were there a lot of places that one could set a trap that would be hidden from view of the road. Even though the line was long, I ran only 60 traps and averaged nearly four coyotes per night for 3 weeks on that line.

When to Trap for Prime Pelts

Coyote pelts become prime at slightly different times, depending upon latitude and local elevation. In most cases, coyotes are at their peak in December and the first part of January. However, I have taken good ones during the latter part of October through the middle of February.

If coyotes are taken too early, the skin side of the pelt has a bluish color. A prime coyote pelt appears almost pure white on the skin side.

Bascially, a coyote has two types of hairs, longer coarser guard hairs and shorter, finer hairs or "nat" found underneath the guard hairs. The guard hairs give the coyote its overall coloration while the nat provides the animal with insulation and warmth.

In late February the mating season is well underway and a coyote's pelt will sometimes be rubbed during this period. Then the fur begins to shed a little later in the year, and the pelt becomes "springy," as fur buyers call it, the guard hairs on top of the shoulders taking on a slightly curled or singed appearance. Later in the spring the nat begins to fall out leaving only the guard hairs, forming a scraggly, coarse pelt.

A fur buyer familiar with pelts coming from his local area can generally determine the time of year, to within a few weeks, when a coyote was taken. Of course, a trapper loses money if he takes a coyote when its pelt is not prime.

The Coyote's Keen Senses

All the coyotes' senses are extemely keen, but, it relies most strongly upon its nose when it comes to staying out of danger. Accordingly anything that's suspicious and smells of man is avoided by the coyote. A trap that has been handled by bare hands, even though buried under nearly 1-inch of soil, can be readily detected by a coyote's nose. If a trap has been tainted with the scent of bait or lure, a coyote is likely to dig the trap out of its bed. Too, it must be said that a coyote's vision is keen and any trap set that does not blend well with its surroundings or appear natural will be readily detected and avoided.

A coyote also has quick reflexes, and if a trap pan travels too far before releasing the trap jaws, a coyote will sometimes jerk its foot out without getting caught. If a coyote is not caught securely by the trap jaws, it may have the strength to jerk out. If the trap stake is not long enough, a coyote's jumping may pull it up, particularly if the trapper is using the short trap chains that have recently become popular.

The most important and frequently overlooked aspect of trapping coyotes can be stated in one word — scent. Keeping traps and trap-setting materials absolutely free of human scent is, in my experience, the single greatest contributor to coyote trapping success. This is one aspect that is too often overlooked or ignored by the beginning trapper and is no doubt the reason that coyotes have a reputation for being difficult to catch. No doubt, it is also the reason that coyotes become readily educated to traps.

Be certain to boil all coyote traps, trap covers, grapnels, and even stake tops to remove any human scent. The details about trap dyeing, waxing, and boiling are covered in a separate chapter and the would-be coyote trapper would be wise to follow those steps closely.

If a rabbit is caught in a coyote set, the trap may as well be pulled and replaced, the set moved a few feet and re-made. Any trap that holds the scent of a prey species is likely to be dug out by the coyote. This may surprise the novice, but it is common knowledge to the experienced trapper. Be careful to keep any trapping scent or lure off the traps so that there is no odor coming from the point where the trap is located.

Though it probably isn't necessary, even traps that

have caught coyotes are replaced with "clean" ones when I'm trapping. It's my feeling that a little blood on the trap *could* arouse suspicion among subsequent coyotes. As a result I prefer not to have any scent whatever on the trap. I've also found it's best to direct the coyote's attention to whatever is intended to attract the animal if an attractor is used. Even if there is none, such as a blind set, it's still best if the coyote has no indication that anything foreign is present.

In addition, when trapping coyotes, I wear rubber soled boots that aren't worn anywhere except in the field and in the vehicle. I place my feet on a clean rubber mat on the floor of the trapping vehicle as well and avoid brushing against bushes when walking from the vehicle to the trap site. In short, it's important to do everything possible to avoid leaving human scent at trap sites. There are inexperienced young coyotes that will be fooled even by sloppy technique, but to catch consistently, *don't leave human scent*. When setting traps, even with the aid of a trap-setting cloth, I avoid kneeling but rather squat on the rubber soles. Clean rubber gloves are used in trap setting and care is taken to avoid contaminating the outside of these gloves with either human scent or coyote lure.

Trap Size and Type

No. 3 or 4 size double spring traps have been the favorites of the coyote trapper for many years. The reason the double spring trap is so popular is that it can come up through a lot of cover, and after its jaws close, the springs have holding power second to none. The trapper must, however, dig a larger bed for the double spring trap than for other trap types, but the advantages are worth it.

In my opinion it's generally best to use a grapnel when trapping coyotes rather than staking the trap solid because a coyote, when caught, immediately lunges and jerks. If a grapnel with a long chain is used the coyote easily jerks the chain and grapnel out of its bed under the trap and then drags the grapnel behind it until it's hooked up in brush. This is in contrast to the staked trap which offers solid resistance and an opportunity for a coyote to jerk its foot out on those initial lunges when it's strong and before the trap jaws have a secure grip.

If the grapnel is properly constructed, the trapper will have no difficulty following the drag marks over soil or snow. Grapnels are also ideal for the trapper who places

MAKING A SCENT POST SET FOR COYOTE

1. The author is shown here looking for a place to make a scent post set along this trail. Coyotes have the habit of urinating upon small bushes along a trail such as this.

his traps close to a road. With the grapnel, a coyote usually gets hooked up in the brush, away from the road, and is not as readily seen by anyone passing by. Furthermore, a grapnel permits the coyote to leave the trapping site and not destroy it. In short, the site can be easily reconstructed and used to catch another coyote. If you are trapping along a trail that leads toward bait, the grapnel allows three or four traps to be placed along the trail, close together. The first coyote caught will run away from the trap site and won't spook others moving down the same trail.

If one is trapping open country, where there is only short grass and nothing for a grapnel to hook onto, a stake is mandatory. The length of the stake used is dependent upon the soil type. If the soil is sandy, a long stake is necessary. If the soil is composed of heavy clay, a short one might be okay. Regardless of stake length, it is important that swivels are used or other provisions made so that the trap chain does not wrap around the stake and/or kink up allowing the coyote to twist off.

There has been some disagreement regarding the length of chain necessary when a coyote trap is staked solid. Some feel that a short chain is best so that a coyote cannot get as much strength into its running jerk. Others say that a short chain contributes to stake pull-ups and that a long one eliminates the chance of this. I have used both the short and long chains on solidly-staked traps and don't believe that it makes all that much difference as long as the stake is of ample length.

In my experience, coyotes do not gnaw themselves out of a trap unless temperatures get well below freezing. When running a trapline after a cold night — say zero or below — it's best to check the line as early and quickly as possible. *Caution:* Avoid getting too close to trapped animals — particularly if they are excited and jumping about wildly. Dispatch any trapped animals as quickly as possible for you cannot be certain if you have a secure hold on them, particularly during cold weather.

On two separate occasions I have had coyotes pull out of a trap *after* I arrived upon the scene. Believe me, shooting at a running animal is more difficult than shooting a trapped one.

Coyote Sets

There are three basic sets that work extremely well for coyote trapping. The would-be trapper can do very

3. With the trap setting cloth in position and the tools on the cloth, the trapper begins excavating the trap bed beneath the bush. The excavated earth is placed upon the "sifter." If the ground is soft a small gardener's spade makes an excellent digging tool, but when the earth is hard, a brick hammer makes the work easier. It's important that the trapper be careful to avoid leaving human scent by brushing against any bushes around the site.

2. Before touching any trap equipment it is mandatory to put the rubber gloves on. The author avoids any chance of contamination by pulling the gloves on with his teeth.

well by perfecting only one or two.

Besides traps, you'll need stakes or grapnels and chain, a hammer for driving stakes, a small spade or trowel for digging the trap bed, trap covers, and a dirt sifter made with ¼-inch wire mesh. I've also found that the sharp head of a brick-hammer works very well for loosening up really tough soil. If you happen to have one, take it along — it may come in handy. A trap-setting cloth is also necessary for standing and placing equipment upon; and, be sure to take a trap basket to carry the tools you'll be using. Clean rubber gloves and boots are necessary, and different types of baits and scents are needed as well, depending upon the set to be made.

Scent-Post Set

One set is probably used by coyote trappers more than any other and is referred to by different names such as scent post, flat set, urinating post, etc. It's based on the fact that a coyote may urinate onto any prominent bush, rock, chunk of wood, etc., along a trail or road. Further, any coyote traveling down a trail will stop to investigate another coyote's scent that was pre-viously deposited.

When making a scent-post set, the trapper artifically reproduces a natural scent post, using a coyote gland lure or urine to fool the coyote. The best place to make a scent-post set is where a coyote would naturally scent a bush or weed — along a jeep trail or cow trail, particularly in open, short grass country. A prominent low bush or bushy weed should be selected — one that's a bit higher than the others but low enough for a coyote to see over. It should be about a foot off the trail. (In the case of a cow trail, this distance will prevent any by-passing cattle from springing the trap.) Some trappers will even go to the trouble of placing coyote droppings at a scenting post. In fact, it's a good idea to make a set wherever coyote droppings are naturally found along a trail.

If you're traveling a jeep trail, the potential trapping site can be spotted from the vehicle. If you're going to set your traps along a cow trail, you'll be afoot. When approaching any trap site, be it in a vehicle or on foot, avoid leaving tracks, particularly in the trail — they could alert a wary coyote. Instead, walk 10 or 20 feet off the trail in the grass when looking for a trapping site.

5. The aluminum screen trap covering is positioned over the trap pan and under the jaws.

4. A completely excavated and properly positioned trap bed beneath the bush. Hopefully a coyote will pass this way to lift its leg on the bush and get caught. This particular bed is excavated for a trap that will be staked solid. If a grapnel were to be used, a deeper hole is necessary.

When walking, be careful not to brush against weeds or bushes; in short, be careful not to contact any of the surroundings with anything except your rubber boots.

After you've located a likely looking bush or weed, spread the trap-setting cloth within easy reach of the bush (in the trail is okay) and place its edge very near the intended excavation for the trap. You can now step on the cloth, being certain to keep all tools *on the cloth* at all times. The trap will be placed between the bush and the cow trail with the center of the trap pan approximately 6 to 7 inches from the base of the bush.

Place the dirt sifter near the edge of the trap-setting cloth, next to the intended excavation. Using the trowel or spade, begin digging the trap "bed" in which to bury the trap. Next, place the loose dirt you've just excavated in the dirt sifter which will be used later to sift dirt over the trap. Don't dig the bed any larger than necessary because, first, it's easier to camouflage a smaller hole, and secondly, it's best not to have any excess loose soil for a coyote to step on before it steps into the trap — it could alert the coyote too soon. My best advice is to dig the trap bed deep enough so that about ½-inch of sifted soil will cover the trap when everything is complete. If a grapnel is used, a deeper hole must be dug so that the grapnel and long chain can be placed beneath the trap. Just dig the bed in the shape of the trap. The long trap springs should be angled toward either side of the bush — not toward the trail where the coyote can step on them.

After the bed is prepared, it's time to set the trap. In case you haven't guessed, a coyote trap is large, and it takes some strength to depress the flat springs. I generally place the trap on the setting cloth in front of me with the trap's trigger facing away from me. The next step is to place a foot on each spring, then depress them while pulling the jaws apart with the gloved hands. If more strength is needed, simply pull on the trap jaws to force the feet down harder. Once the jaws are opened, place the trap trigger in the notch while pushing the pan upward with a hand *under* the free jaw — you don't want to get your fingers pinched.

Now that the trap is set, you'll probably find that the free jaw does not lie flat and has a tendency to cock upward. Just swing the springs toward the trap trigger or dog until they're at about a 45-degree angle to the jaws, and the free jaw will lie flat.

6. (Left) The trap is firmly seated so that it won't tip if pressure is placed upon one of the long springs. The author now pounds the twisted square bar stock stake through the trap ring into the firm soil, using a 6-pound sledge. The stake should be driven in far enough that the top will not show once everything is covered.

7. Sift the excavated earth back over the trap. Sifting prevents stones or sticks of any size from jamming trap jaws once sprung by a coyote.

Now pick up the trap, keeping upward pressure on the pan at all times with one hand, so the trap can't "spring" while you're holding it, and put the trap cover in place over the trap pan and under the jaws. I generally use aluminum screen as a trap cover.

Now, place the set trap in its bed, driving the stake through the retaining ring. Next check the trap to see how it lies in the bed. Wiggle it around to "seat" the base plate and springs firmly in the bed. If this isn't done, and a coyote steps on a spring or trap jaw before stepping between the jaws, the trap could tip out of the soil, revealing itself and alarming the coyote.

Once the trap is seated firmly in its bed with the trap cover in place, pick up the dirt sifter and gently sift the excavated soil over the trap until everything is level with the surrounding earth. If necessary, carefully use the trowel to smooth out the bumps.

Now take the trowel and, a few yards away from the trap site, skim off a bit of sun dried topsoil that is similar to the soil where the trap is located. Carry this soil to the set and sprinkle it on top of the trap to camouflage the appearance of the freshly excavated dirt. If done carefully, it's difficult to recognize where the trap is

when everything is completed. The next step is to place a bit of coyote gland lure or urine on the bush or at its base. I usually insert a small stick into the bottle and withdraw it with some lure, leaving stick and lure both in the bush. Don't get lure on the gloves, and don't touch the stick with the bare hands.

Now put all the tools back in the trap basket, step back, and carefully pick up the trap-setting cloth with the excess dirt enclosed. Step away from the trap site and with a mighty heave, sling the dirt in a fan-shaped direction *away* from the set. Next, brush up the packed-down area where you squatted. A wisk broom or trap cloth works well to dust the area and remove all signs of it having been disturbed. If you're setting your traps along a jeep trail, a few passes with the vehicle adds further realism and camouflage to the set. This completes the "flat" or "scent-post" set. When a coyote comes along the trail, its nose will detect the scent in the bush and it will step off the trail to investigate . . . Bingo, you've scored a coyote pelt!

Blind Sets

Another type of coyote set is used in conjunction with

8. The author applies a lure to the bush to attract any coyotes passing down the trail. In this instance, the lure was made from glands of previously trapped coyotes. Since the stick will be left at the site, it is handled only with the rubber gloved hand. This way, there will be no human scent remaining at the trap site.

9. (Right) With the gland scent placed in the bush, the excess dirt is carefully picked up on the trap setting cloth, as shown here.

(Right) This coyote is held fast in the jaws of a Victor No. 4 double spring trap. It fell victim to the dirt hole set.

the carcass of a dead animal. As most outdoorsmen know, a cow or horse carcass attracts many coyotes. However, many would-be trappers make the mistake of setting traps close to the carcass. After all, that's where most of the tracks are. The problem is that a lot of crows, vultures, and possibly even eagles will also utilize that same carcass as a food source. More often than not, those same birds will spring the traps that were intended for coyotes.

The remedy is to place your traps along trails leading toward the carcass but at least 50 or 100 yards away from it. Even if there are no permanent cow trails nearby, close scrutiny will usually reveal certain points where coyotes approach the carcass regularly, leaving indistinct trails. This is where a trapper is likely to score. In this instance, no sort of scent or bait is necessary.

Bury your traps, using the setting technique described in the scent-post set in the trails leading to the

10. Backing a few steps away from the setting site, the author flings the earth in a wide arc so that it will not arouse the suspicions of any wary canine predator.

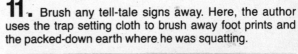

11. Brush any tell-tale signs away. Here, the author uses the trap setting cloth to brush away foot prints and the packed-down earth where he was squatting.

A coyote trapped at a dirt hole set along a cow trail. As can be seen here, the dirt hole set can be constructed where there is no vegetation.

(Left) The dirt hole set can be just as effective for coyote as it can for red fox trapping. Here is a dirt hole set made along a cow trail. The trap is placed right at the edge of the hole between the hole and the trail. The freshly excavated earth is scattered over the top of the trap and cow trail to peak the interest of any coyote passing along this pathway. An egg-sized chunk of tainted meat is partially buried in the bottom of the hole. A food-type scent is placed along the back side of the hole. (Note the small stick back of the hole.) Coyotes are very suspicious by nature and will avoid this side of the hole. All precautions regarding the prevention of leaving scent should be observed when making this dirt hole set or any other set intended to take coyotes.

12. & 13. (Left) Step several yards away from the trap site and carefully skim off ⅛- or ¼-inch of sun-dried topsoil with the trowel. (Above) The sun-dried soil is sprinkled onto the trap for a final surface covering. If carefully done, it is nearly impossible to tell where the trap lies.

carcass. These are called "blind sets," because you aren't trying to get the coyote's attention with any sort of lure, you're just hoping it'll step in the right place. Existing tracks will help you to decide where those "right places" are. For some animals, "stepping sticks" could be placed in the trail to direct the animal's foot to the proper place, but for wary coyotes I prefer to do without them because they tend to alarm them.

If you use a grapnel instead of a stake, a trapped coyote will leave the trail and hook up somewhere else, not spooking other coyotes who will want to use the same trail. Three or four traps can be buried 20 or 30 yards apart along a well-used trail and, if you're fortunate, you may catch several coyotes at the site in a single day.

Dirt Hole Set

A third set that I have found to work particularly well for coyotes has been the standby of red fox trappers for many years. It's the dirt-hole set fully outlined in the section on fox. When using the dirt-hole set I have found that it pays dividends to place it close to a cow trail for coyote trapping. Position the dirt hole so that freshly excavated dirt is thrown across the trail — when completed, even near-sighted coyotes won't be able to resist investigating this type of set.

Place a bit of tainted meat in the bottom of the hole, and put a dab of coyote food lure at the top edge of the hole.

These three sets are all that anyone needs to take coyotes in number. However, I want to emphasize that the trapper should always keep an open mind and be ready to develop a new set for any unique situation.

Pelt Care

A coyote is "case" skinned with all the fur remaining on the pelt except for four "socks" extending about 6 inches above each foot. (Case skinning is detailed in Chapter 15.) Fur buyers do not require that the claws be left on the pelts of coyotes. A No. 6 stretcher is best for coyotes if the commercial spring steel variety is to be used. The dimensions for home-made wooden stretchers can be seen in Chapter 16.

Coyote pelts should be placed on the fur frame, skin side out, until the skin acquires a glazed appearance and feel. In dry desert conditions, this may mean only a cou-

14. With the final touches, only the trapper can tell where his set is. Any coyote that travels down this trail will not hesitate trotting over to the bush and will consequently be caught.

15. Some trappers use a scratching tool to simulate coyote scratches near a trap site. This simply adds a degree of authenticity to the scent post set since coyotes have a habit of scratching after urinating.

The author with a coyote pelt that was properly stretched and dried. This particular coyote was stretched on a homemade wooden stretcher.

ple of hours; if the humidity is high it can mean a couple of days. After the skin is glazed over, and before it becomes too dry and less supple, it is slipped off the fur frame, turned fur side out, put back on the frame, and dried thoroughly in this manner.

Coyotes are not difficult to skin, and the flesh readily separates from the pelt. Coyotes do not *generally* have the layers of fat under the skin that other animals do. If a coyote is skinned cleanly there is very little pelt scraping necessary. Generally, all that is necessary is to pull small pieces of flesh from the skin that cling to the base of the front legs. In those rare instances where coyotes have a layer of fat next to the skin, a fleshing knife and beam are necessary.

As always, when using the fleshing knife (its use is described in Chapter 17), be sure to first remove the burrs from the hair side of the pelt, otherwise, you'll cut holes in the skin.

In the warmer areas of the Southwest, be certain to keep a sharp eye out for blowfly eggs and remove them if they're found. A quick pelt drying will usually prevent any problems that might arise from blowflies. Generally, in such warm regions pelts can be dried more quickly by keeping them skin side out a bit longer on the fur frame and then using a fan in the drying shed to hasten the process. Pelts stretched on spring steel commercial frames seem to dry a bit faster than those mounted on traditional wooden stretchers.

RED FOX

TRAP SIZE: No. 2
BAIT: Tainted Meat
PRIME: December
STRETCHER: No. 4
TRACK:

THE RED FOX *(Vulpes fulva)* belongs to the canine family and has an overall length of about 40 inches with a tail that averages between 12 and 14 inches. The animal generally weighs between 8 and 14 pounds with 10 pounds considered to be the average. The life span of the red is from 8-10 years. There are at least 23 recognized subspecies of the red fox. These dog-like animals generally have a reddish or reddish-yellow color with black legs, a white tail tip and white on the belly. The red foxes' ears are pointed and stand erect. There are, however, three distinct color phases which exist in the red fox: the *red, black,* and *silver.* There is also the *cross fox* which is an intermixture of red and black. Amazingly, all of these color phases can occur in a single litter.

The red fox is distributed widely throughout the United States with the exception of the extreme Southeast and Southwest. The red fox generally breeds between December and March with most matings, according to one New York study, occurring between mid-January and mid-March. After a 53-day gestation period, the young are born, usually in March or April, the litter consisting of from one to 11 pups with an average of five. It is reported that the size of the litter increases until a female reaches the age of 5 to 7 years. Also, litters born early in the season are reported to run slightly larger than those born later in the season. After breeding, a female fox prepares a den — or two — with-in her home range. A typical den is usually located on the sunny side of a slope and may be nothing more than a burrow dug in a hollow log, or in a rocky cavern. The pups are born with their eyes closed but open them by about the eighth day. As with most members of the canine species, the male provides food for his new family.

Young foxes generally leave the den at about 4 to 5 weeks of age and are weaned at the age of 8-10 weeks. Sometimes, before weaning, the young are moved once or twice to new denning sites. At the age of about 4 months, fox pups begin to forage for themselves within the home range of their parents. They then disperse in the fall and are solitary until they pair when breeding season arrives.

Like most members of the dog family, red foxes are primarily nocturnal although they increase their daylight activity during the fall and winter. An adult red fox reportedly occupies a single home range for life, most confining their activities to an area of a reported 10 square kilometers.

Population densities of the red fox average two or three foxes per square kilometer, but in some ideally suited habitat, density may range up to 32 foxes per square kilometer. The red fox feeds primarily upon small mammals, fruits, berries and insects. It should also be said that bird nests built on the ground (such as those of pheasant and quail) are sometimes raided by red foxes.

Prime red fox habitat. The trapper should be able to recognize set locations, even from a distance. Here, the points of brush extending into the field would make excellent set locations. The small fencerow or ravine in the center of the photo will also be investigated by any passing red fox, so don't overlook these areas as being too obvious for sets.

Another example of good red fox habitat—woodland interspersed with farmland.

A red fox pelt is prime when the color of the skin side of the pelt is all red or white. A bluish or black-colored pelt on the flesh side is an indication that the pelt is not prime. Generally, red fox pelts are in top condition through December and January.

The most often-seen sign of the red fox is its tracks and droppings. The red fox track, of course, is much smaller than a coyote's, with the front footprint wider and more sprawling than the narrower, more pointed hind footprint. The red fox print has one distinctive characteristic that shows up if the track being seen is quite clear and shows good detail. The heel pad has an arched raised bar protruding from the hair of the foot that runs crossways on the pad.

Red fox scats (droppings) are much like smaller coyote scats and can be easily confused with the droppings of the grey fox. For this reason, in areas inhabited by both the red and grey fox, droppings are not a clear-cut indicator of red fox sign unless accompanying tracks can be distinguished.

Red foxes frequent open fields that are bordered by woodlands, and in the winter a fox can often be easily seen against the snow. Red foxes also have a habit of

MAKING A DIRT HOLE SET FOR RED FOX STEP-BY-STEP

1. Roy Daniels prepares to make a red fox set in this mowed hay field. Note the bale of winter hay and the strip of weeds in the background. Red foxes hunt these areas at night, seeking out field mice.

frequenting winter meadows where they hunt for mice. They are particularly fond of hunting around haystacks or hay bales in brome or prairie grass pastures where the hay has been left in the meadows for the winter months. Those hay bales attract field mice, hence the presence of the red fox. It will suffice to say that such areas are ideal for trap sets, providing you see sign.

Besides the areas around those hay bales, set locations are generally found along the edges of meadows that border woodlands. Sometimes a brush-choked ditch or ravine will project into a meadow, the apex of the ravine being an excellent place to set for red fox as it forces or "squeezes" them around this point. Pasture fences or gates are other natural places for red fox and should not be overlooked as potential setting sites.

Making the Red Fox Set

The red fox is a scent-wary, trap-wise animal, and all precautions should be taken to avoid contaminating the traps and the setting site with a foreign scent. Be sure to use clean rubber or cloth gloves and stand on a canvas trap-setting cloth that is clean and free of human odors.

The No. 2 trap, be it double-spring or coil-spring, is the generally accepted standard for red fox trapping. The dirt-hole set is also standard and should be dug into the ground at about a 45-degree angle and to a depth of about 5 inches. The diameter of the hole can range from 2 to 3 inches, depending upon the digging tool used. A No. 2 trap (I use the coil-spring variety) is then placed directly in front of the hole below the surface. Some of the dirt that was excavated from the trap bed and the dirt hole should then be sifted over the trap to conceal it completely. The remainder is then deposited at a low angle across the top of the trap and away from the hole — the finished set giving the appearance that a fox or other animal dug the hole. (This freshly dug earth is also an excellent sight attractor.) A small chunk of tainted flesh bait is then placed into the bottom of the hole and is sometimes covered or obscured slightly with dirt and/or grass. Sometimes a bit of food or gland scent is placed at the opposite rim of the hole. When the set is complete, a few drops of fox urine may be sprinkled over the area where the trap is and around the edge of the hole to serve as a suspicion remover. This also serves to further convince the target animal that another fox had already been there and perhaps left a bit

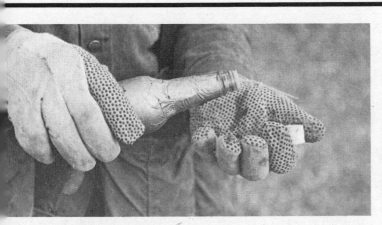

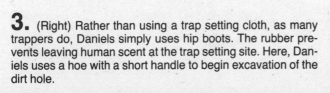

2. Roy prefers to sprinkle his gloves with fox urine prior to setting his traps to disguise any human odors that may be on them.

3. (Right) Rather than using a trap setting cloth, as many trappers do, Daniels simply uses hip boots. The rubber prevents leaving human scent at the trap setting site. Here, Daniels uses a hoe with a short handle to begin excavation of the dirt hole.

of a meal for this fortunate new bypasser. When complete, the set should bear no traces of a human having been there.

Some trappers suggest using a type of backing material behind the dirt hole because foxes are wary of stepping over anything. "Backing" may be a tuft of grass, a small stone, or a stick. This reportedly directs them to the front of the hole where the trap is located. However, if the hole is dug deep enough and small enough, the fox cannot see what's inside without moving around to the front side where the trap has been laid.

During breeding season it's also a good idea to make a second set of the scent-post type about 15 or 20 feet away from the dirt-hole set. This is due to the fact that foxes frequently travel in pairs. A rock, small bush, or other prominent object located in the same immediate area of the dirt-hole set is ideal for the scent-post set. Following the set-up instructions outlined in the section on Coyotes, place the trap next to the bush or rock on the side facing your first set, and spot the trap very close to the urinating post. (The placing of the trap *very close* to the urinating post is the only major difference between a fox and coyote scent-post set.) For this second set, I prefer to use urine only as an attractor. I use a spray bottle, and spray the bush, rock or stick liberally.

Using those two sets has its benefits when two foxes happen along. Here's what can happen: The first fox will see the dirt hole, go for the meat in the bottom, and get caught; the second, in the tension of the moment, generally beats a path around the fox caught in the trap — at a safe distance, of course. In its excitement, the second fox may feel a need to urinate and will immediately be attracted to the natural urinating post nearby. Bingo, you've got them both!

Things might also happen in reverse: Two foxes happen along and spot the dirt hole. One is trap wise and suspicious. Trying to figure out whether the dirt hole is safe or not, the trap-wary fox gets excited. The tension brings on a desire to urinate. It trots over to the nearest natural bush. That takes care of the first fox. The second fox, while hanging around its mate and trotting back and forth, will generally notice the baited dirt hole. Even if it was trap wary at first, the second fox finally decides that there's certainly nothing happening at the dirt hole, and eventually can't resist going for the bait.

4. Daniels excavates earth for the trap bed, and since he doesn't use a trap-setting cloth, discards the excess earth. He prefers to cover the trap with dried earth which he carries with him.

5. After setting and bedding the trap Daniels covers the set with dry earth he carries with him. Since the earth is dry, it will not freeze to prevent a trap's operation.

As with coyote trapping, there's little need for a lot of different types of sets for red fox trapping. There may be some unique situations that will dictate the use of a totally different and perhaps unique type of set. But in most instances, either the dirt-hole or scent-post set can be employed. The trapper who becomes adept at making only these two sets can become successful at trapping foxes if he observes all the trapping precautions.

Roy Daniels is an expert red fox trapper from Iowa and perhaps you can benefit by his experience:

Fox generally stay in the open areas — the farm areas — with a little brush and a few creeks running through where they can den. They also like the open meadows and bluegrass pastures where there are mice, rabbits and squirrels.

Generally speaking, for fox trapping, the best set is the dirt-hole. I wear hip boots instead of using a setting cloth and use the No. 2 coil spring traps with chains cut short. I place the trap dead center in front of and just as close to the dirt hole as I can and use a 14- or 15-inch stake. Some trappers consider this too short but I haven't had one pull out yet. I place a good gland scent around the rim of the hole and a good call scent or bait in the bottom. Then, I sprinkle fox urine over the whole thing — traps and all. I've tried other sets but always go back to the dirt-hole.

When breeding time comes, foxes run in pairs. In Iowa, this is generally about the middle of January, or the first of February. At this time I make dirt-hole sets in pairs about 4 feet apart and angle the holes toward each other.

I took a friend along with me to run my trapline one day during the breeding season. I made six double catches that day — 12 fox. That guy was ready to go home and sell his wife, his house, his car and everything, to get into trapping because he thought it was such a money-making proposition.

I imagine that if I were to ask Daniels about the first fox he ever caught, he could recall it vividly. Catching a wary red fox is an accomplishment for the beginning trapper — I'll never forget my first. When I was a young lad, I sent for a trapping booklet called "Johnny Muskrat's Tips to Trappers," available through the Sears and Roebuck catalog. (At that time Sears and Roebuck bought furs as well.) Though I no longer have the booklet, it seems there were details on the construction of a cubby set for raccoon.

6. (Left) Daniels smooths the dry soil into a natural appearing condition.

7. To form the hole, Daniels uses a pointed hoe handle to poke a hole down into the soft earth.

Using the book's example, I constructed a cubby of dry sticks and bark and then covered it with oak leaves. Then I carefully positioned a No. 2 double-spring trap in front and covered it with leaves. Hoping for a raccoon, I placed a piece of fish, as I recall, in the back of the cubby though the set was not constructed near a creek.

I generally ran my 10 or 12 traps right after school, before my chores. But this day when I came home from school my father insisted I do my chores right away — trapping had to wait. It wasn't until nearly 9 o'clock that night, when the milking was finished, that I was able to go down into the woodlot behind the house and check my traps. I'll never forget approaching the cubby set in the dark and hearing that trap chain rattle. You can imagine my excitement when, as I got closer, I directed the rays of my flashlight onto a prime red fox held securely in the trap.

I remember another time when red foxes began raiding my parents' and neighbor's henhouses. At the time, I had no knowledge of dirt-hole or scent-post sets. In fact, I barely had 2 years of 'possum and skunk trapping experience behind me. However, I figured I could catch those marauding foxes by using the equipment on hand coupled with a little common sense. I put my thinking cap on and came up with a set that seemed to make sense. I'd just take a dead chicken, throw it out in the pasture, and set a trap on either side of it. The first time I checked the traps, the chicken was gone and there were feathers about 30 feet from the trap — that bold fox had eaten it within plain sight of the two traps. (Of course, I hadn't taken any precautions about keeping human scent off the traps.)

The next step was to get another chicken and, rather than just lay it on top of the ground, I wired it to the trap stakes where the two traps were attached. I returned to find that the foxes had somehow managed to free the chicken from the stake and, again take it a short distance away and eat it.

I decided that there weren't enough traps around the chicken and set two more for a total of four, all equally spaced around the bait. In two nights, no foxes visited the set and the securely wired chicken stayed put. On the third night, we got about 2 inches of snow and I

8. A small chunk of tainted meat is poked to the bottom of the hole, and dried grass forced into the hole to partially obscure it.

9. This is the way a dirt hole set should look when complete. Though there is not a lot of freshly excavated earth for a sight attractor and the dirt hole quite small, the keen nose of the red will pick up the scent of the tainted meat from some distance.

thought that, perhaps, the snow and cold would make the foxes hungry. It all made sense to a schoolboy fox trapper. When I neared the set that night, I was surprised to find that my third chicken was missing and again, a fox had eaten it only a short distance away, right on top of the snow. However, the snow provided an education for me because I could clearly see where a fox had circled the four traps, just inches out of reach. The fox apparently figured where the traps were and deduced a safe approach to the chicken. The fox somehow managed to pull the chicken off the wire, and make off with the bait. At that point, considering the amount of "bait" I had used, it was hard to tell who was doing the most damage to the henhouse population!

A short while later, from a more experienced trapper, I learned the value of using fox urine and relatively clean traps. Next winter I employed those techniques, using basically the same chicken-bait set, and caught nine foxes in one week at the single set. The traps were checked twice a day, before going to school and after coming home. On 2 of those 7 days, I had a fox each time. I never did catch a double.

Caring for the Pelt

The red fox pelt is "cased" and sold fur side out, leaving the tail attached to the pelt, slit to its tip. I slit the tail fully because I want to make certain that the fluids drain out the tip. Some trappers recommend slitting it only halfway, saying that it will dry sufficiently without the top end spoiling but I won't take the chance.

A red fox pelt generally pulls off the animal quite cleanly with relatively little fat or flesh left on the hide; this makes it quite easy to handle. A No. 4 commercial wire stretcher is the generally accepted size for red fox. However, if you use a two-piece wooden stretcher be sure to stretch that pelt for length, more so than width. It's easy to make a red fox pelt wider than it should be but fur buyers prefer quite a long pelt. However, be sure that it is stretched wide enough to take the wrinkles out, otherwise it could spoil in the folds.

As a final note, it should be said that a prime pelt from a red fox is one of the most valuable furs in the trapper's bag. Treat it accordingly and you'll make money.

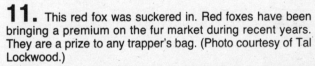

10. (Left) The set completed, Daniels sprinkles additional red fox urine over the entire trap setting area including the rim of the dirt hole. This not only serves to disguise any human odor but also serves as an additional attractor.

11. This red fox was suckered in. Red foxes have been bringing a premium on the fur market during recent years. They are a prize to any trapper's bag. (Photo courtesy of Tal Lockwood.)

GREY FOX

TRAP SIZE: No. 2
BAIT: Tainted Meat
PRIME: December
STRETCHER: No. 4
TRACK:

THE GREY FOX (*Urocyon cinereoargenteus*) resembles the red fox although it is somewhat smaller. An adult grey fox weighs from 7 to 12 pounds and generally measures 35 to 43 inches in total length. It has a greyish back with a rust colored belly and legs, the tail generally black tipped with a line of long stiff black guard hairs running along the top side forming an almost mane-like appearance.

The grey fox range overlaps that of the red fox in many areas, but in the United States, its range extends deeper into the South. The grey fox does not like the extreme cold of the North and seems to prefer the hot dry climate of the Southwest, particularly at elevations between 3,000 and 7,500 feet. The grey fox also inhabits much more densely forested or brushy regions than does the red, its habitat often composed of a mixture of rocks, brush and lightly timbered forest interspersed with small open parks and rocky canyons.

The grey generally breeds in February and March over much of the United States. After breeding takes place, the vixen prepares a den which is usually located on top of the ground. Sometimes the den will be made in a boulder pile, or even in the hollow of a decayed tree and on occasion, lined with grass, leaves or shredded bark. The gestation period for the grey fox ranges from 51 to 63 days whereupon one to eight young (the average is four or five) are born. The young greys generally

remain in the den from 4 to 6 weeks at which time they are weaned. When they begin to appear at the den entrance, the male will start to bring food like most members of the dog family. At the age of about 10 weeks, the pups leave the den to forage with their parents and will remain with them until late winter. After this time they may disperse and establish their own ranges, generally breeding their first year.

Much like the large grey wolves, there seems to be permanency of mating after a female chooses a mate. After the young have separated from the parents, the old male and female generally stay together. Most authorities suggest that a grey fox in the wild probably lives no more than 6 to 10 years.

The grey fox is adept at climbing, frequently running up sloped tree trunks — vertical ones as well! In the course of trapping the grey fox, the trapper who uses grapnels will frequently find the trapped grey 10 or 12 feet up in a tree. During the 1982-83 season I trapped a grey fox which I found 14 feet up a pine tree; that fox was wearing my No. 4 double-spring trap complete with 6 feet of chain and a coyote grapnel. How the fox made it that far up — with the bottom of grapnel hanging 6 feet off the ground — I'll never know.

The diet of the grey fox varies depending upon the season and geographical location in addition to the relative abundance of foods. Some known food items include cottontail rabbits, ground squirrels, cotton rats, deer mice, tree squirrels, snakes, horned toads, grasshoppers, berries, hickory nuts and a wide variety of other food items.

The most frequently seen sign of the grey fox are its tracks and droppings. In areas of the Southwest its droppings are readily noticeable in brushy areas where the foxes are plentiful. In those areas, droppings are frequently left on rocks or trails throughout the brush. It is also common to find grey fox droppings on top of an isolated rock in a sand wash or in the middle of a jeep trail. While the tracks of a grey fox are similar to that of the red, they are smaller by a slight amount. The grey prefers more wooded areas than does the red, and it particularly likes rocky, brushy sections of woodland more than open mature forest areas.

The grey fox is a quick little animal though not particularly difficult to trap. Unlike the coyote, the grey fox is not particularly wary of an unnatural looking set. The preferred trap size for the grey is the No. 2, either double or coil spring. It must be said, however, that grey foxes are often taken in coyote and bobcat sets where No. 3 and 4 size traps are used.

Making the Grey Fox Set

The grey fox can be taken at sets wherever its sign is found, which is usually along old roads or cow trails that run though brushy areas. The grey also has the habit of traveling the sandy bottoms of washes. Fortunately, for the trapper, the grey fox is very susceptible to a gland lure and a flat- or scent-post set. Interestingly, it will also visit, but seldom be caught in flat sets made for coyotes. The reason is that the grey fox, being so much smaller, generally passes between the trap and the scent when it moves in to investigate. When making a scent-post set for greys, you should construct it much like the one made for a coyote; however, make sure that the trap is set in as close as possible to the selected trail-side bush.

The dirt-hole set is another type of set that will take greys. I generally place a small chunk of tainted meat into the excavated hole, spotting a No. 2 double-spring trap in front of it with food scent placed on the rim of the hole. The freshly excavated earth is a natural attractor to any of the canine or feline predators, and the grey fox is no exception — it can't resist investigating.

MAKING A DIRT HOLE SET FOR GREY FOX

2. Trapper Mark Horwath prepares to construct a dirt hole set.

1. (Left) A natural dirt hole dug by an animal makes an excellent set location for grey fox.

One of the most successful grey fox sets, for me at least, is one placed next to the base of a tree or bush. The end of a stick, approximately 4 or 5 inches long, is dipped into a bottle of gland lure and is then leaned against the base of the tree with the lured end up. The trap is then bedded so that the center of the pan is about 10 or 12 inches from the tree base. The most important part of this set, however, is to then brush up the sides between the trap and the sides of the tree so that the small grey fox, with cat-like agility, cannot get its nose close to the gland lure without passing through the opening where the trap is. The trap is generally concealed beneath sifted earth. Even though the base-of-the-tree set doesn't look or sound very natural, the grey fox is suseptible to it.

Stepping sticks also work well for grey fox. They are nothing more than pencil-size twigs placed on the ground next to the trap jaws so that the fox will step over them and into the trap. For me, this set addition has been consistently successful wherever I've located grey fox sign. On the other hand, I must admit that my flat- and dirt-hole sets rarely nab a grey fox, on its first visit unless the sticks are used. Simply put, most greys won't step onto a trap pan unless you herd them into it with stepping sticks.

Even though the grey fox is not as scent wary as some of the other predators, it still pays to make every effort to eliminate human scent from the trap and the setting site. In short, take all precautions to leave only the scent of the gland lure.

Whenever I make a gland lure for the canine predators, it consists of the anus, with a section of skin around it containing the anal glands. I use 4 to 6 inches of the large intestine, including any fecal matter that section of intestine contains. The female and male reproductive organs are included as well. The pads of the hind feet also go into the scent mixture as does the gland at the base of the ear and the gall bladder. This gland potpourri is then ground with urine added to make a paste. The resulting mixture makes for natural scent that cannot be resisted by any of the dog family from which the glands come. I have also mixed together the glands of coyotes, grey foxes and bobcats, using them in the proportion that they were trapped. I have then used this "combo" lure at various sets intended for all three animals and have had excellent results. In fact, I have

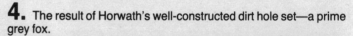

3. (Left) With the trap set, tainted meat placed in the hole and food scent spread on the rim of the hole, Horwath prepares to leave, brushing his tracks out as he goes. Notice that he is stepping on a rock in an effort to avoid leaving any more tracks at the site than necessary.

4. The result of Horwath's well-constructed dirt hole set—a prime grey fox.

not been able to distinguish any increase in success when the various glands are kept separate. It's also more convenient to mix the various predator glands and end up with a single scent that will attract all three animals to any given set. When this three-in-one scent is used, the trapper should be sure to design his set for the most wary predator represented in the mixture.

When grey foxes are traveling sandy washes, the wise trapper commonly places tumble weeds or other types of brush in the bottom of the draw, leaving an opening that's just large enough for this species of fox to go through. A trap is then placed underneath the surface of the sand, in blind-set fashion, in the center of the opening. It will not only take fox, but bobcat and coyotes that may be traveling the dry wash as well. In some regions, these sandy washes serve as highways for furbearers because they're much more easily traveled than the areas of dense undergrowth.

Another good set for greys is what might be termed the "campfire set." Grey foxes have the habit of visiting recent camp sites and inspecting the area, possibly for tidbits of food. They'll also dig in the ashes, particularly where pieces of bacon or eggshells remain. There may

not be an old campfire where you want to make a set but you can easily simulate one.

First, find a spot where there is a small clearing. In the center of the clearing dig trap beds for a pair of No. 2 double-spring traps, keeping them approximately 10 to 12 inches apart from the center of one pan to the center of the other. Attach a separate grapnel to each trap and place the grapnels in the trap beds and lay the traps on top of the grapnels, sifting soil over both. Make sure the completed sets are level with the ground. After you've completed the sets, gather a few sticks and build a fire directly between the two traps. It doesn't have to be a large fire, just enough to leave a small bed of ashes. When the fire is burning well, throw a strip or two of bacon into it and allow it to burn. Let the fire burn itself out and the grey fox campfire set is complete. Be careful not to leave large chunks of unburned bacon, however, as it will only serve to attract scavenging birds that may spring the traps.

Caring for Pelt

A grey fox pelt is case stretched and sold fur out, just like a coyote or red fox. Greys are also relatively easy to

MAKING A SCENT POST SET FOR GREY FOX

1. (Left) The hole excavated for a scent post set, the author beds the trap. Note that, in this case, a grapnel is to be attached to a trap chain rather than a stake. The author prefers grapnels in brushy country because the animal can leave the trapping site and "hole" up out of sight.

2. Dirt is sifted over the trap. Note the large stones, sifted out of the covering material, which could have jammed the trap jaws.

Because the price for grey fox pelts have escalated in recent years, it has become a much sought after furbearing animal in North America.

4. The author skims some sun-dried crust, carries it to the trap site, and sprinkles it on top of the freshly excavated earth. This serves to blend the freshly excavated soil with its surroundings so that the site is not obvious. A gland-type fox scent is placed on a tuft of grass where the hand trowel is pointing. Any passing grey fox will not be able to resist investigating the site and will subsequently be caught.

3. After dirt has been sifted over the trap, it is smoothed out with a trowel or garden spade.

skin, the pelt usually coming off easily with little fat or flesh left clinging to it. In past years, grey fox pelts were not particularly valuable, their fur generally being quite coarse when compared to the fur of the red fox. However, the long-haired furs have become stylish in recent years and the grey fox is now "in" with fur buyers. Today, a grey fox pelt demands a good price on the fur market and consequently grey fox trapping pressure has increased.

Fortunate for the trapper is the fact that the grey fox has a high rate of reproduction. As a result, those areas which are suitable grey fox habitat frequently have the animals in very good numbers. According to one study, grey foxes occupy home ranges averaging about 4 to 6 square kilometers, population densities ranging up to 14 foxes per square kilometer with the average population running about one or two. For these reasons, grey foxes are capable of sustaining relatively heavy trapping pressure, year after year.

(Right) Grey foxes are strong climbers, and are hard to find after being trapped, particularly when they climb into the trees, trap and all.

MAKING A BUSH BASE SET FOR GREY FOX

1. (Left) The author has the trap bed excavated in preparation to position the trap next to the bush. This set is not a scent-post type, but rather is designed for a curious animal to come and investigate the scent which will be placed on a stick inside the bush.

2. Once the trap is in its bed, the covering material is sifted on top.

3. The author carefully places the sticks around the edges of the trap jaws so that an approaching predator will step over the sticks and into the jaws of the trap.

4. The completed set. Though it is suspicious-looking, bobcats and grey fox are very susceptible to it. The scent is placed in the bush back of the trap. The predator must step over the sticks and into the trap in order to get its nose close to the scent it will be investigating.

BOBCAT

TRAP SIZE: No. 3 or 4
BAIT: Fresh meat or
   gland lure
PRIME: January
STRETCHER: No. 5 or 6
TRACK:

THE BOBCAT *(Lynx ruffus)* is a member of the feline family and weighs about 25 pounds on the average although large males have been known to approach 50 pounds. They have a short round face, a very short tail, broad triangular ears with small tufts at the tips, and tufted facial cheeks. The underparts are generally yellowish-white in color and spotted with black, the color of the sides and back ranging from grey or brown to yellow. It may also have subdued dark spots on the back. The eastern and southern bobcats are much darker, in general, than those found in the West. The spotting also varies considerably, being pronounced on some and subdued on others.

Found throughout the United States, bobcat numbers may vary from region to region according to local topographic and vegetation features. They are capable of living in areas of heavy brush as well as relatively barren short-grass country.

Bobcats generally breed anytime between January and June, sometimes a little later, with peak breeding activity usually running from late January to April. Females may breed twice a year and, after a 63-day gestation period, one to seven kittens are born, an average litter generally numbering three. A bobcat den can be a rock cave, a hollow tree, or a hollow log and the kittens stay in the den until they're about 5 weeks old. However, they aren't generally weaned until they're about 2 months old. While the kittens are young, the female brings them food — the male offering no assistance with this domestic chore. (In fact, it is reported that the adult male will sometimes kill the young kittens!) When the kittens are approximately 3 to 5 months old, they begin following the female while she hunts for food, and when they're about 8 months old, they generally disperse. However, litter mates may travel together for some time after leaving the female parent.

Females generally defend their territories from other females although they permit males to establish ranges within their territory. On the other hand, males are tolerant of others of their sex, their ranges frequently overlapping. Bobcats may live 10 to 14 years in the wild, and not surprisingly, the mountain lion is one of the few major predators the bobcat has to worry about.

The bobcat's diet, like that of many animals, varies not only with the season, but with the geographical region, and the available prey species. Bobcats are known to eat rabbits, hares, fawns of both deer and antelope, and a variety of rodents and birds.

Many trappers have said of bobcat habitat that "rocks" are synonymous with these animals. While it's true that bobcats roam rocky canyon rims and ledges wherever they're found, they also inhabit forested and brushy areas.

The sign of the bobcat generally consists of tracks, droppings and scratches. The tracks are generally more rounded than those of the coyote and, unlike the coyote or dog, bobcat tracks show no claw marks. However, this can be confusing because imperfect tracks of coyotes and dogs may show no claw marks either. The ball pad of the bobcat is distinctive from any member of

In recent years, bobcats have brought a premium price. A cat such as this one could fetch $300 to $400.

the dog family in that the anterior portion on both front and hind feet have two lobes, rather than one. The major difference between front and rear footprints of the bobcat is the slightly smaller ball pad of the hind foot.

Bobcat droppings, according to some trappers, are quite different than those of a coyote. In the arid Southwest, this is true as the droppings tend to be segmented or marked off through constriction, and, unlike the scats of coyote, are usually deposited as short pellets. However, in very humid areas such as the coastal Northwest, bobcat scat (excrement) can easily be confused with that of coyotes and dogs. For this reason, it's often necessary to find other types of sign near the droppings in order to verify bobcat presence. For example, like most other members of the cat family, bobcats tend to cover their scats. Sometimes, there is no actual covering of the droppings, just merely scratches nearby. If you notice scratches in conjunction with droppings, you can assume that it is from a bobcat, not a coyote.

In some sections of the West, bobcats are known to leave their sign in very specific areas. Generally, these cats travel along the top rims of canyons, and if there are juniper trees in the area, bobcat sign can be found in the duff under them. When bobcat droppings age they generally become bleached out and are readily noticeable under the trees mentioned above. In some instances you'll find an amazing number of bobcat droppings under a single tree. Frequently, there will also be scratches which consist of no more than a slight depression in the juniper duff not much wider than the paw of a bobcat, and sometimes not much longer. A small pile of juniper duff will generally be at one end of the scratch. These types of scratches, found on the ground in conjunction with droppings, are not to be confused with scratches on the trunk of a tree — yet another type of bobcat sign. Another interesting aspect of bobcats is the fact they seem to prefer to leave their scratches and droppings under certain types of trees, particularly those which have juniper duff or pine needles around the base of the trunk.

Unlike coyotes, bobcats generally travel a given section of country according to the lay of the land. Canyon rims are one specific route of bobcat travel, but when it comes to a mountain range, a bobcat will generally cross over the saddles, sometimes leaving sign under a prominent tree on its way through. When a bobcat is

MAKING A LOG CROSSING SET FOR BOBCAT

1. This is a log a bobcat might use to get across the stream. Such stream crossings are few, making this an ideal set location.

2. First, a notch or flat spot must be chopped into the log so that the trap will be flush with the top of the log after it's bedded and covered.

confronted with a long low hill that tapers off on the ends, it will generally travel down the ends and sometimes scratch and leave droppings under a tree coming off the point of the hill, particularly when timber and brush are on the hill and the flat is relatively barren. When long lines or "fingers" of trees project from a main body of forest into an open grassland, tracks, scratches and droppings will frequently be found under a tree at the outermost point of one of those lines.

These felines also have a habit of frequenting dead trees that are particularly prominent — no doubt in search of mice and pack rats which are known to inhabit dead timber. The brush at the bases of such trees will also harbor pack rat nests and those of other types of rodents. Look for bobcat sign here too. Sometimes you'll find lone, prominent trees in grassy flats surrounded by forest; here again is another place that may be frequented by bobcats in search of food.

The pelt of this species generally comes into prime condition about January or February (a bit later than coyotes). However, I have received top dollar from cats taken as early as November and as late as the last week in February, when I usually stop trapping these animals.

A bobcat is particular about where it places its feet. They are like any other cat, including house cats, in this respect. Knowing this can be to the trapper's advantage or disadvantage depending upon how he makes a set. Bobcats are curious animals, but once their curiosity is satisfied they may lose interest. It is my feeling that if a bobcat is lured in to a set and checks it out, but is not caught, it may not come back a second time. Therefore, I feel it's important to nail it the first time through, if at all possible.

This particular feline prefers *fresh* meat — tainted meat holds little interest for it other than from a curiosity standpoint. Also, unlike the canine predators, the bobcat is much more sight oriented, its hunting efforts dominated by eyesight. The olfactory gland of a bobcat is not nearly as well developed as a coyote's but it does use its nose contrary to what some trappers think.

However, given the lack of olfactory gland development it is not surprising that the bobcat is not particularly scent wary. Believe it or not, even the scent from traps handled with bare hands doesn't seem to spook this feline predator away from sets. Even a suspicious-looking set, which would alert even the dumbest

3. A trap bed is chopped out of the log and the trap positioned in the bed.

4. The trap is in position and covered so that an unsuspecting cat will place its foot on the set. Guide sticks placed just before and just after the trap might direct the cat into the trap, but they shouldn't be so high as to make it difficult for the cat to approach the set.

coyote, is very likely to catch a bobcat if it's made properly in other respects. However, due to the fact that coyotes and foxes frequently inhabit bobcat country, and due to the fact that coyote and fox pelts are also valuable, the trapper might as well take scent precautions when making bobcat sets. There's no telling when another of these predators might happen along and get into a bobcat set.

Making the Bobcat Set

The animal's curiosity, combined with its habit of hunting by sight, has been the downfall of many a bobcat. One of the more popular bobcat sets involves the use of some sort of sight attractor near the trap. The sight attractor may consist of nothing more than a bird wing, a piece of dried rabbit hide, or a ball of cotton suspended from a tree limb by a string. A trap is then placed underneath the sight attractor on a mound of earth. If this technique is used, be sure to suspend the wing or cotton ball low enough to attract the attention of bypassing bobcats; however, be sure the object is high enough to force the cat to reach up to get it.

Some sets only utilize a sight attractor to lure a bobcat into a set that has been baited with gland scent or food. This technique preys upon the cat's full array of senses, and is usually successful. It's really quite simple.

The dirt-hole set will also take bobcats consistently; the construction of which is detailed in the section dealing with fox and coyote.

A variation of this approach consists of a dirt-hole set with an aluminum pie plate or tin can lid suspended over it. When making this set, I generally use a piece of monofilament fishing line to suspend the object; the clear quality of the line, from a distance, giving the impression that the object is floating, not suspended from a tree limb. This will hopefully appeal to the bobcat's curiosity and lure it in from distant ridges or other far away vantage points. The suspended pie plates and can lids are sensitive to any breeze — they flash around and are hard to miss seeing, particularly on a bright moonlit night.

Generally Nos. 3 or 4 traps are used, some trappers preferring the coil spring, others opting for the long-spring or jump trap.

MAKING A TREE SET FOR BOBCAT

1. For the tree set a No. 4 double-spring trap is bedded with the center of the pan approximately 14 inches from the base of the trunk. Evergreen branches are placed on either side of the trap to prevent a bobcat from entering the set at the sides.

The bobcat is susceptible to a number of different types of sets, depending upon the trapping situation at hand. They can be taken with cubby sets, dirt hole sets, or log crossing sets — all of which will serve double duty for the trapper since they will also take most of the other predators.

The Cubby Set

To make a cubby set you must first find a natural hole in a rock pile or log located in an area having fresh bobcat tracks. If tracks are present, but there's no natural structure to build a set in, you can create your own. A "cubby" generally resembles a small den or house — something that an animal must enter. Cubbies have the advantage of keeping snow, or even rain out so that a trap keeps on working, even in adverse weather. Trappers often build them out of logs and rocks with some type of bait and lure placed inside with a trap set at the entrance. The trapper-constructed cubby should be large enough to encourage a bobcat to enter it, thereby duping it into stepping on the trap in the process. Just put the bait or lure far enough back in the cubby so that the bobcat cannot get to the bait without passing the trap.

The Log-Crossing Set

In making the log-crossing set, the trapper will sometimes find tracks indicating that a bobcat has been crossing a narrow draw or stream by walking across a fallen log. Even if there is no sign of anything crossing the log, a set made at a natural log crossing may pay off as bobcats tend to travel along the edges of ravines, inspecting those log crossings as they go. It's sometimes difficult to predetermine where a cat will jump up onto the log and, for this reason, the trap is usually placed in the middle.

To make a log-crossing set, use an axe to chop out a trap bed on the log. The trap is then positioned, bedded firmly, and securely attached to the log or a branch by heavy wire. Now you can cover the trap with dry moss, leaves, rotted wood or snow. However, when you cover the trap be sure the area directly above the pan is very smooth, and completely free of sticks or stones. A bobcat is almost eager to place its foot in a nice smooth spot — it'll avoid sticks and stones like the plague.

2. Large cow chips, serving as umbrellas to protect the springs from moisture or snow, are placed on the trap springs and stepping stones are positioned in front of the trap next to the jaws.

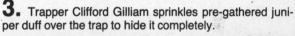

3. Trapper Clifford Gilliam sprinkles pre-gathered juniper duff over the trap to hide it completely.

Here's the front foot of a bobcat in relation to a No. 4 double-spring trap. The wide jaw spread of the trap allows it to get a grip above the cat's footpad.

The Tree Set

I have had very good luck with one unusual type of bobcat set and generally construct that set wherever I find bobcat droppings and/or scratches. Other trappers use this set, but I'm not sure if it has a name. I call it the "tree set." It consists of nothing more than placing a trap with the center of the pan approximately 14 inches away from the base of a tree where scratches and other sign are found. Scent made from ground bobcat and fox glands is then daubed on the tree trunk about 8 or 10 inches above ground level. The trap is positioned with the trigger next to the tree trunk with the springs of a double-spring trap angled toward either side. Then, sticks, branches and other "fencing material" is placed between the trap jaws and the outside of the tree trunk to prevent the cat from entering the set from the side, missing the trap. For this reason, a wide tree trunk is better than a slender one. The trap should then be very carefully covered with sifted dirt or other surrounding material and stepping sticks placed right next to both trap jaws. I have used such a set not only next to the base of a tree, but up against a thick bush; the set is constructed in basically the same manner.

4. Though the completed set is obvious, and wouldn't trap most wary predators like the coyote, it's deadly on bobcats. The important thing is to have a very smooth spot directly over the trap. Bobcats are particular about where they place their feet, and they seem almost eager to place a foot on smooth surfaces.

5. Bobcats do not have keen noses like the canine predators. For this reason, it is important to have the set well-scented. It should be re-scented every 3 or 4 days, if possible.

In some instances, the trapper may not be able to find bobcat sign though he knows through sightings that there are bobcats in the area. This is when the bobcat trapper might do well to simply place sets according to the lay of the land. I have done this repeatedly, knowing there were cats in the region, and upon finding a "catty" looking setting site, I've placed a trap and have, in many instances, been successful.

Clifford Gilliam, photos of whom accompany this chapter, is one expert bobcat trapper. As you will see, Clifford makes an unusual type of bobcat set. The trap is positioned much as in the tree set, but instead of stepping sticks, Clifford places small stones forming a circle around the trap jaws and almost touching them. The bank of stones is approximately 2 inches wide around the trap. Gilliam knows that a bobcat will not step on these stones but will place its foot inside the jaws of the trap just to get its nose close to the gland lure. Due to the aluminum trap cover, a foot placed anywhere inside the stones is going to spring the trap and catch the cat.

Another important feature of Clifford's cat set is the use of large dry cow chips over each of the trap's double springs. Clifford generally uses a No. 3 Victor double, long-spring trap for bobcats. The cow chips are lightweight and are easily thrown out of the way when the trap is triggered. The chips form a natural umbrella over the trap springs in case of rain and also provide, to some extent, enough insulation to keep the trap springs from freezing in cold, foul weather. In many instances, the cow chips serve to keep the traps working when other traps are frozen in.

Bobcat Lures

Regarding the best bobcat lures to use, I prefer natural gland lures, and in many cases, nothing else. Bobcat urine, particularly when taken from a female in heat and used during the mating season, is a real tomcat killer. It must be said, however, that urine can be effective any time during the year. I do feel it important when employing only urine as a lure to use plenty of it — particularly for bobcats. There are instances, however, when a trapper can use too much of a good thing, especially when it comes to gland lures and particularly those spiced up with plant extracts. When it comes to using urine as a lure for bobcats, however don't be bashful with it. In order to have a sufficient quantity on

MAKING A TREE SET IN JUNIPER DUFF

1. (Left) This juniper has an excellent scratching location underneath it with bobcat droppings all around.

2. Trapper Clifford Gilliam sets the No. 3 Victor double-spring trap and simply wiggles it into position in the duff under the tree. No real trap excavation is necessary.

hand, I collect urine from cats I've trapped. When using urine as a lure, I prefer to dispense a couple of tablespoons at cat sets, generally pouring it down the side of a tree trunk at the "tree set," beginning about a foot or 14 inches above the ground and letting it run down. I also pour a little on a dried cow chip, or small chunk of rotten wood (if a piece is handy), and place it next to the base of the tree underneath the other urine. Being absorbent, the rotten wood or cow chip will hopefully, hold the scent longer. One problem with using urine as a lure is the fact that it, like other liquids, tends to evaporate. Of course, evaporation could probably be retarded by adding a bit of glycerine to the urine. This would also help prevent it from freezing in bad weather. You are welcome to try a few drops of glycerine to alleviate any of the above problems; however, I personally don't use it because I've had such good luck without it. Bobcat urine has a very musky odor that I'm able to smell at a set for several days. I have even caught large male cats at sets that have not been re-scented for a week. However, when using straight urine, it's no doubt best if the urine can be "freshened up" every 5 days or so.

If you visit a set where a trap was attached to a grapnel and the trap is missing, you'll probably find the bobcat hooked up in the nearest bush; however, there are times when bobcats travel a little farther — you'll simply have to go looking for them. Trapped, grapneled bobcats, unlike coyotes, will sometimes lie low in the brush when a trapper approaches; and, more than one trapper has been alarmed by finding himself inches from one of those feline buzzsaws before realizing it was there. I've had this happen to me quite a few times. Frequently, when the trapper unknowingly gets "too close," they'll slap out, much like a house cat slaps a dog that has infringed on its territory. Considering the fact that a bobcat can kill a full grown deer, I don't want to stand still for a slap from a bobcat. For this reason, be extremely cautious when looking for any trapped cats dragging a grapnel. Here's some more advice: If you find a bobcat in a trap, and it's sitting up looking at you like a big calm pussycat, don't assume it's as tame as it looks. A bobcat can lunge and slap in an instant *without warning*. I once narrowly missed a severe scratching when a trapped bobcat sprang and slapped at me. Fortunately, the trap had a good foot hold and jerked the cat back just as I jumped away.

3. He then takes large, flat dry cow chips and places them on top of the trap's long springs. This serves to keep them dry if it rains or snows, and prevents them from freezing. Gilliam is not particularly concerned about leaving scent at the site for bobcats are not particularly scent wary.

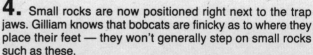

4. Small rocks are now positioned right next to the trap jaws. Gilliam knows that bobcats are finicky as to where they place their feet — they won't generally step on small rocks such as these.

Caring for the Pelt

Bobcat pelts are "cased" much like a coyote or fox pelt and they're sold fur out. There are a number of fur buyers who grade bobcat pelts according to length as measured from the tip of the nose to the base of the tail and, for this reason, it's good idea, when stretching a bobcat pelt, to opt for length over width. However, once you've pulled the pelt down snug for length, there's no reason not to swing the two-piece stretching boards for width. If you're using a wire or spring steel stretcher, don't be bashful about pulling the grippers snug to get a little extra length. Bobcats have very good fur all the way down their legs and, for this reason, I generally leave the fur on the pelt right down to the toe-nails.

The bobcat, like most felines are clean animals, the fur being beautiful and soft to the touch. They usually skin easily and cleanly, with little fat and flesh remaining on the pelt. For this reason, they're a pleasure to handle. However, if there is any fat or flesh left on the pelt after skinning, it must be removed — this holding true for any animal pelt.

The prices of bobcat pelts — $300 to $400 at this writing — have soared in recent years, making for keen trapping competition when it comes to these feline predators. The trapper who knows how to read bobcat sign and scouts for it long before the season starts will have a jump on the competition.

One advantage to bobcat trapping is that once caught they rarely escape. This, of course, is assuming that you have a solid foot hold. They are strong animals but they don't usually twist out or bite themselves as some fur-bearers do. Finally, I must again emphasize the beauty and the value of the bobcat pelt. Handle it with care and treat it with respect — it's a true trapping prize.

5. Pre-sifted juniper duff is sprinkled onto the trap. Gilliam carries the pre-sifted duff in a plastic jar where it can be kept dry and ready for instant use.

6. A gland-type of bobcat scent will be placed on the tree branches behind the trap. However, the set is not complete; a bobcat could reach the scent by walking around the trap rather than stepping into it.

8. When the set is complete, this is how it appears. The bobcat must now step over the rocks and into the trap in order to get a good sniff of the scent placed on the tree branches beyond the trap. The side "fencing" of the pinon branches prevents the bobcat from entering the set from either side.

7. To prevent a bobcat from walking around the trap, Gilliam places tree branches, along either side.

chapter 12
SMALL FURBEARERS

RACCOON

TRAP SIZE: No. 1½ or 2
BAIT: Fresh fish
PRIME: December
STRETCHER: No. 4 or 4½
TRACK:

THE RACCOON *(Procyon lotor)* is a stocky, medium-sized, short-legged, bushy-tailed animal that is most easily recognized by the dark patches of fur around its eyes, giving it a masked appearance. This, combined with its bushy, ringed tail of alternating black bands interspersed with a brownish fur are distinguishing features of the raccoon. The raccoon varies widely in color from greyish brown or greyish black to a dull yellowish grey. Some specimens are very dark, almost black. The hair of the raccoon is usually darker along the back with many of the guard hairs black tipped, giving the coat a grizzled appearance. The underside of the raccoon is generally dull grey or silver colored while the face is usually lighter than the rest of the body with the exception of the "mask."

The raccoon is found throughout the lower 48 states although it generally avoids the drier desert. It mates in late February, March and April with the young being born in May and June after a 64-day gestation period. There are generally one to five young in a litter, all born blind and covered with thin hair. The female is reported to care for the young raccoons by herself until they are about 3 weeks old. At that point the male may start to help out. The young raccoons generally begin to eat solid food at about 7 weeks of age although they are not weaned until they are about 3 months old.

Raccoons generally develop their adult fur by about 3 months of age and remain with their parents through fall. Sexual maturity appears to be attained at 1-year of age. Yearling males usually become sexually active later in the spring than do the adults and, for this reason, the yearling males probably do not find unmated females. Raccoons do not pair permanently, and a male raccoon may mate with more than one female. About half of the yearling females produce litters their first year. The female raccoon is very devoted to her young and will fight savagely to protect them.

The raccoon is omnivorous and, like most furbearers, its diet varies with the season and the geographic locale. They are frequently found near water and eat fish, crayfish, frogs, mice, muskrats, birds, grasshoppers, all sorts of berries and insects, fruits, corn and other garden vegetables.

Probably the most frequently seen sign of the raccoon is its tracks, generally in the mud along any body of water such as a pond, river, stream or small brook. A raccoon track is very distinctive and easily identified. They walk in a flat-footed manner, producing a front footprint that somewhat resembles a hand with long toes. The rear track is more elongated and also has long toes. Once you become familiar with raccoon tracks, they won't be mistaken for anything else and will be readily noticed; not only along the edges of creeks and other bodies of water, but also on occasion in the mud under the surface of the water.

A raccoon sometimes picks up mud on its feet and then tracks it over rocks or logs, where the tracks can be readily noticed by the observant trapper. Raccoon droppings can be found on these rocks and logs as well. Those droppings contain primarily berry matter when these fruits are available; and, like other furbearers, the raccoon sometimes leaves a number of droppings in the same small area. Though the raccoon is frequently found near bodies of water, it often travels over land and sometimes denning trees can be found some distance from water. Denning trees are generally large old

Note the raccoon tracks along the edge of a very small creek. It is, perhaps, these tracks which most frequently reveal the presence of this nocturnal furbearer. Raccoon tracks can easily be distinguished by the long toe marks.

hardwood trees that have cavities in the trunks. The cavity must extend downward within the trunk to be ideal for raccoon denning. Raccoons are primarily nocturnal and spend the daylight hours high in their den trees. Where there is a paucity of hardwoods, the dens will be found in rock bluffs or simply dirt burrows — it depends upon the available habitat.

On a number of occasions while squirrel hunting I have found raccoons high in their den trees. Frequently a raccoon will make the mistake of allowing its tail to hang out of a crack in the tree, exposing its presence. In hardwood forests that have raccoon populations, the trapper or hunter only needs to "look up" to find them. This indicates a prime area for raccoon sets.

The raccoon pelt becomes prime earlier in the fall than do some of the other furbearers. These animals are not particularly difficult to trap although there are several things a trapper needs to know about raccoon in order to be successful. First of all, the raccoon is not especially trap wary, even though it has very keen eyes and a keen nose. It is no doubt more trap wary than the skunk or opossum although not as wary, for instance, as a coyote. The raccoon is also a reaching animal and has stolen the bait from many a trap site simply by reaching in from the side or around the corner and removing the bait without getting into the trap. However, this animal is particularly curious and always hungry. It is also easily "fenced" or directed into a trap.

Generally, Nos. 1½ or 2 size traps are recommended for raccoon, and I strongly suggest using double-jaw or Stop-Loss type traps. Though relatively easy to trap, the raccoon, a strong fighter, can be difficult to hold, tending to twist, wring and chew its way out of a trap. For this reason, a drag or clog attached to the trap chain to prevent the raccoon from getting a solid tug on the trap, at least for the initial lunges, is an excellent idea. The body-gripping killer-type traps are also an excellent choice for the raccoon and the 220 Conibear series is generally considered to be the proper size. When it comes to the body-gripping traps, raccoons are generally trapped on land, or at least above the surface of the water and, as a consequence, the trapper should be careful about where he uses them. He certainly wouldn't want to place them where there is the possibility of catching a non-target animal. A drowning set, where feasible, is perfect for raccoon.

MAKING BLIND TRAIL SETS FOR RACCOON

1. (Left) One of the most effective sets for raccoon is the blind-trail set on the bottom of a shallow creek. It's best if the banks are steep on either side. Here, Roy Daniels is shoving sticks into the creek bottom in order to block the raccoons' passage. The idea is to leave only a single gap, right in the middle of the creek, where the raccoon normally travels.

2. The creek is almost fully blocked except for the gap in the middle where a trap is placed. It isn't necessary to make an impassable barrier, only "guide" sticks to direct the animal into the trap.

Blind-Trail Set

As mentioned earlier, raccoons are fond of frequenting bodies of water which are naturally some of the best places to trap them. The set to be constructed depends primarily upon the specific site. One of the best, most efficient sets for raccoons is a blind-trail set, particularly in very small brooks or streams.

To make this set, the trap is simply placed in the middle of a stream. Of course, the size of the stream will vary, but I've had good luck making blind-trail sets in streams no wider than a foot or two. Once the trap is in place, sticks are poked into the mud, vertically, along either side. The sticks should protrude 8 or 10 inches above the water or bank to block the raccoons' passage down the stream and guide it to the only open passage where the trap is located. The trap should be completely submerged in water with no more than about 3 inches of water covering the trap pan. It is not generally considered necessary to camouflage a trap for raccoon as long as it is set below the surface of the water. However, if a trap is placed in still water, the effectiveness of the set might be improved by a camouflage of various materials. I generally place water-soaked or water-logged leaves over the trap springs, and use one leaf to cover the trap pan, large enough to hide the pan but small enough to fit inside the jaws. Bottom silt is then placed on top of the leaves to make everything blend in.

A raccoon trapper should beware that when he places gobs of water-logged leaves on top of a trap there are two problems he will be confronted with. One is that the large leaves may jam a trap; second, the slippery leaves may sandwich themselves between the trap jaws and the raccoon's foot, making it possible for the raccoon to pull out of the trap. A raccoon's foot is tapered and, when it's slippery and wet (and muddy as well) the slippery leaf coating over the trap jaws may be all it takes for a raccoon to pull its foot free. For these reasons, the trapper should use common sense when it comes to covering traps set under the surface of the water.

The Pocket Set

Another very popular set for raccoons is the pocket set, one frequently used for mink. It consists of a hole dug at a sharp upward angle into the bank of a stream at

3. Another example of the blind-trail set. Though the guide sticks used are very thin and wispy, they will still direct the raccoon into the trap. It simply isn't necessary to use heavy sticks which would only serve to block a raccoon's vision and probably cause it to notice something unusual about the stream bed.

4. This raccoon was caught in the blind-trail set and pulled the long slender stick clog about 20 feet.

THE POCKET SET

the water's edge. The hole should be constructed so that water runs into the cavity. When the trap is placed at its entrance the trap pan should be sitting under 2 inches of water. A bait is then placed up in the hole above the surface of the water. A good bait for this set is a fish, crayfish, or a chunk of muskrat meat.

The raccoon does prefer fresh rather than tainted bait. For this reason, it's a good idea to obtain your bait before the season, cut it into chunks, and freeze the chunks for future use. When needed, the frozen chunks can be easily thawed out. When setting a trap, some trappers prefer to wrap such baits in wet grass or leaves to preserve the freshness and keep them from drying out. What ever you do, be sure to attach the bait securely by pressing a stick through it or wiring it to a stake. As mentioned earlier, a raccoon is a reacher and grabber and has a tendency to remove baits without getting caught.

Other 'Coon Sets

Clyde Tryon, a trapper from Perry, Kansas, has devised a special set to nab reaching raccoons. The set is constructed along a creek or river where raccoons have been traveling the banks. To make it, find a place where the bank is exceptionally steep, steep enough to force the raccoons into the water. If the bank is not steep enough, and generally it isn't, take a spade and cut a 4-foot wide section straight up and down right to the water's edge.

A SPILLWAY SET FOR RACCOON

(Left) Raccoons frequently investigate spillways in farm ponds such as this one. This is an ideal location for a raccoon trap. In this case, Roy Daniels places one of his double-spring raccoon traps under water alongside the culvert next to the bank. The trap chain is attached to a clog made of a stick approximately 3 inches in diameter and 4- or 5-feet long.

This well-made set paid off.

Allow the excavated dirt to simply drop into the water and, if necessary, rearrange the dirt to form a shelf in front of the bank about 4 inches below the water. Then, with the use of a pointed stick (Clyde uses a pointed broom handle), three holes, spaced about a foot apart, are punched back into the freshly exposed edges of the bank.

Make the holes about 2 or 3 inches in diameter, nearly 6 inches deep, and about 3 inches above the water level at a slight downward angle. The holes will contain chunks of fish or other baits which will be dropped into them. Then, a trap is placed in front of the center hole on the shelf built of bank dirt, with the center of the pan about 5 inches from the bank and with about 3 inches of water over the pan. The trap should also be staked in deep water for a drowning set.

Frozen fish can be used as a bait. However, be sure to shave off very small pieces not large chunks; it'll take longer for the raccoon to get it all. Also, the fish should be poked back into the hole to prevent the raccoon from getting it out too quickly and easily.

According to Clyde, trap-wary raccoons may be a little cautious when getting the fish out of the first hole they come to. However, after they've eaten the fish out of the first hole, they're convinced that this is an easy meal. By the time they get to the center hole, where the trap is, they've thrown caution to the wind, thinking they'll clean out this hole just as easily.

Since raccoons are so fond of traveling small sand or mud bars along creeks, stick fences devised to direct them into a narrow opening in the middle of the sand bar can work very well. Just place a trap in the opening. Next, add a bait or gland lure to one of the sticks near the trap, and the set becomes even more appealing.

Another type of set that works very well for raccoon can be constructed at a place where a log has fallen into the creek and is resting at a slight upward angle. Here, a trap bed is chopped into the log so that the pan will be approximately 2 inches below the surface of the water. A piece of fish or other bait is then nailed onto the log, above the edge of the water, and a bit of call lure is placed on the log just above the bait.

There are three things to keep in mind when trapping raccoon: (1) a raccoon is hard to hold once you catch it; (2) you can build stick fences to direct them where you want; (3) the raccoon is very susceptible to the use of food baits. If a trapper keeps these things in mind when trapping raccoons, he can use common sense to construct a set to fit any situation.

Anywhere that a stream forces a traveling raccoon into a narrow passageway works to the trapper's advantage. Besides guide sticks, stepping sticks also work very well. Just place the sticks so that the rac-

coon has to step over them into the trap. Stepping sticks can be shoved into the sides of a steep bank or two of them can be shoved into the bottom of the creek to form a low cross near the trap. Raccoons generally travel very close to the water's edge along large bodies of water, but when it comes to small streams and brooks, just inches deep, they may travel right up the middle.

One popular method of catching raccoons is to attach a shiny object, such as a piece of tin foil or perhaps a mirror, to the trap pan. The trap is then placed under shallow running water. (A good location would be a riffle near the water's edge where raccoons are traveling.) Some trappers suggest cutting the tin foil into the shape of a fish, but the 'coon is curious by nature and will generally attempt to handle the foil, no matter what shape it's in.

Raccoons have the habit of going into metal culvert-like spillways in farm ponds; traps near or inside these entrances can be effective.

Land-Trapping Raccoons

Though raccoon sign is generally found near water, there are times when these animals leave the water for lush berry patches and mast crops on the higher ridges. Yes, 'coons can be trapped in these areas as well. When trapping "upland" 'coons, the dirt hole set can be highly effective. Just use a natural raccoon bait in the bottom of the hole and a gland scent around the edge of the hole. I would also suggest a bit of 'coon urine, just as if you were making a fox set. If you take all the precautions that you would normally take when making a dirt hole set for fox, the set may also take foxes and bobcats that happen along.

The cubby set also works when it comes to land-trapping these animals. Make the cubby deep enough and the walls tight enough so that a raccoon cannot reach the bait from the outside. Place the bait in the back of the cubby with a lure at the entrance.

Natural cubbies are readily located in most raccoon habitat at the bases of large trees, in small rock ledges, etc.; so, you may not have to build one, or expend a great deal of effort in modifying a natural one for trapping. Generally, a wooden limb drag or clog is used for land trapping. It should be a piece of solid dead wood 2 or 3 inches in diameter and about 4 to 6 feet long.

The raccoon usually holes up during cold weather and will lay up for long periods of time. However, when the weather warms up for a night or two, it'll be out roaming the hills again. For this reason, don't expect to catch a lot of raccoons when it's extremely cold. There are exceptions, but as a general rule, you'll have the most action when a warm foggy winter night comes along.

Certainly, the raccoon trapper will have a higher degree of success when the season opens if he has done his pre-season scouting homework. In my opinion, pre-season scouting for raccoons is a must because the warmer early season nights are when they are moving most — not later on when the season's in full swing and the weather's cold. In order to get plenty of action before the cold weather hits and raccoons hole up, some serious trappers not only pre-scout areas but also pre-bait sets. Cubbies are commonly built and baited long before the trapping season, just to get the animals used to coming in to them. It's advisable to cover the future trapline every 3 days or so and pitch a piece of bait into the cubby, pocket set, dirt hole set, etc. Then, when the season opens, all that's necessary is to place the trap and attach the bait securely. The raccooms are now conditioned to the set site — catching them will be a snap.

Today, raccoons are generally cased and sold skin side out, the tail having been left on the pelt and generally tacked out flat to dry. A raccoon pelt usually has a lot of fat and flesh remaining on it after it's removed from the animal. Some trappers prefer to leave a freshly skinned raccoon pelt in a cool area for a day or so before fleshing. This way, the fat breaks down and is easier to scrape off the pelt. Generally, the No. 4 or 4½ wire stretcher is recommended for raccoon pelts. These masked bandits of wood and stream fame are certainly worthy of the trapper's time and effort.

A dirt-hole set accounted for this raccoon. Like many other furbearers, 'coons are quite susceptible to dirt hole sets. Once made (just like it's made for red fox), and positioned in the 'coons' line of travel, your chances of taking one are very good. (Photo courtesy of Tal Lockwood.)

A raccoon pelt stretched on a commercial spring-steel stretcher should be quite long and rather narrow—the preferred shape among raccoon buyers. Note how the pelt gripper is placed quite a ways down on the raccoon's tail rather than directly on the base of the tail. This helps to hold the tail skin stretched open so that it can quickly air-dry.

SKUNK

TRAP SIZE: No. 1 or 1½
BAIT: Tainted Meat
PRIME: December
STRETCHER: No. 2 or 4
TRACK:

THE STRIPED skunk (*Mephitis mephitis*) needs little physical description. Of course, the skunk is best known for the obnoxious scent that it sprays from two anal glands at the base of its tail. For those who care to know, the striped skunk has a long bushy tail and generally two white stripes running along its back. A male striped skunk weighs about 6 pounds with a female averaging slightly less. The feet of the "wood pussy" have long claws which are used in digging for food and excavating a den. When being approached by an enemy, a skunk will generally stamp its forefeet or scratch the ground rapidly while the tail stands erect, the body hair standing on end. It's this classic "pose" that has been known to make strong men moan.

The fluid is ejected from two "nozzles" exiting the anal glands, the two fine streams of "perfume" converging into one. Generally, skunks can spray the fluid about 6 to 10 feet although large skunks have been known to throw it a distance of 20 feet. For these reasons, it's always best to approach a skunk from upwind and don't get too close. Contrary to what some trapper's tales would have us believe, a live skunk *cannot* be safely carried by its tail for it can spray in any position.

Various subspecies of skunks are widely distributed throughout the United States and Canada. Skunks generally breed in February and March with the males competing for receptive females, a single male often breed-

ing with more than one. During the breeding season males will frequently fight, vying for the rapt attention of the female which is sexually receptive for only a short period of time. If a female breeds and does not become pregnant, she will again become male-receptive approximately a month later.

Gestation may vary from 62 to 75 days with the average about 63. From two to 16 young are born although the average is about six or seven. When the kittens are born, they're sparsely haired with eyes and ears closed. The ears reportedly open about 3 to 4 weeks after birth, but the eyes do not open until the fourth or fifth week. The young skunks have glands which contain musk at birth, but they don't develop control of the glands until they are about 2 or 3 weeks old.

By the sixth week, the young are able to come to the entrance of their burrow, and by the seventh week, they're ready to leave the den and feed with the mother, often following her in single-file fashion. Female skunks are capable of breeding at 10 months of age and, as you can see, they have a high rate of reproduction. This, combined with the fact that skunks are the object of few predators, reveals why a healthy skunk population is capable of sustaining high losses.

Skunks, like most furbearing animals, are nocturnal. They do not hibernate, in the strict sense of the term, but during cold weather they do spend considerable

Believe it or not, these two skunks have been caught in a double! Most skunks are caught as incidentals to trapping other furbearing animals. Due to their low pelt prices in recent years (and the foul odors associated with skinning and stretching them), few trappers pursue this furbearer for its pelt value. Perhaps more trappers attempt to catch skunks simply because they're pests. At any rate, skunks are not difficult to catch and can be baited into a trap with any sort of tainted meat. Even a trap placed in the open, on top of the ground, will catch a skunk. They're just not trap shy at all.

time in the den. Although skunks usually den in a solitary manner, they may share winter dens with ten or more other individuals, frequently utilizing modified badger dens or abandoned woodchuck or fox burrows for their winter quarters.

The striped skunk is omnivorous and though it tends to like meat, insects frequently make up a large part of its diet. Another major portion of its diet will be plant material, but they've been known to eat rats, mice, carrion, bird eggs, fruit, berries, frogs, earthworms, corn and a variety of other foodstuffs.

The sign that a skunk leaves may consist of its "diggings" where it has been searching for insects and grubs, or its small irregular droppings. Also, a skunk's tracks can sometimes be seen in dry dust alongside a road although the skunk itself is probably seen or smelled more often than its sign.

These amazing little animals are highly adaptable and can survive practically anywhere, from wilderness areas to the interiors of small cities. On a number of occasions, I have seen skunks on the main street of downtown Prescott, Arizona — a town with a population of approximately 20,000 people. The skunks were always seen at night, but nonetheless, it's a sign that they are surviving in the back alleys and small woodlots within the city.

There are thousands of skunks trapped every year,

most of them in sets which are intended for other animals. As a result, it's generally considered a nuisance to the trapper, many simply released if caught. In short, trappers don't want to go to the trouble of skinning the smelly animals for the meager price they bring.

Skunks do have a quality fur however, and in the past they have been worth relatively more money. I have skinned a good many skunks myself and, when trapping full-time a few years ago, I skinned every one I caught. As a full-time trapper, I wasn't specifically trapping for skunks, but my trapping area was so heavily infested with these animals that they kept getting into my coyote and fox sets. Rather than fight 'em I decided to skin 'em; at the end of the season, I had a good collection of skunk pelts which, if I remember correctly, netted $8 apiece. Those "pests" ended up paying for my gasoline and more during that year of trapping. During that period I also collected the scent from those skunks and sold it to the various trapping supply houses, frequently getting more than the price of the pelts! When it comes to gathering scent, the trick is to get skunks with a lot of "essence" remaining in the glands. Unfortunately, trapped skunks expel much of their scent when caught, and you may find, after skinning one, that the glands are practically empty. Scent collection is, however, another way to maximize trapping profits.

Today, skunk pelts bring only a fraction of what I received for them a few years ago. I skinned several during the 1982-83 season and was offered only $2 apiece for excellent prime pelts taken from the high country of northern Arizona. From an economic stand-point, it should be said that skunks with the most black and the least white have traditionally brought the most money.

Interestingly, the skunk is one of the first furbearers to acquire a prime pelt in the fall. When caught late in the season, skunk pelts are often "den burned" or "springy" which means that the hair is relatively coarse and scattered in spots over the pelt. To eliminate catch-ing this type of skunk, trapping efforts should be con-centrated before late January.

Skunks are not wary of any type of set and are very easy to trap, even with a trap on top of the ground, with no covering whatever! Just place a bait (any smelly foodstuff will do) near the trap — that's as complicated as it gets. I think the reason that I have caught so many skunks at predator sets is due to the fact those sets were sprinkled with gland scent. I should add that the dirt-hole set, wherein a bit of tainted meat is placed in the bottom of a hole, is a real skunk taker. However, it is not necessary to go to the trouble of making a dirt hole set to take skunks. Generally, traps for skunks consist of the No. 1 or 1½, or 110- to 220-size Conibears.

One of the easiest and most effective sets for skunks was passed along to me by trapper Jim Nolan. You may find his information helpful:

A skunk is not at all afraid of an open trap. One of the easiest ways to catch skunks is just take some roofing tacks and nail some strips of bacon onto a tree about a foot above the ground. Set a trap under the bacon on top of the ground and throw a few leaves over it.

The best bait for skunks is a food bait; they are vora-cious when it comes to eating. A good food-bait mixture is peanut butter and anise oil. You can just wipe it on a tree, and it sticks and stays forever. Rain doesn't seem to affect it a great deal and the anise oil will give off fumes for a long time.

There is a way to kill a skunk so that it doesn't spray. Use a 22 caliber rimfire pistol with 22 Short ammunition and shoot them just behind the front leg through both lungs. One shot will usually do it. A lung shot with a 22 Short is not so traumatic to them so it doesn't cause them to tense up their muscles and spray. A lung shot doesn't hit any nerve centers; all it does is stop the breathing. Nine times out of ten, they won't spray.

A TRAP SET FOR SKUNK

(Left) Tack a strip of bacon to an old stump and position a trap beneath it. (Above) Cover the trap with leaves or duff.

If you trap a skunk and it sprays the set area thoroughly, the stench will only serve to improve the set for future use. In fact, even the trapper who is *not* wanting to catch skunks but who catches one in a good setting location will very likely catch more of what he's not after if he simply re-sets the scented trap, right where it is, and does not move the set to a new location.

Traps placed at den entrances which are being used by skunks are practically a sure thing. Cubby sets using both foot-hold or body-gripping traps will also work very well — just place a chicken head, a piece of tainted meat, or skunk scent in the back of the cubby; you'll catch the first skunk that comes along and decides to investigate the set.

A skunk should be case skinned and sold skin side out. A skunk, in my experience, spoils very quickly. I once caught one in the Arizona desert mountains, shot it, and left it in the trap until I returned from checking a few other traps. It was lying in the sun and the tempera-

Here is a skinned skunk pelt. Like other animals with fatty skins, skunks are stretched cased with the fur in.

REMOVING THE SCENT GLANDS

(Left) Skunk essence is one of the most sought-after ingredients for trapping lures because it has a carrying capacity second to none. To remove the glands, which are located at the base of the tail, a cut is made at the base of the anus. Once the glad is exposed, it can be gently pulled out and the tissue around it cut away with a sharp knife to free it.

The glands are almost entirely free. Be careful not to cut into the scent-containing glands which would release the valuable essence.

ture was about 60 degrees. I returned less than an hour later and when I reached down to pick it up by its hair, the fur pulled out freely. The hair was already "slipping," indicating the pelt was ruined. Any skunk that is killed should be skinned immediately unless the temperature is very cold (preferably around the freezing mark, or lower).

When skinning a skunk, be careful not to puncture the scent glands around the anus. Those glands can be removed and sold separately as mentioned earlier. Once they are removed, there's no danger of getting skunk essence on you when you skin the animal. If you so choose, the skunk can be carefully skinned first, enabling you to see the scent glands more easily, and then you can remove them.

The tail should be left on a skunk pelt, split to the tip, and tacked out flat when the pelt is mounted on a solid wooden stretcher. If the pelt is placed on a commercial wire stretcher, the gripper will hold the tail open to dry.

A skunk is generally a very greasy animal although it is relatively easy to separate the fat and grease from the pelt by scraping on a fleshing beam. A No. 2 or 4 commercial wire stretcher is recommended for skunks, depending upon the size of the animal.

There have been a lot of tales regarding the difficulty in removing skunk odors. However, I have found that gasoline will take the odor out very well. When I'm skinning skunks, I use rubber gloves as I do when skinning all furbearers. Then, once the skinning is completed, I walk outside, away from any open flame and run a little gasoline over my gloved hands as I rub them together in a hand-washing manner. Those gloves are then washed in soap and water to remove any final traces of skunk. The washed gloves may have a trace of gas odor about them that will remain for a while, but the smell will, in an hour or two, dissipate in the air.

There you have it — everything you ever wanted to know about trapping skunks, and more!

OPOSSUM

TRAP SIZE: No. 1½
BAIT: Tainted meat or fish
PRIME: November
STRETCHER: No. 2, 3 or 4
TRACK:

THE OPOSSUM (*Didelphis marsupialis*) is about the size of a house cat and can weigh 10 pounds or more. It is best identified by its large rat-like appearance and hairless prehensile tail (meaning it can grasp objects with it). It also possesses opposable big toes which allow the animal to balance and cling to branches. Like a rat, the opossum's face is long and pointed, the ears hairless. Opossum fur is made up of long, white guard hairs which overlie softer under fur of black-tipped hairs. The female of the species has a pouch on the underside or belly where the young are carried after birth.

The term "playing 'possum" comes from the animal's habit of going limp and motionless when threatened with danger. The animal is so good at this trait that it frequently fools dogs—and young trappers—into thinking it is dead.

The opossum is widely dispersed over much of the United States and is reported to be in all the lower 48 states. I have not seen one in the desert Southwest, although I have seen them in the hills of southern California.

The opossum is quite prolific with breeding generally taking place in January and February and, after a short 13-day gestation period, from 3 to 17 young are born. Shortly after birth, each new-born opossum crawls into the female's pouch and immediately attaches itself to one of the 12 or 13 nipples normally present. Any newborn in excess of the number of available nipples will die quickly with only seven young generally surviving. Their eyes don't open until they're 8 weeks old whereupon they let go of the nipples but still continue to nurse from the pouch. At about 3 months of age they start to eat solid foods and accompany the female by holding onto her fur and tail with their tails and feet. Young opossums generally leave the female at the age of about 3½ months; a second litter often being born in May or June. However, in states farther north, one brood per year is generally the norm.

The opossum is omnivorous but may eat more insects than anything else. They have also been known to eat corn, mammals, birds, fruit, berries and carrion. Often carrion, sometimes badly decomposed, makes up an important part of the opossum's diet. They are also reported to spend a considerable amount of time in trees seeking out bird eggs and young birds.

The most frequently seen sign of the opossum, which is readily distinguishable, is its tracks. The opossum has a very peculiar hind foot wherein the "big toe" is slanted inward or even backward. There are five front toes, of which the middle three remain in a close group, separate from the others. Opossum scats are quite irregular in appearance, but these are seldom found.

Preferred opossum habitat includes mixed woodlands and farmlands. Exposed roots on stream banks may provide den sites as do rock crevices and abandoned woodchuck dens. An opossum generally doesn't dig his own den but moves into any convenient abandoned hole.

This marsupial's pelt is generally prime from the first of November through the end of February, and, like the skunk, the opossum has no strong points relating to its difficulty of being trapped. Again, like the skunk,

A TRAP SET FOR OPOSSUM

1. (Left) Get a jar, punch holes in the lid, and then insert rotted fish or sun-rendered fish oil.

2. Dig a hole just large enough to accommodate the jar so that the top of the jar will be flush with the surface of the earth when the hole is completed.

this animal is usually taken in sets designed for other furbearing animals, particularly when those sets are baited with meats or other foodstuffs.

When I was a young lad, just beginning to trap, I remember making an opossum set at an abandoned woodchuck den at the top of a rock bluff. As I recall, I placed a No. 1½ single long spring Blake and Lamb trap just inside the den entrance and scattered a few oak and elm leaves over the top of it. At that single set, I took five 'possums during the next week. In fact, I used the same set at the same den for several years in a row with the same type of success. Over the years, some of my best 'possum sets have been made at such dens. Of note is the fact that 'possums seem to use such available dens frequently in the fall and winter; and, traps set at these den sites will need no bait or lure.

An opossum is not wary of a trap, in any manner, whether it be by scent or appearance. In short, a trap laid on top of the ground is all that it takes to trap a 'possum. However, as when setting any trap, it's always best to camouflage it from any possible trap thieves. Any of the No. 1½ or 2 size traps are excellent for 'possum as far as the foot-hold variety goes — they are also not difficult to hold in a trap.

A trap set practically anywhere that opossums frequent, (fencerows or small streams), and baited with tainted meat produces good results. The tainted meat can be tacked onto a tree, several inches above the ground, with a trap placed directly below the bait and covered with a few leaves or dry grass.

A fishy smelling bait or scent such as sun rendered fish oil is an excellent 'possum lure, its foul-smelling odor easily detected by these animals from some distance. I once caught a good many 'possums at sets intended for coyotes. Those sets included a jar of tainted fish parts buried underneath the surface of the earth, holes poked in the jar lid to let the odor escape. It didn't do much for coyotes, but it was a real killer of a 'possum set.

Opossums are case skinned and sold skin-side out. Since their tail has no hair or fur on it, it is cut off and discarded with the carcass. A wire stretcher of No. 2, 3 or 4 size is generally the best bet for stretching the hide. These animals generally have a lot of fat next to the hide which must be removed with a fleshing beam and scraper.

4. Dirt is filled in around the jar, and a covering of light material used to camouflage the set. The smell will exude from the jar lid for a long time, making this a long-lasting possum set.

3. Then place traps on either side of the jar. This way, the possum will be taken if it approaches from either direction.

Opossum pelts, though they have been sold by the thousands in this country, have always brought a relatively low price. As a result, many trappers don't feel they're worth the skinning and stretching effort. For this reason, there seems to be little current interest in trapping opossums. Frankly, most trappers would rather know how to keep them *out* of sets! Of course, one way to keep them out of other sets is to avoid the use of tainted meat or other foul-smelling baits. Even with that precaution, 'possums will blunder into all varieties of sets.

Given the ease with which these marsupials can be trapped, they should be considered a prime candidate for the young or beginning trapper. In short, they serve to bolster confidence and provide valuable skinning experience that is easily transferred to larger, more valuable animals.

This furbuyer is holding up two 'possum pelts which have been improperly stretched, fur-out. Note also that some unknowing trapper left the tail on the 'possum pelt at the right. This is incorrect. Opossum tails should *not* be left attached to the pelt and they should be stretched skin-out and fur-in.

BADGER

TRAP SIZE: No. 3 or 4
BAIT: Meat
PRIME: December
STRETCHER: No. 5
TRACK:

THE BADGER *(Taxidae taxus)* is a short-legged, wide-bodied carnivore with powerful front legs and long sharp claws. It is built something along the lines of the wolverine with the average adult running about 28 inches long and weighing 15 to 20 pounds. However, some of them have been known to weigh as much as 30 pounds!

A badger's fur is predominately grizzled grey on top of its back with a yellowish tinge to the fur on the belly. There is a white stripe that runs from the animal's nose up over the top of its head and down the back of its neck, the length of which, of course, is dependent upon the individual animal. The legs of the badger are dark brown or black.

The animal is widely distributed over most of the plains and prairie country west of the Mississippi River. Its range extends into the prairie provinces of Canada to the North and into Mexico to the South. The badger usually prefers the arid open plains and foothills and generally shuns densely forested timber country and wet lowlands.

Badgers mate when the female becomes receptive in late summer or early fall. Following fertilization, the embryos undergo development which ceases during the winter months and resumes again in February with one to five young born in April or May after an 8-month gestation period.

The young have little fur at birth and their eyes remain closed for about 1 month. At about 2 months of age, the young are weaned and travel with the mother, learning to hunt and forage for themselves. By early fall they're hunting alone, generally leaving the mother's home range in October. Females are usually a year old before they start breeding although that is not always the case; some may breed in the fall when only 5-6 months old. Males do not breed until the second year.

The badger's powerful front legs and long claws are well equipped for digging and, indeed, this is how adult badgers survive — by digging out ground squirrels, prairie dogs, and other rodents. There are few animals that can outdig the badger. Young badgers which have not fully developed the knack of catching some of the large rodents feed on insects until they learn. Besides subterranean rodents, badgers also eat rabbits, snails, worms, snakes and eggs of all sorts.

The most frequently seen sign of the badger are the burrows left by the animal in its search for rodents. The burrow, indicative of the badger, is generally wider than it is tall to correspond with the badger's low, wide body build. Frequently, there will be a great many of these burrows in a small area, indicating a lot of activity by both hunter and hunted. Sometimes, a badger will burrow into a nest of ground squirrels, consume the entire lot, and then rest there during the heat of the day before venturing out again at night.

A badger is pigeon-toed and, if its tracks are seen, they clearly reveal this characteristic. If a short-legged badger crosses a snowy area, the drag marks of its body can sometimes be seen in the snow. One of the best places to look for badger sign is along dry sandy washes where it hunts for food. However, anywhere that fairly open, dry, treeless plains or rolling hills are found, one is likely to find badger sign.

Badger pelts generally prime in mid-winter although primeness of the pelt is less dependent upon season or fur quality as it is on the fur type of the individual badger. These animals are generally classified into either "fur badgers" or "hair badgers" by fur buyers, each term describing the fur quality. Badger guard hair, 2 to 3 inches in length, was once used in shaving and paint brushes or sometimes for pointing other furs.

Because it is such a strong digger and fierce fighter,

Badgers, once they've been caught in a trap, will dig up the area. Though it is possible for a badger to dig a long trap stake out of the ground, it is unlikely. They generally reach as far as the trap chain will allow before beginning their excavation. (Photo courtesy of Tal Lockwood.)

the badger usually digs a considerable amount when caught in foot-hold traps. Sometimes, it'll dig a 12- to 18-inch deep trench all around the trap stake and could very probably dig out even a long trap stake. Therefore, even when trapping them in open country, it's a good idea to snap a grapnel and a long chain onto the trap chain, even if the trap is staked solidly. This way, if the badger does dig the stake out, you'll still be able to track it up by following the grapnel marks in the soil.

A badger, being built low to the ground, and having its feet spaced widely apart, may sometimes walk over a trap and spring it with its chest. The trapper should keep this in mind when setting his traps. Also, when a badger exits a den where it's been digging rodents, it sometimes pushes a mound of earth in front of it which could spring a trap.

However, a badger is susceptible to being trapped, particularly when baited with a chunk of meat or when the trap is set at the mouth of an occupied den. Generally a No. 3 or No. 4 trap is used for badger and, if properly set, these will retain a good hold on the animal's short strong legs.

A few years ago a good quality "fur" badger was quite valuable on the raw fur market though the price has dropped considerably in recent years. For this reason, badger trapping activity isn't very great. Generally, badgers are caught in sets designed for coyotes or other animals that inhabit the open rolling grassland country. Since they are fond of meat, it is usually a dirt-hole set devised for a coyote which nabs them.

The dirt-hole set is actually very good for trapping badgers if you are pursuing this furbearer specifically. However, when making this set, it's a good idea to use two traps instead of one, slightly offsetting each trap in front of a dirt hole to account for the animal's wide leg spread.

Clyde Tryon holds up a fresh badger pelt prior to stretching. This particular badger was caught at a den entrance in a snare, rather than a foot-hold trap. It had been digging up a farmer's alfalfa field and Tryon was doing the farmer a favor to rid him of the pest.

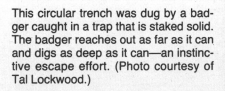

This circular trench was dug by a badger caught in a trap that is staked solid. The badger reaches out as far as it can and digs as deep as it can—an instinctive escape effort. (Photo courtesy of Tal Lockwood.)

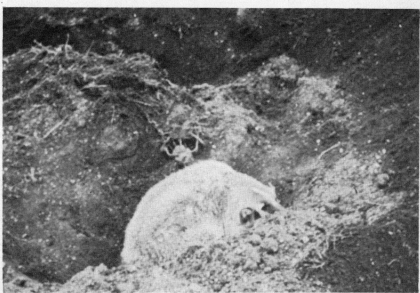

Another excellent set for badger is at the entrance to an occupied den. Again, it's a good idea to use two traps and place them side by side at the den entrance. Burrows are generally quite deep and a lot of earth is excavated which makes trap setting convenient. It's generally a simple matter to conceal traps below the soft, fine earth in a recently used burrow.

A body-gripping Conibear-type trap is also an excellent method of trapping badger at a den entrance although in some states it is illegal to use the larger-size 220 or 330 Conibear trap on land. Badgers have also been snared at den entrances — just be certain to set the bottom of the loop very close to the ground so that the animal doesn't pass underneath the noose.

If there is no badger den in the immediate area, just make an artificial one in a bank. Make the set in an area known to be inhabited by badger and dig a hole about 2 feet deep and 1½ feet wide. Place a chunk of meat bait such as prairie dog or jackrabbit at the back of the hole. A strong-smelling food lure, similar to that used for coyotes, can be placed above the den entrance to work as a call lure and further enhance the set. As when setting at a den entrance, use two foot-hold traps side by side. Attach grapnels and bed everything below ground, sifting dirt over the traps with trap covers in place.

A badger's pelt may be sold either open or cased although there seems to be an increasing demand for cased pelts. The pelt should be sold fur side in. A badger generally has a lot of very tough gristly fat next to the skin but this can be removed with a fleshing beam and knife. One advantage to skinning a badger in a cased manner is so that the head end of the pelt can be slipped over a fleshing beam and it can then be fleshed much easier than if the skin is handled "open."

Sometimes, a trapped badger will be asleep when the trapper approaches. Don't for a moment think that the badger is dead or even docile if this happens. I remember trapping a badger shortly after I began working badger country. When I approached the animal, it appeared to be asleep. Obviously, it was tired for it had already dug a circular trench all around the trap stake, as far as the chain would allow, and just as deep as it could reach. The only problem was, this one wasn't smart enough to dig where the stake was. (They seldom are.) The badger was evidently sleeping soundly for it

A SET FOR BADGER

1. This is a freshly dug dirt hole, constructed by a trapper.

didn't wake up until I reached out and tapped it on the head with the barrel of my .22 rifle. It didn't awaken with a sleepy yawn and stretch, but instead with a sudden snarling, hissing and biting. It bit the muzzle and front sight of my rifle barrel a couple of times before I even knew what happened. That's the last time I ever tapped a sleeping badger on the forehead!

Badgers are generally thought to be pests by ranchers because of the many large holes that they leave in pastures. For this reason, a rancher may welcome a badger trapper who is adept at catching the diggers. This just might be what the trapper needs to get his foot in the door for trapping other more valuable furbearers.

(Right) Badgers can be stretched either "open" as was the one on the left, or "cased." There seems to be little preference among buyers the author talked to regarding which method was preferred.

2. Here is the proper positioning of two traps with screen coverings in position. Note the manner in which they are offset or staggered to accommodate the badger's wide body.

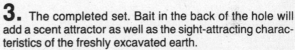

3. The completed set. Bait in the back of the hole will add a scent attractor as well as the sight-attracting characteristics of the freshly excavated earth.

MARTEN

TRAP SIZE: No. 1 or 1½
BAIT: Meat
PRIME: December
STRETCHER: No. 1½
TRACK:

THE MARTEN *(Martes caurina)* is a member of the weasel family. It has a long slender body, slightly smaller than a house cat, with short limbs. During the mid-winter the bottom of a marten's feet are heavily covered with hair so the toe pads do not generally show in a track. Toward the end of winter, however, and during the summer, the toe tracks do appear. The soft pelt is usually a shiny yellowish-brown intermixed with dark brown hairs. However, the color may vary among different individuals. Generally, the legs and tail are darker than the rest of the body, and the underparts are lighter with an irregular spot of buffy yellow on the throat and chest.

Marten are born in late April in the nest of a hollow tree or, on rare occassions, in a burrow in the ground although the tree nest is most common. The young number up to five in a litter, are blind and helpless for the first month. By fall, the juveniles closely resemble their parents and have learned how to hunt by themselves. It is at this time that the family generally splits up.

The marten is primarily a tree inhabitant though it does take some of its prey on the ground. It is extremely agile and able to escape many of its enemies though many marten are reportedly killed by lynx, its cousin the fisher, and the great horned owl. The marten lives primarily on squirrels, chipmunks, mice and rabbits, though it will occasionally kill a grouse or other bird, a few reptiles, frogs, and insects. Nuts, fruits and berries are also part of its diet.

Commonly seen sign of the marten are its tracks in the snow or its small scats or droppings. However, marten scats can easily be confused with those of the mink, its cousin, for the animals are similar in size and body structure. However, evidence of berries in the droppings is a pretty sure indication of marten. At certain times of the year, the marten favors a diet of berries, particularly if mountain ash or blueberries are in the area. If one finds sign of this in the droppings, it can generally be assumed to be marten, for mink and weasel do not eat these fruits. Sometimes, several marten scats will be found in the same area indicating their preference for leaving droppings where others have been left, as many other animals do.

Generally, the sign of the marten will be found in heavily timbered high country from 4,000 feet to timberline. It prefers the wilderness and shuns the presence of man which may give some indication regarding where the best places are to begin looking for marten sign.

This is a very quick animal with a keen nose, and though it is extremely wary of man, it's not the least bit trap shy. Even a trap placed uncovered on the ground or on a log will serve to catch it. Generally, a No. 1 or

1½ trap is recommended for foot-hold types. If a body-gripping trap is to be used, the size generally used for mink and muskrat will work fine for marten — Conibear traps of the 110-120 series.

One of the most popular sets for marten is a body-gripping, leaning pole set. To make the pole set, find a dead tree limb or trunk about 12 feet long and 5 or 6 inches in diameter. If it has any branches, remove them, at least from one side. Lean this pole, smooth side up, against the trunk or branch of a standing tree, or spike or wire it to the side of the tree. The pole should contact the tree about 5 or 6 feet off the ground or snow, and the end of the pole should extend well beyond the trunk of the tree.

A piece of meat bait is placed at the upper end of the pole and a trap is placed next to the main part of the tree. A body-gripping trap works very well at this set, and a 120-size Conibear can be positioned so that a marten running up the pole will have to go through it to get to the bait. If preferred, bait may be placed on the trap's trigger.

If a foot-hold trap is used, it may be necessary to chop a flat trap-bedding spot on the pole. Position a No. 1 or 1½ trap, and tie it in place with light string. Attach the trap chain securely to the pole with wire. This way, a trapped marten will break the light string, and both the trap and marten will fall off the pole to a dangling position. Here the marten's efforts to escape are fruitless, and it will generally be found frozen in this position, well out of the reach of predators and rodents. A marten trap on the pole does not have to be concealed for these animals are not trap shy.

Another type of leaning pole set can be made wherein a larger diameter pole is leaned against the main part of the tree trunk so that it butts into it. A foot-hold trap can be placed on the top of the leaning pole and the bait (a prey species of the marten) can be tied or tacked above the trap.

The advantage of the leaning pole set is that it keeps the trap out of the snow for, in country where marten are found, the snows frequently get quite deep and traps at ground level will sometimes become inoperable.

It's always a good idea to position marten traps under overhanging branches of evergreen trees to protect them from heavy snows. If necessary, a shelter of pine

A LEANING POLE SET FOR MARTEN

1. Jim Nolan illustrates how to build a leaning pole set for marten. They generally inhabit the high country and frequently are trapped where several feet of snow may be on the ground. Nolan simply pulled a small size fallen tree over to the larger standing one and leaned the large end in the crotch formed by a small branch.

2. A Victor Conibear 110 trap is placed on the top side of the leaning pole right next to the trunk of the larger tree. When a marten runs up the pole, it has to go through the trap and trigger it. Nolan usually places the trap trigger off to one side of the opening to make an apparent clear passageway for the marten to pass through.

branches can be built over a marten trap to keep the snow off it.

A marten is case-skinned and stretched fur out. Most trappers recommend skinning a marten right down to the feet.

Due to the habitat where marten are found it generally takes a trapper with a lot of stamina and endurance to trap them in the high snow-covered wilderness areas.

This furbuyer holds two marten pelts. The one on the left shows the belly side, the pelt on the right shows the backside of pine marten. Both have been properly stretched.

3. A bait is placed out on the end of the pole to attract marten. Fish baits, such as sardines, work very well with this method.

4. Here's the marten's view of the bait. It appears that there is nothing to block its way to the bait except for that skinny "twig" which can apparently be brushed aside. So much for the marten's thinking. Conibears are very effective in running pole sets for marten, but not absolutely necessary. A foot-hold trap can also be placed on top of the log, preferably after chopping out a notch in the log for solid trap placement.

WEASEL

TRAP SIZE: No. 0 or 1½
BAIT: Bloody meat
PRIME: December
STRETCHER: No. 1½
TRACK:

THE WEASEL *(Mustela frenata)* is a small slender animal with a long neck and body, short legs, and rounded ears set close to the skull. There are 36 species and subspecies of weasel widely distributed throughout North America. They are usually brown in summer with a light colored underside though some turn white in the winter with a black tail tip. Pelts taken during the winter in this color phase are frequently referred to as ermine. However, they are not really ermine in the true sense of the word.

Weasels are extremely blood-thirsty, carnivorous animals and often kill more than they can eat. Their normal diet consists of mice, rats, shrews and moles although they will also attack larger animals such as rabbits and squirrels. On occasion, a weasel has been known to enter a henhouse and kill all the occupants. It generally kills by biting the back of the neck or the throat of its victim and then will suck the blood of its prey from a main artery.

The weasel is a very prolific animal that breeds once a year, but has five to 14 young in a single litter. The young are born in a burrow lined with leaves and fur. Some species breed in July and August after which the fertilized eggs develop for a little more than a week, then cease development for about 7½ months. At that point the embryos resume growth and the young are born 27 days later. According to one source, the gestation period of the weasel is between 205 and 337 days with an average of about 280. The newborn are blind

and unfurred although they soon develop a soft white coat which is replaced in about 3 weeks by adult fur. Their teeth are evident by the fourth week, and their eyes open at about 5 weeks when weaning begins. The female of some weasel species may breed at the age of only 3 or 4 months while males may not be sexually mature until the year following their birth.

The best time to look for weasel sign is during the winter when their tracks can be seen in the snow along grassy ditches, cattail swamps, or in the high weeds and grass along fencerows where field mice and other small prey can be found.

Though the animal is extemely high-strung, active and a fierce fighter, it is not the least bit trap shy and a trap placed on the top of the ground will catch them. A weasel, as mentioned earlier, is a very small animal, and the small No. 0 foot-hold trap offers light treadle resistance for easy springing. Due to the weasel's quickness and light weight, slight pressure must be all it takes for the trap to spring.

Some trappers prefer to use a larger trap such as the No. 1½ which generally ends up working like a body-gripping trap on the small weasel, catching it high on the body across the shoulders and lungs so that the animal suffocates. Conventional body-gripping traps also work well when placed with the bait on the trigger and on top of the snow wherever weasels travel. The bait should consist of bloody meat — the bloodier and fresher the better. Meat baits may include mice, rats, rabbit, or any other prey species of the weasel.

Baits placed in cubby sets made in rocks or hollow logs are very effective. Artificial wooden box cubbies are frequently built with a hole in one end to let the weasel into the trap. The advantage of this type, and most cubby sets, is that they protect the trap from the snow.

Weasels should be case skinned and sold skin side out. They can be stretched on a No. 1½ adjustable wire stretcher made for mink although most trappers generally stretch weasels on solid wooden forms, sometimes made from a shingle.

A CUBBY SET FOR WEASEL

(Left) A rock and wood cubby constructed by the trapper provides a small opening because weasels like to investigate and squeeze through small places. (Above) Though a weasel is not the least bit trap wary, the addition of leaves can prevent a trap thief spotting the set.

MINK

TRAP SIZE: No. 1 or 1½ or 110-220
BAIT: Fresh meat
PRIME: December
STRETCHER: No. 1½
TRACK:

THE MINK (*Mustela vison*) belongs to the weasel family *Mustelidae* and is generally distinguished by a long slender body, short legs, and toes equipped with non-retractile claws. It has a thick coat of light to dark brown fur with a small white spot or spots on the throat, chest or belly. The mink resembles its close relative the weasel in both form and gait, but is larger, heavier bodied, and darker. The mink is generally about 24 inches long, including a fairly bushy tail that accounts for about one-third of its length. The mink's head and ears are on the small side in relation to its body. Its ears are rounded and nearly hidden in the fur. The legs of the mink are short, but the neck is long. Male minks are generally heavier than females with the males weighing from 2 to 4 pounds and the females generally going from 1 to 2 pounds. Mink are found in all parts of the United States, Canada, and Alaska, the exceptions being the arid regions within that range.

These animals generally begin breeding in late January and continue through mid-March, and a male will mate with any available female. Gestation occurs over a period of about 51 days though immediately following fertilization the embryos cease development for about 21 days. Three to six young are born with the average being about three or four. The young, born in late April or May, are blind, and the kittens are almost without fur. Their eyes open at about 25 days and at this time the female begins to bring solid food to them. They are generally weaned at the age of 6 weeks. By 8 weeks they're accompanying the female while she hunts, and they leave the family unit in late August or September. The females reach adult size at about 4 months and are sexually mature at 12 months; males are full grown at 9 to 11 months and are sexually mature at 18 months.

Mink are carnivorous, feeding mostly on mammals such as moles, ground and tree squirrels, rabbits, mice, and birds. However, mink are frequently found in or near water where the food generally includes such items as crayfish, muskrats, mollusks, fish, frogs, and snakes. They are also known to eat various types of insects but they rarely eat vegetable matter.

The male mink is generally a wanderer while the female spends most of her entire life within ½-mile of the den. It is reported that a mother mink will sometimes make a meal of her newborn, and if a mature male finds a nest of young mink, he may even fight the mother in an attempt to kill the young ones.

The most common sign of the mink is its tracks, and it sometimes takes close scrutiny for the trapper to recognize them. Usually, the tracks will be seen in the soft mud along a stream's edge and consist of a main heel pad separated from the widely spaced toes. There will sometimes be evidence of hair marks in the track, between the animal's toes.

145

Mink dens are difficult to recognize for they frequently use muskrat burrows, holes in logs or stumps, and other ready-made shelters. However, whenever a mink makes a nest, it will usually be lined with leaves and even feathers if they're available. Mink droppings can sometimes be seen along the creek bank on rocks and logs and will sometimes have fur, feathers, fish remains, etc., in them. It is not uncommon to find muskrat fur and bone in the droppings.

A number of trappers scout for mink sign around creek bridges because they can be checked rather quickly and simply by parking the automobile, and walking down to the creek below. There is frequently a good bit of dead or dried grass which has grown around these bridge abutments in the fall and winter months, and this provides a good habitat for rabbits and other types of small rodents, all prey species of the mink. As a consequence, mink frequent these areas, and if many of them are traveling through, their sign will be easily noticed.

Though mink are seldom seen in the daytime, I once had the opportunity to see one about 2 o'clock in the afternoon, at a distance of no more than 15 feet. There was a drainage ditch running through the middle of a sudan and cane grass field, with cattails and dense swamp grass growing along the ditch. It had been a wet summer, and the field had been too wet to cut for some time. Finally, in the early fall, I decided the field was dry enough for a tractor, and I began green-chopping the sudan grass for cattle feed. While finishing the last strip with the cutter, a monster of a mink ran out of the standing grass. It turned to face the side of the tractor, as if to challenge it for intruding. I stopped, and the mink bounded off toward the ditch.

The pelt of the mink generally becomes prime by the first of December, but usually begins to molt and fade in color in February, depending upon the region. The pelt also becomes damaged due to vigorous mating activities in late winter. For the best mink pelts, they should, generally speaking, be taken before the middle of January.

Mink are thought to be very difficult to trap although the reason for this might be because they are widely scattered. If there is no mink sign in the immediate area, they simply may not be frequenting the area. Also, unlike many of the other water-dwelling furbearers, the mink is scent wary. If a mink becomes suspicious of a set location and, in addition, smells the scent of man around, you're not likely to catch it. For this reason, it's important to observe all the precautions regarding the leaving of scent.

The effectiveness of mink bait is up for debate among trappers. Some say it is practically worthless, others say it is valuable. In either case, the mink generally prefers

This is prime mink habitat — a small winding stream that is heavily wooded and inhabited by muskrats. Mink are bloodthirsty animals and kill muskrats, small game, and rodents to survive. With this in mind, the wise trapper will select set sites accordingly.

fresh meat, and this should be kept in mind when placing bait for it. Aside from bait, many trappers value the use of a good lure when making a mink set, and it is frequently used to lure a mink closer to a set or, at least get its attention so that it doesn't pass by.

Mink have the habit of investigating every den or hole in a creek bank, around log jams, hollow logs, small feeder streams, etc., and experienced trappers utilize this knowledge to design mink sets.

The No. 1 or 1½ and Victor No. 11 series of foot-hold traps are considered the proper size for mink, whether they're of the long-spring, coil-spring, or jump variety. A mink will fight savagely and attempt to twist and chew out of a trap. For this reason, it's an excellent idea to make a drowning set for them whenever possible and to use a Stop-Loss or body-gripping Conibear 110-220-size trap on land.

One set that is popular for mink is the pocket set. It

consists of digging an artificial hole or pocket into a steep bank of a stream or pond at the water's edge. The dimensions and slant of the hole varies considerably from trapper to trapper although the principle remains the same. Some prefer to dig a relatively small 4-inch diameter hole into the bank at an upward-slanting angle, while others prefer to dig a hole straight back into the bank with a small entrance and a big cavity behind so that water covers the bottom of the pocket.

In any case, a trap is set at the entrance of the hole under about 2 inches of water and a stick with a good lure is placed in the bank just above the hole. Sometimes a second lure is placed inside the hole above the water level. The second stick with lure on it is thus protected from the elements. If the lure on the outside stick gets washed away by rain, the one on the inside is still effective.

Sometimes, a bait consisting of a piece of bird, rabbit, muskrat, etc., is placed inside the pocket and this should be kept fresh. An additional sight attractor, added to the outside of the pocket increases its effectiveness. For instance, if a piece of bloody muskrat meat is used inside the pocket, bits of muskrat fur scattered at either side of the pocket will seldom go unnoticed, even by a mink on the other side of the creek.

When making this type of set it is very important to approach it from the water, either entering the stream some distance from where the set will be made and staying in the water while making the set, or doing it all from a boat. In either case, it's important not to leave any human or other foreign sign on the bank and allow only the rubber-gloved hands and trowel or spade to touch the earth. After the pocket is dug and before luring it, splash water all over the interior of the hole and the surrounding area in an effort to remove any trace of human scent that might have been left.

When trapping for mink it's a good idea to wiggle the trap around on the bottom of the creek so that mud settles over the trap to help obscure it. A leaf over the trap pan and water-logged leaves over the springs, may also help to conceal it. Some trappers don't add any camouflage at all, thinking it isn't necessary for a trap placed under the surface of the water, even for mink. However, any precaution that a trapper can take, particularly if it requires little time and effort, might serve to add a few extra pelts to the fur frames during the winter.

Some pocket sets are not baited. If the pocket is constructed properly, it forms a natural refuge for minnows, crayfish, and other aquatic life to enter the hole naturally. This is why a mink investigates a pocket or hole in the bank in the first place.

Similar to a pocket hole, mink are fond of investigating areas underneath overhanging tree roots. When narrow passageways are formed by them along steep

Trapper Roy Daniels in a section of prime mink stream. It doesn't take large streams for mink to be present. Even very small water-courses only a few inches wide may be frequently traveled by this member of the weasel family.

banks, it is a natural place to make a set. Whenever trapping for mink along a creek, it's always best to place the trap under the surface of the water if possible, including the trap chain, wire, and stake. This is further insurance that the animal won't detect the presence of the foreign object.

Sometimes, narrow passageways may be formed at the water's edge for other reasons. For example, a log or tree that has fallen along the bank might make a small inlet and this might be the place to make a set. Or, an area where the bank has caved in might leave a narrow strip of water between the newly exposed bank and the caved in portion; this is the place to set for mink.

Bridge abutments, as mentioned earlier, are an ideal set location for mink, and in mink country, particularly when trapping from an automobile, all these abutments should be covered with sets. Sometimes, the water may be a foot or more deep running through the concrete
(continued page 150)

1. Roy Daniels digs a hole back into a steep bank, using a short-handled spade. The hole, extending back into the bank a foot or so, should have a narrow opening, with a wide pocket in back.

2. Water should be about 1½-2 inches deep at the mouth of the artificial "den" or pocket. Daniels sets a mink trap for placement at the pocket mouth.

ROY DANIELS ON MAKING A POCKET SET FOR MINK

"Before I trap an area for mink, I check for tracks; to scout an area, I drive the roads and walk down under each bridge to look. By the time the season starts I have a pretty good idea about the mink that are there. But you can't always tell how many animals are on a creek by how many tracks are at a given spot for the simple reason that those old male mink are travelers. They'll roam up here and down there and you might not see its track in a given spot but once every 25 or 30 days. Mink will come back over their same path however, and this is something to keep in mind.

Besides tracks, I look for droppings on any prominent log or rock along its line of travel. I look for frogs at the edge of the water that have had their rear ends bit off. That's a good sign of mink. You'll also find fish scales left back up under the rock shelves along the water.

Lots of times you can't find mink sign. For instance, you may drive up to a bridge and the water underneath is 6 or 8 inches wide but each bank is covered with grass growing right down to the water. Mink are traveling there and it's a "minky-looking" spot. When I come to a place like that I make a pocket set on each side of the creek.

I like a pocket set that has a smaller entrance than the inside; the inside may be 2 feet across and the entrance only 6 or 8 inches wide. I make the pocket with a spade so there is about 2 inches of water in the entrance but the water is deeper inside the pocket. After the pocket is dug out, I reach down onto the creek bottom, pull up a handful of silt and throw it inside the bottom of the pocket to make it look even more natural.

The minnows, frogs, crawdads, etc., will go back into a place like that and you've got a self-baiting hole. Once in a while, I throw a muskrat or rabbit carcass back in the pocket. Then, I place a trap in the entrance and stake it out in deep-water. For mink I use a No. 1 Blake and Lamb double jaw with two springs. I buy the No. 1 traps and then send to the factory for extra springs. Then I pop the jaws and put a spring on the other side of the trap to make it a No. 1 double-jaw, double-spring.

The extra spring gives the trap more speed and holding power for mink, and for those of you who are worried about a raccoon if it comes along, this trap will hold any raccoon that walks. The double jaw, combined with the small trap size, prevents 'coons from chewing and pulling out. I've found that the small No. 1 trap grabs the mink just above the foot, not up the leg where a bone is likely to break. Mink are real fighters in a trap, and if they break a bone, they're more likely to escape.

I always wear hip boots and shoulder-length gloves when I'm after mink, and after I complete

3. (Left) This is where the trap should be positioned in the mouth of a pocket set. Note the long gloves worn by Daniels — they not only help to keep him warm, but also mask human scent.

4. (Below) The completed pocket set with a trap in place at the mouth of the hole looks natural. Any mink traveling along the stream bank will stop to investigate holes, such as this, particularly if there is a piece of fresh meat bait in the back of the pocket.

5. Just in case a mink misses seeing the pocket, Daniels uses a bit of mink gland lure placed just above the pocket entrance. Mink have keen noses and can pick up the scent of a lure from some distance.

the set, I slosh water up on the bank all around the set. This helps to weather the set and make it look more natural; at the same time it takes away scent.

After that, I add a gland lure over the entrance of the hole. The only mink scent I ever use is natural. I use the glands attached to the anus and the anal opening. I add mink urine and glycerine to keep the lure from freezing. I've seen mink tracks in the snow where they've come down to this lure even from high on the creek bank and bang! I've got 'em.

After the streams freeze, mink seem to be looking for small patches of open water such as springs or feeder streams. Sometimes open water can be found in a riffle where the creek is wide and shallow and the swiftly running water keeps it from freezing. In any of these cases, I take a forked stick and tie a muskrat carcass in the fork. Then, I wrap the muskrat in dried grass and tie the grass on so that it ends up looking like a big drumstick. Then I shove the small end of the stick down into the creek bottom out in shallow open water so that the top of the muskrat carcass is out of the water. Then I place a trap on either side of it.

I've read where you can't crowd a mink with guide sticks, but I've found this to be anything but true. Guide sticks are very important and with them you can make a mink go wherever you want.

I skin a mink a little differently than most people. I lay it on its back and cut down the *inside* of the hind legs straight across the belly to the other hind leg, rather than cutting to the vent. Then, from this initial incision I make a second cut to the anus or vent. After it is stretched it can make the difference between a Large and Extra Large graded pelt. I do raccoon the same way and gain 2 inches in pelt length over the conventional method.

It's important to get the hair of a mink perfectly dry before putting it on the solid wooden frame or it will spoil. I use a rag or wadded up newspaper and just rub it until it's dry before stretching it. **"**

Ken Dederick, another Kansas trapper, added the following tip for trapping mink under ice:

"Sometimes, the water level on a creek will fluctuate. The top of the creek might freeze, and then the water level may drop. The ice next to the bank stays where it was but since the water level has lowered, there is now a kind of tunnel underneath the ice next to the bank. This area is heavily traveled by mink looking for muskrats, or anything else that might be found there. This is an excellent place to construct any type of baited set for mink. Just find a natural break in the ice next to the bank, or break one, and make the set under the ice and then cover the hole.**"**

This pocket set is constructed at a small inlet of a small stream and has accounted for a number of prize mink. They frequently seek out rodents living along these banks.
(Left) Culverts or spillways in pond dams are frequent paths of the wiley mink. They are fond of nosing into any hole and a culvert pipe is no exception. In this instance, the trap chain is wired tightly around the pipe so that it won't slip over the ribs of the steel. The trap is placed just inside the mouth of the culvert. This particular set has accounted for several mink.

culvert and a mink, traveling the stream, will have to swim through.

Usually the stream narrows when going through a culvert and then widens slightly on either side of the road. The concrete abutment is generally faced to form a sharp corner where the culvert exits. When a mink enters the water to swim through the culvert, it goes in right next to the abutment, swims around the sharp turn, and exits the water the same way on the other end. The best place to put a foot-hold trap is in 2 or 3 inches of water, right next to the abutment-facing at the nearest point a mink can exit the water.

Even when there's a sharp right angle facing to the bridge abutment, the mink will generally make this turn and swim directly in to the bank. This set location has accounted for a good many pelts. If mink are inhabiting the area, there are usually four such entrance and exit points coming and going through the concrete culverts, and it's not a bad idea to cover all four of them. A trapper will generally find that only one or two of the four sets will take all the mink. Since he has no way of predetermining the travel pattern, it's best to cover all of them, or at least both sides of the stream on one side of the road.

Because these bridge abutments are located along roads, the wise trapper will be secretive when making and checking sets so he won't be seen by passing motorists. The traps should be well camouflaged for the same reason. It's very easy for people walking along the road, or youngsters stopping along the bridge, to spot traps in the water below, so it's a good idea to apply a bit of waterlogged material or bottom silt to the traps.

However, don't place a lot of coarse vegetable matter, and particularly slippery leaves, over the trap jaws. A single leaf over the pan that fits inside the jaws can serve to camouflage the trap, but too much of this material not only clogs the jaws but also makes a slippery surface to allow the mink to pull its foot out. Sometimes, these set locations can be obscured by overhanging grasses, weeds, brush, or even the bank itself, so that they may not be seen from the road above — so much the better.

Any small feeder stream 6 or 8 inches wide that enters a larger creek is a natural spot for a "blind" set wherein a trap is placed in the bottom of the narrow feeder stream at its mouth with no bait or lure whatever.

Small rivulets or areas where water passes through

marshy areas are other excellent places to make blind sets for mink. These water passageways sometimes form a tunnel underneath the cattails or marsh grasses and mink travel these areas in their search for food. Frequently a rivulet of water running through marsh grass will connect two larger bodies of water, and this is a good place for a blind set. Just place a Stop-Loss trap in the small stream under the surface of the water.

A hollow log about 8 or 10 inches in diameter and half submerged in the water is sometimes investigated by mink, particularly if some sort of bait is secured midway inside the log. The log should be a couple of feet long, and a trap placed at either end.

Mink will generally investigate log jams along the banks and by simply kicking a hole through the sticks and leaf debris at the edge of the water makes a natural passageway for them. A trap placed at the edge of the water at each end of this hole is also a natural blind set for mink. As with many other sets, the mink trapper must use his ingenuity to adapt the construction of the set to the situation at hand.

Perhaps more important than outlining a number of specific sets, is to relate the habits of the animal. For example, the mink has a habit of investigating holes, feeder streams, traveling along the edge of creek banks, etc. It is carnivorous and likes muskrat meat. Combine this with the fact that it is attracted to the smell of other mink, but is afraid of human scent, and common sense with a little thought will turn up all sorts of ingenious mink sets.

But, this is true when trapping any animal. The more a trapper learns about the animal he's after, the more effective he can be in utilizing nature and the animal's own traits to catch it. The various sets devised and used down through the years do nothing more than make use of the basic animal habits. There are hundreds of variations which can be made on the basic mink trapping techniques.

Once in the bag, a mink is case skinned and generally sold skin out. It's important not to scrape a mink pelt too thin but rather to only remove the fat and flesh that is easily scraped off. In most cases, there will be a "saddle" of flesh and membrane lying close to the hide and the trapper should not attempt to remove this.

The No. 1½ wire stretcher is the generally accepted size for mink stretching although most experienced trappers prefer the solid wood drying form with a wedge inserted under the belly side of the skin. The tail is usually tacked out flat with push pins, or it can be held flat by a piece of screen which is subsequently tacked at the edges or held in place by a couple of rubber bands wrapped around the fur form.

(Above and left) Places where streams are narrowed down to run through concrete culverts are excellent set locations for mink. Here, Daniels places a trap at an ideal location. The water here is deep enough that a mink traveling the stream will have to swim through the culvert. When it emerges, it makes a sharp left turn and follows the concrete wall around to the stream bank. Lure or bait isn't necessarily needed.

chapter 13
WATER DWELLING FURBEARERS

BEAVER

TRAP SIZE: No. 3 or 4,
   or No. 330
BAIT: Sticks, twigs or
   gland lure
PRIME: February
STRETCHER: Steel hoop
TRACK:

THE BEAVER *(Castor canadensis)* is the largest of North American rodents. It is a compact and heavy-set animal with soft brown fur and short legs. The tail is very broad, flat and scaly and the ears are small, rounded, and set close to the head. The hind feet are webbed with the forefeet smaller and more slender. The average length is about 45 inches, counting the 10- to 15-inch tail and the weight averages 30 to 40 pounds although it can vary considerably according to conditions and the time of year. Some adult beavers may weigh no more than 30 pounds while some old males may exceed 60, 70 or even 80 pounds. The beaver is found over most of North America although its distribution is pretty scattered and spotty.

Beaver generally breed in January and February and after a 115-day gestation period three or four young are born in May or June. The kits are born furred with eyes open and incisor teeth erupted. In 6 to 8 weeks they begin to wean and remain with their parents until they are sexually mature, usually 2 years later. The adults, yearlings and kits constitute a family unit. The beaver is found in rivers, lakes, and marshes where there is running water.

This large rodent leaves so much sign that, in most instances, it's difficult to overlook its presence in an area. Generally, cuttings from felled trees, and dams and lodges are the signs a trapper sees first. There will usually be slides leading down a steep bank to the water's edge and sometimes bank dens, in addition to or instead of lodges, in the water. Beavers dam up even small trickles of water to form sizable ponds. The ponds serve as a means of transporting trees or sticks to build huts that will protect them from predators.

Here's an example of a beaver slide with a tree above it that beavers have felled. This very steep slide leads directly to a feedbed below as can be seen by the tree branches protruding from the water. When the water freezes, the beaver will use these branches under the ice for food—a natural food locker!

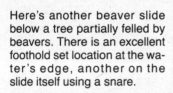

Here's another beaver slide below a tree partially felled by beavers. There is an excellent foothold set location at the water's edge, another on the slide itself using a snare.

In some areas, particularly on the larger rivers, beaver sign may not be as obvious; their felling of trees will be spread out over a much larger area and they will be living in bank dens rather than stick lodges. The beaver prefers to eat softwoods such as aspen, willow, cottonwood, etc., and if a trapper finds these cuttings, other sign, such as tracks and droppings will be noticed.

I can remember two instances, both of them involving fairly small streams, where I was not aware that beaver had been working the area. However, I saw a couple of peeled sticks with the familiar teeth marks, revealing their presence, and an upstream scouting turned up their location.

When a trapper scouts for beaver, he's not generally trying to find where they are so much as he is trying to find places to make sets. It is definitely beneficial to locate dens, feed beds, runways, etc., in advance of the beaver season and certainly before freeze-up. It takes a little looking, for the feed beds, runways and den entrances are all under water. One way to find den entrances is to probe likely-looking spots with a long stick.

The most experienced beaver trappers will have dens and runways located and marked so that if the water freezes during the season, it's a simple matter to cut a hole through the ice in the precise spot and lower a trap into position. Beaver aren't particularly difficult to trap using proper techniques.

For the most part, beaver prime late in the year. In my home state of Kansas they aren't fully prime until about the 15th of February and, when prime, the flesh inside the pelt is white. A pelt graded as No. 2 will be bluish on the flesh side when dried and the coat will be hairy. A No. 3 has a coarse coat and short underfur.

These rodents were once much sought after for their valuable pelts and, as a consequence, intensive trapping severely depleted their numbers around the 1800s. However, with the advent of sound wildlife management practices, beaver became protected, and in recent years, they've increased to numbers never before known, even becoming serious pests in many areas. However there are strict laws governing the manner in which beaver traps may be set, and it is a good idea to check local laws thoroughly before trapping season.

For example, in some states it is illegal to place a trap within a certain distance of a lodge, or to disturb a beaver dam. In other states it's common practice to trap inside the dens and lodges and even to destroy dams.

Most experienced trappers feel that young beaver generally stay close to the den during the winter months. For this reason, if traps are set some distance away from the den the larger, older animals will usually be caught. However, in some instances, where there is overpopulation and depredation of an area, the trapper may be doing a service to take every beaver he can by

The trapper really has to look sharp to find den entrances like this one near the twin trees. Such finds should be marked before freeze-up.

(Left) Trapper Kent Dederick examines stumps where trees were felled by beaver. Such sign can give an experienced trapper some indication about the size of the beaver that are working the area. The height that the stumps are cut above the ground provide one clue, the size of the teeth marks where the stump was gnawed, another.

trapping runways, den entrances and lodges.

Since these animals are very strong, the trapper is wise to make drowning sets. The generally recommended trap sizes for beaver are the No. 3 and 4 foot-holds or the No. 330 Conibear body-gripper. Some trappers feel that since a beaver's front foot is small and it's wise to catch it by the front foot anyway, a No. 2 trap is all that is needed. However, because a beaver can vary so much in size and weight, I prefer to use at least a No. 3 or 4 to insure trapping success.

Beaver Sets

Basically two classes of sets are used to take beaver — those made in open water, and those made under the ice. Though the techniques for both are somewhat different, the basic applications are more or less the same. For example, setting a trap at a den entrance is the same whether in open water or under the ice. A body-gripping trap is placed over the den or runway in such a manner that the beaver will have to pass through the trap opening to enter the den. In this case guide sticks can be used to manipulate the animal into the trap. A foot-hold trap could also be used here, positioning it in 5 to 8 inches of water.

A good food bait for attracting beaver usually consists of the tender finger-size green twigs and sticks of the preferred tree species of the area. Most trappers

shave some of the bark from the bait sticks to expose the light cambium layer, making the bait more noticeable. An ear of corn is another excellent food bait for beaver.

In many areas, beaver seasons open late in the winter when pelts are at their best and when beaver ponds and rivers are ice covered. One of the most popular sets for under-ice trapping, besides the den or runway set, is the pole set. The trap and bait are attached to a large seasoned pole, about 6 inches or more in diameter. A platform is built and attached to the pole to hold a foot-hold trap with bait sticks wired above the trap. A hole is cut in the ice, usually near a feed bed, and the pole, with the trap and bait attached, is shoved through the hole and stuck into the bottom of the pond or river. The top of the pole should project well up through the ice.

Sometimes the trap may be a body-gripper wherein the springs encircle smaller-diameter poles. The pole itself should always be made of a peeled, seasoned wood that will not appeal to a beaver's appetite.

In many instances, snares placed underwater at den entrances or around feed beds have been successfully employed. They can also be very effective at beaver slides coming down a steep bank into the water.

One old trick of beaver trappers is to make a break in the beavers' dam. The animals will respond by trying to repair the leak during the night. Place a foot-hold trap

Beaver dams are strong and they're capable of damming up sizeable bodies of water and even flood roads, fields, etc. Consequently, it sometimes becomes necessary to trap the little darlings out of the area. The trapper can make valuable use of this otherwise nuisance rodent.

(Right) Kent Dederick probes for a runway leading to a bank den. Sometimes, such den entrances can't be seen—they must be felt.

in the break, under the surface of the water, with a drowning wire or heavy weight attached for a drowning set.

Rather than going into detail about techniques involved in catching beaver myself, I'll let recognized beaver trapping expert Kent Dederick do it. He holds a degree in natural resource management from Kansas State University and has worked for the Kansas Department of Fish and Game in the area of beaver depredation control. Dederick has an uncommon interest in beaver, and is known as one of the best beaver trappers in the country:

Trapper Dederick here examines a beaver dam closely. One type of set is made by tearing out a spot in the dam so that the water will begin draining out of the pond above. Beavers will come to repair the break at night, and traps placed at strategic locations will catch them.

‟ For trapping beaver you first need a hatchet or an axe, for cutting and driving stakes, notching logs, etc. You also need wire. I usually use 12-gauge at a minimum. However, when you get as large as 9-gauge, the wire is heavy and hard to work with. You need a pair of wire cutters, such as fencing pliers, diagonals, lineman's pliers or whatever it takes to twist and cut the heavy wire. You also need some sort of slide lock. I prefer to use a beer can opener, but a piece of angled bar also works well. It helps to have a trap basket or something with which to carry your equipment.

For a foot-hold trap I prefer the No. 4 Blake and Lamb; for a body-gripping trap I use a 330 Conibear. A 220 Conibear just isn't big enough to kill a beaver quickly, but a 330 shouldn't really be expected to be reliable on beaver exceeding 60 or 70 pounds. If a beaver is bigger than that its head will hardly go inside the jaws without jarring the trap one way or another or it'll hit a spring or jaw. Beaver as large as 110 pounds have been taken from my area.

For lure, I use gland lure, made from beaver castors and add a little anise in a glycerine base to

KENT DEDERICK ON TRAPPING BEAVER

help sweeten the smell. I prefer to break up two castors and put them in a quart jar, then cover them with glycerine. I then break up whole anise seed, and add a teaspoon to a quart. I let it sit until the castor dissolves into the glycerine, turning to a rich brown color. The longer you let it sit the better it gets. This is a natural smell to a beaver.

Open Water Trapping

Scent Pack Set

All beaver, both male and female, go along a creek and deposit their scent from a castor gland located at the base of the tail. They do this for two reasons: To mark their territory, and, during the mating season, to locate the opposite sex, male or female. During the mating season they will generally push mud and debris into a pile, sometimes on the bank and other times in shallow water, and leave their scent on this. When they're finished, it looks like a big mud pie. It may be no larger than your fist or it could be 3 or 4 feet in diameter. The scent pack has a musky smell that is readily detected by the human nose.

If another beaver comes along it'll sometimes try to cover up the other one's scent with mud, and then put its own scent on the pack. Obviously, this is a very good place to trap beaver, and if you can't find one of those packs, you can make an artificial one and use the lure mentioned earlier to scent it. Even though the scent pack may be on land, I always place a foot-hold trap under water and make a drowning set. Just place a trap near the water's edge near the scent pack. When trapping near a scent pack, it probably won't be necessary to use guide sticks.

Other Beaver Sets

When I'm making other types of sets where beaver come and go from the water, there is a little more to it. Whenever I place a foot-hold trap near the water's edge, I try to anticipate where it will come *out* of the water. It may be coming to a slide or a run, where its route of travel is predetermined. If there is no clear-cut exit point, I'll use guide sticks and perhaps a lure to make it go where I want.

I don't try to catch beaver going *into* the water, especially when they're coming down a slide because they're too easily missed there. They may be going so fast, with their feet tucked in that they'll slide right over a trap, springing it. You'll get either a poor hold, or none at all. The exception is with the use of a snare which I frequently use to catch them going down a slide, but I'll get into that later.

To catch a beaver coming out of the water with a foot-hold trap, I place the trap in 6 to 8 inches of water. I then whittle points on some small stakes

and jab them into the muck on the pond or creek bottom in front of the trap (on the open water side). They're angled outward with their sharp tips about an inch above the trap and about 3 inches from the nearest jaw of the trap.

The beaver will swim toward the bank, with its front feet tucked up next to its body. Then, when it gets poked in the chest by the sharp sticks it'll lower its front feet, hopefully to walk on the bottom and get over the sticks. One of its front feet should then contact the trap pan. There's no danger of the sharp sticks diverting a beaver's direction because it is used to getting poked by them anyway in its natural habitat.

Pocket Set

A type of pocket set can also be used to apply this principle. The pocket may be nothing more than an indentation in the bank. Place the lure on the bank back in the indentation and set the trap at the entrance to the pocket. Just make certain the water is the proper depth. If you consistently have foot-hold traps sprung with few catches, you need to set them in deeper water.

Den Entrance Set

Another type of set is at a den entrance, which can be trapped in several ways. One utilizes a Conibear at the mouth of the den. No bait is used here. Bend the Conibear trigger wires apart so they're lying next to the trap jaws. This allows small beaver and muskrats to go through without

A Victor number 330 Conibear trap is recommended for beaver trapping. The thin wires near the top of the trap jaws are the triggering device. Most beaver trapping experts bend the trigger in this manner so small beaver and other animals won't touch it off.

(Right) Dederick holds onto vertical sticks, marking either side of an underwater den entrance. The sticks will support the Victor Conibear trap shown resting on the tree in front of him.

The circular openings of the spring ends are slipped over either of the vertical sticks. This serves to support the trap in an upright manner over the opening to the den entrance. The trigger is on the upper jaw when the trap is set.

getting caught. Use guide sticks to narrow the den opening, if necessary, and place the trap's trigger on the top of the trap frame when it's set.

Another den set for bank beaver is with a No. 4 foot-hold. This trap generally is placed up inside the den at water level. You may have to put the trap on a flat stick to reach up into the den and place it where the water meets the den entrance. This can be at the bank or it may be 3 or 4 feet back into the bank. I try to keep the trap in 6 to 8 inches of water and offset it 2 or 3 inches from the center of the beaver's expected path. Remember to attach a drowning wire to this or any other foot-hold set. This catches the beaver going either in or out.

A Run Set

Another type of Conibear set can be built at a run. A run is an underwater travelway, and it may have to be "fenced" to direct the beaver into the trap. Fence the runway by poking a series of long sticks into the bottom mud, forming "Vs," one on either side of the runway with the apex of the "Vs" facing each other. Stake the Conibear at the apex. The idea is to funnel beaver into the trap from either direction along the runway. Then, once the beaver is inside the funnel it's committed and won't generally try to back out or go around if the Conibear looks like a tight hole.

The trigger latch should be on the top side of the trap jaws, and the top of the jaws may be level with the surface of the water. If the trap is placed in a deeper run, it can be placed next to the bottom, and heavy sticks placed in a horizontal position over the trap to make any high-swimming beaver dive into the trap. Be sure to use sizable sticks or small logs to do this so a beaver will dive, rather than push through them.

Ice Trapping

So far, I've covered primarily open water trapping. A lot of beaver trapping is done through the ice after everything has frozen over.

There are several extra pieces of equipment that you'll need for trapping under the ice. First of all, you need something to cut the ice. I use a plain old double-bladed axe. Another tool that can be used is an ice auger. It can be either a manual-type or power driven, popular with serious beaver trappers up north.

You have to be cautious on the ice because it can be very hazardous. You may think, "Hey, this ice is fine and there's not much water here." However, in beaver habitat you never know whether you might be standing over a run or den where the beaver have dug channels in the bottom mud and the water can be quite deep.

One time I thought I was standing over about 4 feet of water; I chopped a hole for a pole set, stuck the pole down in it and couldn't touch bottom. I later checked it out and found there was 12 feet of water there!

I feel that it's important to carry something like a long stick or pole when walking over ice. I carry a long stick that I call a "beaver stick" which I use to probe for dens and runs. If you happen to go through the ice the pole will hang up on the ice and provide some help for escape, so don't let go of it.

Reading Sign Under Ice

It really helps if you've scouted the area, and know where dens, feed beds and runways are before freeze-up. If this hasn't been done, there are still things to look for even after the water is frozen. Any animal that moves under the ice leaves bubbles, because air is trapped within the fur and as it moves through the water these bubbles are released. There will be trails along the bottom of the ice where they've been traveling underneath. At times the bubbles can be mistaken for decomposing organic matter as that action also releases a

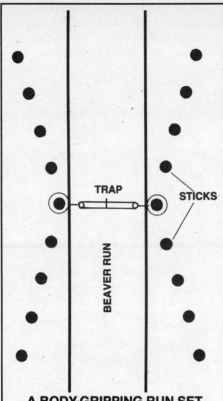

A BODY-GRIPPING RUN SET

A funnel is created with sticks placed in opposing "V" forms on either side of a beaver runway. The 330 Conibear is staked at the apex of the "V"s.

SETTING A FOOT-HOLD RUN SET

A trapper doesn't have to use the body-gripping Conibears to trap beaver in runs. Here, Dederick is setting a foot-hold trap.

(Below) Dederick positions the foot-hold trap in the run. Note that it's offset slightly and will be placed under several inches of water.

(Far left and left) Dederick stakes the trap in deep water, shoving the long stake into the bottom of the pond. The top of the stake is left just above the surface of the water. A freshly-cut stake is light colored and will readily show up. For this reason, Dederick pulls mud from the bottom and smears it onto the stake top.

(Above) Dederick examines an underwater beaver run with his foot. This is an excellent set location for a Conibear trap.

(Right) Scouting can be risky. Beavers dig channels under water which an unsuspecting trapper can step off into. In other instances, the trapper may find that he has to traverse a beaver-built stick jam.

(Left) This beaver feedbed can be seen under the ice. It is given away by the tree cuttings and the air bubbles.

gas. To tell the difference, follow a string of bubbles, and if the string leads to a feed bed, a den, or between the two, that's generally a good spot to make a set.

Another thing to look for is a feed bed. These can be recognized generally by the green branches sticking up through the top of the ice and the many air pockets or bubbles trapped in the ice. The air pockets and bubbles are caused both by the decomposition of the vegetable matter and the many animals coming to the area. However, you can't always tell by looking.

One of the most important things to learn when trapping under the ice is how to recognize sign. You may be walking along the ice and see bubbles, thinking maybe there's a runway underneath. You have to be able to chop a hole in the ice and tell whether it is indeed a run or not. I step down into the hole and feel around with my feet, looking for a well-defined run, but you have to know what you're feeling for. Sometimes it's very difficult, mainly because you'll probably be wearing chest waders and several pairs of socks. For this reason you don't have a whole lot of feeling in your feet. But you have to learn to recognize the contours of a run, or den entrance.

When it comes to setting traps through the ice,

you don't usually need a very big hole for you seldom get down into the water. The hole generally has to be big enough to get a pole set through. If you're using a No. 4 trap with a platform, you need about a 10-inch diameter hole to drop the pole, with trap, through the ice.

If you're trapping in a den, you need a hole big enough to lower the trap down through the ice, with enough room for your arms to fit as well. If you're using a Conibear, the hole will have to be elongated. For a foot-hold trap at a den, even under the ice, you also have to run out a drowning wire. Generally that's accomplished by cutting a narrow slit with a saw through the ice for the wire, or by cutting a second hole, and running the wire under the ice from the second hole.

Remember, a beaver won't drown at a den set without a drowning wire, even under the ice, because it can go into the den or along the bank for air. At other times, if the water level has dropped, you may have a pocket of air under the ice. It may be only a couple of inches, or a couple of feet, and a beaver can move into that area without drowning. With a beaver, the weight of the trap is not enough to hold it under water. You need more weight to pull the animal down, such as a rock or bag of rocks tied to the trap chain.

Pole Sets

Setting under-ice traps in dens and runs is pretty much the same as setting in open water. With ice you just have to cut a hole to do it. But there are other types of sets, designed especially for trapping through the ice. One of the most popular is the "pole set."

To make a pole set, I find a long piece of peeled seasoned wood about 4 inches or so in diameter. I then cut a hole in the ice and find the depth of the water where the pole will be placed. If a pole set is made along a runway, don't place the pole in the runway, place it off to the side.

After determining the depth of the water, I pull the pole back out and make a trap platform on the pole so that the trap will be 1½ to 2 feet below the ice. The top of the pole should project well up through the ice.

I build the platform out of scrap lumber (beaver aren't the least bit wary of traps or foreign materials) and make it so that the trap will be sitting level. Then I set a foot-hold trap, place it on the platform and drive a single nail *beside* the frame to hold the trap wedged into position. I don't want beaver knocking it off before getting caught. The trap isn't actually nailed to the platform so that when it springs, the trap is free.

I wire the trap chain to the pole under the trap, and wire a bundle of bait sticks above the platform. Then the pole, with the bait sticks and trap

Constructing an Under-Ice Foot-Hold Pole Set

(Above) By cutting through the ice and determining water depth, the trapper then knows where on the pole to build the platform so that the trap will be the proper distance below the surface of the ice. Here's the rear support for the platform.

(Above right) Scrap lumber is used to build platforms for the pole sets. They don't have to be pretty—they just have to work.

(Right) The platform base must be large (deep) enough to hold the trap, so keep that in mind when gathering lumber. The pieces can be pre-cut at home. Here, Dederick positions a 16-penny nail just underneath the base board to support the backside of the platform. Without it the board could easily tip.

attached, is shoved into the pond or creek bottom. A heavy stick is laid across the top of the hole and is wired to the setting pole. This way, a beaver can't pull the pole under the ice.

When a beaver sees the bait sticks, it will go for them, trying to place its feet on something firm while it feeds, or while it tries to free them. This is why the pole and platform set works so well.

If the water freezes hard and fast during a time when there's little or no wind, the ice will be a clear sheet you can look through. When you have ice like this, it may be an advantage to check traps after dark because you can see under the ice much better at night using a flashlight than you can see in the daylight. You can see whether the trap has been sprung, whether it's undisturbed, or whether you've caught something—all without having to chop through the ice. This may be an ideal situation for the trapper who works a full-time job in the winter, and traps on the side. The days are short, and it may be dark before and after work anyway.

Ice Safety

Be careful about walking on ice. Be sure it's plenty safe to walk on before trapping through it. Many times ice will soften up during the day. You may be running traps early in the morning when everything is fine, but by mid-morning, if the sun is out, the ice can get too weak to walk on.

A single nail, located next to the trap frame, holds the trap in position on the platform. The trap is simply wedged in place so that it won't be easily kicked off the platform when a beaver merely steps onto the platform in order to reach the bait.

Voila! The completed platform. The set will be used under the surface of the ice and a trap will be placed on the platform.

Here's how the whole outfit looks with a foot-hold trap in place. The trap chain is attached to the pole for drowning the beaver. Generally, aspen, willow, etc., is tied around the pole for bait.

I once went through a thin spot of ice on a creek. I had been trapping on the creek for several days with no problem. Little did I know that there was a riffle under the ice in one spot, making it real thin over this moving water. Besides that, the water level had dropped a bit, so it was pocketed. The water was about 4 or 5 feet deep, and when I was walking along, the ice broke and I went clear under. I banged my rear end on the bottom and luckily caught the edge of the ice with my hands so I didn't go on down the creek underneath the ice. It was about 0 degrees out, and there was about 6 inches of snow on the ground. I had a heck of a time pulling myself out because my chest waders were full of water. As soon as I got out on the ice, I stripped down and wrung out all my clothes, redressed, and made it back okay.

One other time I didn't think I was going to make it back. I was running traps on a big marsh where the ice was about 3 inches thick. It had been 20 degrees the night before, but the sun was out and it had warmed up to 50 in the afternoon. I hadn't thought about the fact that I had been running traps in a shaded area most of the afternoon when I finally worked my way far out into the sunny part of the marsh. All of a sudden, I broke through. Fortunately, the water wasn't deep, but I couldn't get up on the ice because it would break and I'd fall through again. It was too thick to break by forcing my knees up under it yet it wouldn't bear my weight. Fortunately, I had an axe and broke a path back to the bank. **"**

Constructing an Under-Ice
Body-Gripping Pole Set

The Conibear is attached to a slender pole and positioned so that the top jaw will be about 8 inches below the bottom surface of the ice. It is generally baited with tender shoots of aspen, willow, etc., tasty morsels favored by the beaver.

Dederick uses a Conibear trap-setting tool to compress the very stout coil springs of a Victor No. 330 trap. The safety-locking devices for each of the two springs should be left in place until the trap is fully positioned in its bed, then unlatched.

Pelt Skinning and Stretching

A beaver is one of the few animals which is stretched open rather than cased. Also, remember not to make cuts up the backs of the legs as is done with most animals. Before skinning, simply lop the four feet off at the hairline and make a single cut running from the tail up the center of the belly to the chin. Then work the skin either way from this center cut until the entire animal is skinned. When finished, there should be four small legholes in the pelt. A beaver is one of the most difficult animals to skin because its pelt doesn't readily separate from the flesh as is the case with most furbearing animals. The pelt generally has to be cut from the flesh a good portion of the way.

Beaver pelts are generally stretched round or oval depending upon the furbuyer's preference, and stretching is accomplished by lacing the pelt onto a hoop, or tacking it out on a flat sheet of plywood. Even the side of a barn will do fine. When tacking a beaver pelt to a flat surface, be sure to tack it skin side out, otherwise it will spoil. Some trappers also slide long slender sticks underneath the fur side of the pelt to hold it away from the flat surface and allow air to circulate, helping it to dry more quickly.

Some trappers prefer to skin beaver cased, without the back-of-the-leg slits, and the central belly cut made only partway. Then, after fleshing, the belly slit is completed as mentioned before. This way the pelt can more easily be worked while on a fleshing beam than when it is skinned open.

Dederick (sans beard) holds a 62-pound beaver as caught in a Conibear trap. It's easy to see that an animal of this size would have a hard time squeezing through the opening of even a 330 Conibear. (Photo courtesy of Kent Dederick.)

MUSKRAT

TRAP SIZE: No. 110
or No. 1 and 1½
BAIT: Carrot or corn
PRIME: February
STRETCHER: No. 1
TRACK:

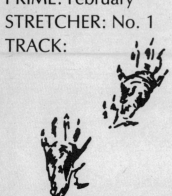

THE MUSKRAT *(Ondatra zibethicus)* is a rat-like rodent with a hairless tail, flattened vertically rather than laterally. It has very short ears, a thick body with small front feet and hind feet with partly webbed toes. These animals are generally about 24 inches long and weigh 1½ to 3 pounds. The fur is soft dark brown on the back and paler, often greyish, on the belly, with a very glossy appearance.

The hind feet and tail are what gives this aquatic rodent its propulsion through the water. The front feet, not generally used for swimming, are for digging, holding food while eating, and for constructing dwellings.

A prolific breeder, this rodent produces two or three litters per year with from two to nine young per litter, the average being about six. The gestation period for muskrats is about 30 days. Born with eyes closed and bodies hairless, the young soon develop a coat of hair, within 14 days their eyes open, and they're capable of swimming and feeding. They are weaned in a matter of 3 or 4 weeks and in 6 months are the same size as the adult. Sexual maturity is reached at the age of 1-year.

Muskrats are primarily vegetarians when there is ample food of this nature available. They eat roots, bulbs, stems and leaves of various aquatic plants although some muskrats acquire a taste for farm crops such as corn. In addition to consuming aquatic plants such as cattails, lotus, and bullrush, muskrats will also eat clams, crayfish, snails, etc. If food becomes scarce and muskrats become overpopulated, they become cannibalistic. Since they are so prolific and widely distributed, nearly any stream river, lake, pond or marsh with suitable habitat is going to maintain a 'rat population.

Muskrat sign is not difficult to find and, depending upon the habitat, the sign will vary. Like beaver, they live in two basic types of dwellings — a lodge of cattails or other reedy aquatic plants built in shallow-water marshes, or a bank den commonly found in ponds or streams; the preferred dwelling type is dependent upon the habitat.

Den entrances in banks can readily be detected if the trapper knows what to look for — a well concealed entrance below the surface of the water. In low water periods, the entrance can sometimes be seen by looking along the edges of streams; if high water has come, or if the water is exceedingly dark, they can be difficult to spot.

(Left) A muskrat "push-up," seen here in the foreground of this drainage ditch. Though this may not look like much of a muskrat stream, 20 of them were caught in a short time in this area. A "push-up" is a spot where muskrats have left piles of vegetation extending above the surface of the water.

Muskrats inhabit large bodies of shallow water and particularly prefer waters with a good crop of cattails or other reedy vegetation which is used to build winter houses or huts. Note the hut (arrow) in the upper left corner of the photo.

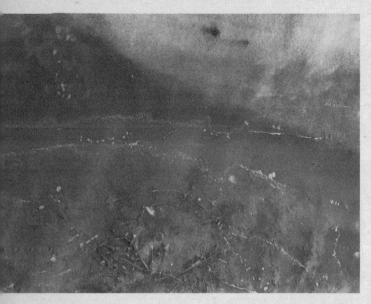

Here's what a muskrat run looks like through thin ice. Because 'rats continually keep the water agitated near den entrances, it is slower to freeze in these places. For this reason, a knowledgeable muskrat trapper can spot den entrances by observing such "sign." Here, the trapper would simply place a trap in the runway.

(Right) This is a very excellent example of a muskrat run which has prevented the ice from freezing where the animals are traveling. This one leads into a den entrance and would be an excellent spot for trap placement.

Other signs include muskrat droppings, signs of their feeding along the bank or aquatic vegetation which has been cut off from the bank and dragged into water. In a marsh or slough where the water is shallow and there is plenty of aquatic vegetation, muskrat "houses" can be easily spotted. In some instances, in a sizable marsh, there may be a great many of these dwellings. The average den, whether it be a reedy "hut" or a bank den will contain from three to five 'rats on the average. The tracks can often be seen along the muddy edges of the water or on points of land that extend into the water.

Muskrats have many predators — almost as many as the cottontail rabbit — and the same animals that prey on rabbits prey upon muskrats. The mink is one very notable predator and, indeed, a large 'rat population provides an ideal habitat for mink. In addition to mink, foxes, coyotes, and bobcats, as well as hawks and eagles prey upon this aquatic dweller. For this reason, the muskrat is a wary animal, spending the daylight hours in the water, under overhanging banks, or working at night.

The muskrat's pelt, like the beaver, generally becomes prime late in the season. In fact, the pelt may not be completely prime until late February or March. Un-

fortunately, primeness and mating season overlap, thus many pelts taken during these 2 months are damaged due to the heavy fighting among males. The early trapper usually has the advantage of trapping open water, while the late trapper, waiting until the pelts are prime, has to contend with frozen streams and marshes.

A muskrat is actually an easy animal to trap because it isn't the least bit trap or scent wary. Primarily a water-trapped animal, a trap 1 or 2 inches under the surface needs no camouflage whatever.

In recent years, the body-gripping traps have been readily adapted to trapping muskrat at den entrances, runways, etc. However, the foot-hold trap is still an excellent choice for muskrat trapping.

The 110 Conibear is the preferred body-gripping trap size while the No. 1 and 1½ — whether long spring, coil spring or underspring — are the preferred foot-hold traps. It is important to note that a muskrat has relatively tender legs, particularly the fronts, and is, therefore, quite prone to wringing out of a foot-hold-type trap. To prevent this from happening, a foot-hold trap should always be a drowning set. A muskrat is not difficult to drown; simply staking the trap in deep water generally does it. The weight of the trap alone is usually enough

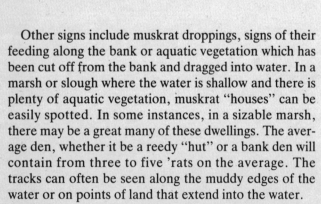

Muskrats are fond of climbing out of the water onto objects; in this instance, that means this old tree stump. Daniels has placed a muskrat trap in the center of the stump just under the surface of the water.

(Right) This set really works and here's a just-trapped muskrat. Common sense and imagination in constructing a set pays off. Though a few basic set types can be outlined, it's more important that the trapper know animal habits and use this information to his advantage.

to drown a muskrat. A second stake, placed 6 or 8 inches from the first, ensures that it will drown. I have trapped muskrats along small streams where the water was little more than a foot deep and have had no problem drowning them using this method.

If, the trapper is not absolutely certain the set will drown the animal, it is essential he use a Sure-Hold or Stop-Loss trap. The Stop-Loss device holds the animal's leg outstretched, causing the trap to turn with the animal's leg so that no twisting results.

Most muskrat trappers use blind sets, and in my own experience, these work as well as baited ones, particularly early in the season. First, it is quite easy to place traps in den entrances or in the den whether it be a bank or "hut" den. If a den is built into a bank, just place the trap on the bottom of the river, creek or pond at the den entrance — the same can be done if it is a reed "hut." A muskrat lodge or hut out in open water generally has three or four entrance and exit holes — you'll want to cover them all.

One good way to spot a den entrance is to look for a light colored streak on the creek bottom where the animal's feet, belly, and tail have been scraping when it comes out of the den. After freeze-up these entrances

The fact that muskrats like to climb out of the water onto floating objects can be used to the trapper's advantage. Some trappers prefer to build their own floating devices like this one consisting simply of two planks with a platform nailed to the bottom side. The trap is placed in the wide part of the "V." Sometimes a bait is placed back in the narrow portion of the "V". However, bait isn't always necessary.

This is another type of floating muskrat trap. Here, it is intended that the muskrats go inside the float at each of the four corners. Each opening can be covered by a 110-size Conibear trap for a sure catch. It should be attached to the bank by a long chain or wire so that it won't drift away.

can sometimes be located by a string of bubbles under the ice. The den generally has an underwater entrance which curves upward, leading to living quarters above water level. Sometimes, there are lateral tunnels underneath the bank connecting several den entrances. This network of entrances helps the muskrat elude its land-dwelling predators. If a lot of this information sounds similar to beaver trapping, it is in many respects. The same basic set ideas work for both animals.

Trappers skilled in working heavily populated marshes or streams specialize in getting a lot of traps out in a hurry; some can set as many as 100 traps in a single day. This feat is accomplished by considerable pre-season preparation. Experienced professional trappers have scouted and mapped many areas in advance of the season and know exactly where the animals are. It's best to scout just a few weeks prior to the season because muskrats are known to move from summer feeding areas, now depleted of food, to more suitable marsh for the winter. It is also an advantage to have several muskrat marshes, or stretches along creeks and rivers, located prior to the season just in case another trapper moves into one area before you do.

Of course, all traps and equipment are prepared in advance of the season, and stakes for attaching the muskrat traps are cut in the spring and allowed to sea-

son all summer. The stakes should be variable in length from perhaps as short as 2 feet to as long as 6 or 8 feet, depending upon the area and water levels. If the water level is known to fluctuate considerably during the trapping season, a very long stake is an advantage. The stake marks the trap location, and if a stake is submerged under muddy water, trap location can be difficult if not impossible to ascertain. Some trappers tie brightly colored ribbons around the top of their trap stakes while others dip stake ends in paint so they can spot them from a distance. However, in an area where trap thieves are a problem, it may be better to be a little more discreet. Keeping a logbook of all trap locations and camouflaging the traps may be the best solution.

In some areas where water levels fluctuate regularly, floating-type muskrat sets are about the only means of keeping the trapline in constant operation. Basically, these involve the use of a floating board or log onto which the baited traps are placed. This way, the float can raise or lower with the water level. However, in my experience, conventional sets, made at dens, runways, feed beds, underneath overhanging banks, etc., are more productive than floating sets. If conventional sets can be made, this is the best way to go.

A muskrat can easily be directed into a trap by the means of "guide sticks." For example, if there is a water passageway connecting two sloughs, and the passageway is too wide for a trap, narrow it down by jamming sticks into the mud and leaving an opening just wide enough for a trap. Some trappers also use stepping sticks so that the muskrat will have to step over them and directly onto the trap pan.

Professional muskrat trappers are so skilled in their pre-season preparation that not only are trap stakes cut in advance but trap supporting devices are prepared for body-gripping traps. When using one of those, a support is necessary to keep the trap from falling over or getting knocked aside. This can be accomplished with sticks and reeds, but that takes extra setting time. There are commercial trap supporting devices which serve very well to quickly attach and "seat" the trap in the bottom of a den or runway. However, if you find yourself without a trap-supporting device, a body-gripper

can be set in position by placing a stake through the ring of the trap spring, and positioning a second small stick at an angle between the upper corner of the jaws on the opposite side, pushing this stick into the mud.

In many cases, muskrat dens are located on steep drop-offs, and rather than using a shovel to rearrange the bottom mud into a supporting shelf for a foot-hold trap, some trappers have pre-made, bent U-shaped wires which can be stuck into the bank to serve as a support platform.

It's generally not difficult to figure out where muskrats have been feeding, and simply by placing traps in shallow water around these feed beds, a trapper can have good success. If the water in the feed bed is too deep, bend the vegetable matter over, stomp it down into the water, and place your traps on top of it.

As mentioned earlier, muskrats are fond of spending

(Right) It's easy to see the feedbed grasses which have been dragged into the water and left. This is an excellent place for trap placement.

Roy Daniels points to a muskrat feedbed. Muskrats in this pond have been coming up to the pond bank, cutting off grasses, and other vegetation growing along the edge of the water, dragging it out a ways, and leaving it.

Trapper Daniels is shown here placing a trap at the edge of a feedbed. Note that the stake for holding the trap chain is in fairly deep water so the muskrats caught here will drown.

time underneath overhanging banks, and foot-hold or body gripping traps, depending upon the specific setting site, can be used to good advantage in these places. In fact, I prefer to cover every overhanging bank with some type of set. Underneath overhanging tree roots is also an excellent trap site for muskrats and, if necessary, use guide sticks to force the animal into the trap.

In some areas, muskrat slides will be found along stream or pond banks. A trap placed at the bottom of such a slide is practically a sure thing for trapping success. Muskrats are also fond of going through small culverts, and a trap placed at the mouth or just inside the culvert under water can be a good bet.

For automobile trappers, the bases of bridge abutments are particularly good sites because the stream usually narrows to go underneath the road. Traps placed along either side of the bridge abutment base are generally a good bet. Some trappers use guide sticks to "fence" the entire stream running under the road, leaving narrow openings for foot-hold or body-gripping traps.

When placing body-gripping traps at den entrances, the trap is nearly always submerged. However, when using this trap type at other locations it's usually best to have the top just barely under the surface of the water. If the water is too deep, block the underside of the trap with sticks or vegetation.

Droppings spotted on logs slanting downward into the water or logs where 'rats have dragged acquatic grasses up to feed on are excellent places for sets. Just chop a notch in the log under the surface of the water for a trap bed, or tack a trap in place with nails to hold it until a 'rat gets into it whereupon the trap will be free and the muskrat will fall off and drown. Just be sure to tack the trap securely enough so that the 'rat won't knock it off before getting caught. Again, stake the trap in deep water for a drowning set.

The same basic types of den and runway sets can be made under the ice as well as above the ice — the trapper only has to chop through or look through the ice daily in order to check his sets. As with beaver trapping,

scaled down pole sets can be made for muskrats. Bait them with a piece of carrot, apple, or an ear of corn.

Again, professional muskrat trappers specialize in getting lots of traps out and the efficient trapper who puts a lot of steel into an area can take a lot of 'rats in a hurry. Such trappers may trap a given area only a few days and will then move on to a new location. The hobby trapper, on the other hand, who runs just a few traps in an area may gain more satisfaction in working a smaller marsh, pond, or creek for a longer period of time. Whichever method the trapper decides to employ, the important thing is not to over-trap the habitat. It *can* be done, for the muskrat is not difficult to trap. It is said that two thirds of a muskrat population can be removed from a given section of stream or marsh every year with no harm whatever to the stability of the population.

Muskrats are case-skinned with the hairless tail cut off the pelt; the pelts are sold skin side out. A muskrat is very easy to skin. Just separate the legs where the fur ends and try to make sure that the hair side of the pelt is dry before stretching it. Generally, the hair will be dry by the time you get it home. If not, wipe it off with a towel or rag and allow it to dry before skinning — it really doesn't take that long, and it will help prevent it from spoiling.

After you've skinned the animal, you'll notice that there is quite a bit of flesh clinging to the pelt. There are basically two layers of flesh to a pelt, and it is important not to scrape it too much. Many beginning trappers over-scrape. What actually appears as a thin layer of fleshy membrane next to the pelt should *not* be scraped off. If it is, the roots of the hair will very likely be exposed. With it, this layer will tan properly and is actually desirable to the furdresser. The No. 1 wire stretcher is the recommended size for most muskrat pelts. As it's drying on the stretcher, an oil film, or oily droplets will form on the pelt, but this isn't an indication that the pelt has not been scraped enough. Leave the oil on the pelt until you're ready to sell the fur. Then wipe it off with a burlap bag or grease rag, and the pelt is ready for sale.

chapter 14

DISPATCHING THE QUARRY

ONCE YOU'VE trapped a furbearing animal, the next step is to somehow dispatch it if it isn't already dead. If you've made some sort of a drowning set for a water-dweller, all you have to do is lift the trapped animal out of the water, release the trap from its foot, and put it in the bag while you reset the trap. Obviously, it's the same when a body-gripping trap is used.

However, in most land-trapping situations, the animal will still be alive when you return to check the trap. The main concerns here are to kill the animal quickly and humanely with as little pelt damage as possible, and without getting a lot of blood on the fur. There is one animal where there's no risk of doing damage to the pelt because it can be dispatched quickly and humanely with relatively little effort—the lowly 'possum.

I'll never forget the first 'possum I trapped. I was probably no more than 8 or 9 years old and had set a trap at the entrance to an abandoned groundhog den, camouflaging the trap with leaves. I returned to find a big fat 'possum in the trap. My English shepherd and rat terriers ran up to the 'possum whereupon it did what came natural and played "possum." I wasn't aware of this characteristic at the time and thought the dogs had killed the animal. I released it, reset the trap, and

proudly walked ½-mile back home, toting the 'possum by its tail.

Upon reaching home, I proudly displayed my catch to my father who asked me how I killed it. I told him the dogs had killed it in the trap. He laughed and said the 'possum wasn't dead yet. Of course, I knew better and laid the "dead" animal on the ground beside the barn while I did my farm chores. My Dad said something to the effect that it probably wouldn't be there when I came back. Not really thinking much about it, I returned 30 minutes later to pick it up and found, to my surprise, that the 'possum had disappeared. My father's only consolation was, "I told you so," and a chuckle. He then explained to me the ways of the lowly 'possum. It was hard to believe that a wild animal would play dead after getting bitten by dogs and being carried home by the tail.

A few days later, when we were doing the chores, we spotted a 'possum making its way around the corner of the chicken house. Fortunately, the dogs spotted it too, and ran it down and grabbed it by the scruff of the neck. The 'possum did the same as the one before, curling up and playing dead. I picked it up by the tail and took it to my father who then showed me how even a small boy

A trapper should beware when approaching any trapped animal. They can be dangerous. Here, the author is showing a sharp bobcat claw. Bobcats have the habit of slapping at intruders, and they're known to do it without warning. As this claw illustrates, these cats are capable of dealing severe damage in the blink of an eye.

The author approaches a trapped bobcat which will be dispatched with the .22 rimfire rifle. The .22 is an excellent choice for dispatching any of the large predatory furbearers such as coyotes, bobcats, and foxes. A single shot to the head usually kills them instantly.

could kill one without a gun and without a club.

He found a stout stick about an inch in diameter and a foot or more long. He then grabbed the 'possum by the tail and turned it belly down on the ground. He laid the stick across the back of its neck, and placed his feet on the stick, one foot at either side of the 'possum's head. He then grabbed its tail and pulled upward. There was a bone popping sound, and the 'possum went limp. It was dead, with a broken neck.

The next time I caught a 'possum in a trap I tried the same technique and found that, indeed, it worked quite well. Neck breaking was the best way to kill a 'possum—no blood and no holes in the pelt. What's more, it's quick and humane.

However, this works *only* with a 'possum. Most animals won't allow you to put a stick across the back of their necks nor will they allow you to grab them by the tail without a fight. Any trapper who tries it may be severely bitten.

There's another method of dispatching an animal without any blood. First, stun it with a firm blow to the base of the skull. If it's a coyote, it can be stunned by a blow across the bridge of the nose. After it's stunned, you can stretch out the front legs and place your foot back of the forelegs and step heavily and quickly downward. The quick, heavy pressure on the rib cage will result in an almost instantaneous death. This method works well with coyotes. However, I don't recommend this method for the novice trapper.

I've dispatched a good many coyotes in this manner, but there can be problems for the inexperienced trapper. First, some animals become more frantic when a human approaches, and there's a chance they may pull out of a trap, if it doesn't have a good hold.

Secondly, there is some personal risk involved. When approaching a trapped animal staked in the open, it will usually move away from the trapper in a direction directly opposite the stake. The trapper may then have to step within reach of the animal in an attempt to strike the stunning blow. If you miss, the animal may be the one to strike the first blow. You have to acquire the knack for stunning.

I much prefer shooting the animal from the size of a raccoon on up, including skunks, with a .22 rimfire rifle or handgun. A bullet from a .22 Short, when placed in the ear or forehead kills quickly. Any blood that does get on the pelt can generally be brushed out when it has dried. I prefer the .22 Short over the Long or Long Rifle versions because it, affects less damage and results sometimes in less bleeding. No doubt this is a result of the Short's lower velocity and lighter bullet weight.

Sometimes a trapper will happen upon a water dwelling furbearer that has not drowned for some reason. In this instance a body-gripping trap can be set and attached to a stick 3 or 4 feet long. The trap is then extended with the stick, placed onto the trapped animal's head, sprung and the stick used to hold the animal under the water until it has expired.

One question many trappers have is how to dispatch a skunk without the animal releasing its obnoxious odor and valuable scent. Some recommend shooting a skunk in the heart with a .22 Short; others recommend shooting it in the brain. However, I have found neither of these methods to be completely satisfactory. Jim Nolan,

A trapped animal characteristically moves his head from side to side. The author prepares to make a shot. However, he's waiting until the bobcat has its head turned directly toward him so that he can shoot it between the eyes and slightly above — into the center of the forehead. This kills the cat instantly. This is the proper shooting angle; the bullet, if it does penetrate, will go down the cat's neck, rather than exit. There's no sense in getting a second hole in the pelt. The first one, where the bullet enters, is enough.

in the section on skunk recommends a lung shot. From my experience, this is the best though you may find that many skunks will have already released their scent by the time you arrive.

Some trappers recommend attaching a skunk trap to a long pole so that you can grab the other end and drag it over to a water hole or creek where the trap, skunk and all, can be put under water until it's drowned. This seems like a lot of trouble to me, and it assumes there will always be a water hole nearby. I certainly don't want to be grabbing a pole with a live skunk at the other end unless it's about 40 feet long and I'm on the upwind side. The best thing I know to do when a skunk is trapped is to just shoot it in the lungs, and hope for the best.

When an animal the size of a coyote, bobcat or a fox is dispatched with a shot to the head, even from a .22 Short, there will sometimes be a lot of blood left at the trap site. Some say the smell of blood at a set will frighten many predators away. Others feel that the area torn up around a staked trap is a very good attractor for subsequent animals. Generally, however, a staked animal will dig up the area so much it is difficult to reconstruct a natural looking set anyway. Consequently, I move the set a few feet and make a new one. It is my thinking that any animal visiting the area will be enticed into the second set even if it is initially attracted to the old set site. Also, I generally use a trowel to scoop up any bloodied soil and fling it some distance away. I don't know whether this helps or not but I prefer taking the precaution.

Roy Daniels is shown here trying to maneuver a trapped raccoon into position for the killing shot with a .22 rimfire handgun. Raccoons can bite and scratch and so the trapper should be cautious when handling an animal in this manner.

173

One thing to remember when shooting any animal is to make certain it's dead before removing it from the trap. I remember trapping a good number of red fox during my high school years. One morning before school I walked down behind the house to one of my fox sets and found that a large male red had been suckered in. Using a .22 rifle loaded with Short ammunition, I quickly shot the fox in the head, took it out of the trap and hurriedly began remaking the set for I didn't want to be late for school. All of a sudden the fox began to move and almost immediately was up on its feet. I practically fell on the fox, grabbed it by its hind legs, swung it around in the air and whacked its head against the ground, all in one quick motion. I was a lot quicker and more nimble in those days, and I didn't want to lose the pelt. I never gave personal danger a second thought, but there was every chance the fox could have bitten me.

When I skinned the animal, I found that the bullet had hit it between the eyes as intended, but due to poor shooting angle and my being in such a hurry, the bullet did not penetrate to the brain; it passed underneath the skin and out the ear opening. The initial shot had done little more than stun the fox for a few seconds.

I remember another time when I was running a trapline and saw an untrapped coyote. I shot it in the neck, flung it over my shoulder, and headed back to my vehicle. Halfway back the animal regained consciousness and tried to bite me. You can imagine what a coyote might have been thinking when it woke up to find itself hanging by the hind legs over some human being's shoulder. It certainly wasn't pleased with the idea, but I didn't waste any time letting go of that one. A second shot to the head completed the job that I had started.

Once a scent-wary animal is trapped, I prefer to pull that trap and replace it with a clean one, not using a trap that has held an animal until it has again been boiled, dyed, and waxed. I certainly don't want any telltale blood scent to tip off the next furbearer that this site was associated with another animal's demise.

Also, I generally don't skin animals on the trapline but rather save the skinning until after I get home or back to camp — which is usually after dark. I prefer to use the daylight hours for setting, resetting and checking traps rather than for skinning animals. For this reason, it's also necessary to have some sort of provision in the vehicle for carrying the dead animals in a way that will keep them separate from the other equipment. It's important not to get blood on any of the clean traps, grapnels, or stakes that are intended to be set later.

Here, Clifford Gilliam prepares to dispatch this trapped bobcat with a .22 revolver.

chapter 15

TRANSPORTING AND SKINNING

WHEN YOU HAVE a valuable furbearer that you've trapped and killed lying on the ground in front of you, what do you do next? You'll probably either skin it on the spot, or take it to camp or back home where you'll skin it later.* But before you even touch the animal, you should be aware that furbearing animals are known to harbor a number of diseases which can be passed on to humans such as rabies, mange, plague, and various types of fungus. Although thousands of animals are skinned each year by trappers and rarely is there a case of a disease contracted from a furbearer, it can and does happen. Studies undertaken recently in northern Arizona, for example, indicate that more than one-third of the coyotes have plague antibodies in their blood. This means that those coyotes have been exposed to that disease at some point in their life.

Rabies, or hydrophobia, is a dangerous disease carried by a number of furbearers in the wild and serious outbreaks have occurred from time to time. Mange is an affliction of the skin and fur caused by mites; it general-

*Before transporting trapped animals in a vehicle, especially if it means crossing state lines, check the state laws governing the transportation of such game.

ly causes a good portion of the animal's hair to fall out or be pulled out by the animal as it bites at the irritated areas.

Skunks sometimes contract a fungus which is the causative organism of histoplasmosis, a respiratory disease often confused with tuberculosis. A few other infectious diseases that are known to be harbored by furbearers are tetanus, encephalomyelitis, enteritis, distemper, tuberculosis, and tularemia. Please don't allow all this to dissuade you from trapping, but I do feel that a trapping book would be incomplete if the reader were not at least made aware of the disease possibilities and some precautions to prevent these afflictions.

Some of these diseases are contracted through various types of vermin such as fleas, ticks, or mites. Particularly here in northern Arizona where the plague is ever present in furbearer populations, it is recommended that trappers avoid fleas associated with coyotes and foxes. In many areas, these animals are heavily infested. The various health agencies recommend spraying a recently dispatched furbearer with a powerful insecticide before transporting it anywhere. It's not a bad idea to put the animal in a plastic bag and liberally spray the inside of the bag with an appropriate insecticide, then

The author carries a fine bobcat out of the woods. It's important to prevent the dead animals from coming into contact with other trapping equipment such as traps, grapnels, etc. However, with bobcats, this isn't as important as it would be with a coyote, which is extremely scent-wary.

Clifford Gilliam hauls a just-trapped bobcat back to his vehicle. Furbearers have been known to carry diseases which can be transmitted to humans and domestic animals. For this reason, it's wise to take precautions as mentioned in the text prior to handling them.

close it up for 5 or 10 minutes. With some of the better, more potent insecticides the animal can simply be sprayed right where it lies.

Even if the animal isn't carrying some form of a disease, the fleas themselves can be a particular nuisance to the trapper. If a flea-infested animal is thrown into a vehicle without being sprayed, the trapper will soon become host to the small "bugs" looking for a warm-bodied home. Though a human being is a poor host for most fleas, a poor one is better than none at all as far as they're concerned. It's a bit unpleasant, to say the least, when you find the little buggers crawling through your hair and in behind your ears. Wives and mothers are especially prone to excited reactions when this happens.

If you decide to skin the animal on the spot, immediately after it's been killed, one that is flea-ridden can be very unpleasant to skin. Once its hung up and you begin skinning it, the fleas will start hopping on your arms, up your sleeves and pant legs, etc., and, in general, just make your life miserable.

There are documented cases of trappers contracting such serious diseases as the plague from furbearers. Fortunately, with today's antibiotics, curing the plague and most other diseases, isn't difficult. However, if not caught in the initial stages complications can enter the picture. The first symptoms of the plague resemble a case of the flu or a severe cold. As a consequence, the disease may progress for some time without being treated. If allowed to go too long, things get serious. Again, a good insecticide can rid the animals of the fleas and is well worth the extra few minutes needed to apply it.

I recall trapping coyotes in the desert of southeastern Arizona which were ghastly looking due to mange and fleas. When I put the .22 bullet between their eyes, I felt like I was doing the animal a favor by putting it out of its misery for it was obviously suffering more discomfort from the mange mites than it was from being caught in a trap. Whenever I come across such an animal in a trap, I keep my distance. I shoot it, pull out the insecticide and spray it *thoroughly*. I then leave it lie until the next day around the trapline.

On another occasion I recall catching a coyote in northern Arizona which had clusters of tiny fingerlike projections growing all over the inside of its mouth, lips and gums. Though the coyote appeared to be healthy otherwise, it had a terrible looking mouth. I took photos and found out, from a wildlife biologist, that this was the result of a fungus which can be transmitted to man. In this particular instance, since the coyote was otherwise healthy looking, I skinned it though in retrospect that may not have been a wise thing to do. I didn't suffer any after effects probably because I used a good pair of rubber gloves with no holes in them for the skinning job. In fact, I wholeheartedly recommend the use of rubber gloves when skinning any animal, *especially* if the animal behaves strangely before I kill it, or if there is anything unusual about its outward appearance. A healthy animal looks healthy, a sick/diseased critter will usually show some signs of trouble. Nowadays, I usually skin with gloves, but not always. I buy gloves used for washing dishes, and now, after having skinned hundreds of furbearers with them I don't like to skin one without them. Remember to take a couple pair of them into the field with you, just in case one gets a hole in it.

Though the gloves make skinning a bit clumsy at first, you'll soon find that it's easier to grip a slippery hide with the rubber gloves on. It's a pleasure not to have to come into direct contact with the animal. Once you've finished the skinning job and remove the gloves, your hands are clean — free from blood and fat.

Probably one of the best reasons for using rubber gloves is to avoid direct contact with the animal, its saliva, and its blood because it's entirely possible for bacteria or virus to enter the human body through any tiny scratch or cut. As a trapper, tiny hand cuts seem to be ever-present.

After you've sprayed the critter to get rid of the vermin and have your rubber gloves on, you've taken just about all the precautions you can, as a practical matter. From this point on you take your chances, although with these simple precautions you'll probably be in good shape.

Now you're ready to skin the animal. There are a number of different methods for skinning but most people prefer to hang the animal by its hind legs or at least attach its hind legs to some solid object so that the fur can be pulled off. My method of hanging an animal is somewhat unorthodox but it's quick and simple.

I loop a small stout nylon cord around one of the animal's hind legs, then throw the other end of the cord over a tree limb, pull the animal up to the proper height, and tie the free end. With only one of the animal's hind legs attached, the animal is easier to turn for complete access to all sides. For the larger predatory animals, and most of the other furbearers, one hind leg offers enough support to resist skin pulling pressure.

A more orthodox method involves the use of a skinning gambrel, a device with one hook on each end of a bar for hanging and securing the animal by each hind leg and holding the legs apart for easier skinning. Skinning gambrels are available in different sizes for different animals. Other trappers prefer to make the starting cuts, then stand on the animal's hind legs and tail and use an upward-pulling motion to remove the pelt. The hides of some animals such as muskrats and skunks pull off quite easily, and this method is probably faster than taking the time to hang the animal up.

Although they use a skinning gambrel, some trappers prefer not to hang the animal but rather pull the hide off in a horizontal pulling motion. Slim Gilliam, a western predator trapper, has a metal skinning gambrel attached to the bumper of his four-wheel-drive trapping vehicle. It is made from a bent piece of ½-inch rebar material, pointed at the ends so they can be slipped through the hind leg gambrels. Slim then places his foot against the bumper for additional leverage in pulling the hide off in a horizontal manner.

There are basically two different methods for skinning any furbearer. One is the "case" skinning method, and the other is called "open" skinning. When an animal is "case-skinned" or "cased," this means that cuts are made along the back or inside of the animal's hind

Here's a homemade skinning gambrel hanging from the ceiling. The hooks at the lower end are inserted into the hind legs of the animals between the leg gambrel and the bone for support.

legs and low around the front legs. The skin is pulled off much like one would pull off a sock, letting it turn inside out. When an animal has been case-skinned, the pelt will end up resembling a tube with the animal's mouth being one end and the hind leg cuts being the other end. The only other openings are those where the fur was cut around the front feet. When an animal is "open" skinned, it is slit up the entire length of the underside — from the chin to the vent or the base of the tail.

Most animals are case-skinned including weasel, muskrat, skunk, raccoon, otter, mink, fisher, marten, fox, lynx, bobcat, wolf, coyote, and wolverine. Today, only the beaver is requested by fur buyers in an open-skinned condition.

At one time, it was common practice to handle raccoon "open," the furs stretched into a very square shape. This practice has pretty much gone out of favor with most fur buyers. Also, some people handle badger pelts in an open manner. A check with several local fur buyers turned up no real preference one way or the other about badger pelts. Their primary interest was that the animal be well fleshed and stretched in a uniform manner.

When a beaver is skinned, there are no back-of-the-leg cuts. The only major cut is a centerline slit down the belly from the chin to the base of the tail. Then, the fur is cut away from the scaly portion of the tail and around its circumference with a very sharp knife. The forefeet generally are cut off at the fur line. *There are no cuts going from the centerline cut to the legs.* Instead, each of the four legs is worked out of the pelt through the cut made at the foot hairline, resulting in four small holes in the finished pelt where the legs were. The pelt is removed from the flesh by pulling back the skin from the central cut, all the way to the back. Beaver flesh has a tendency to cling to the hide and must practically be whittled from the meat most of the way. It's a tedious process to the inexperienced trapper for at first it's difficult to tell where the meat ends and the skin begins, with the result generally being a lot of holes inadvertently cut in a pelt. It's the type of thing that requires a lot of trial-and-error experience before a person gets good at it.

Some skinners grasp the pelt in a fist-making manner, with the fur side next to the knuckles, and the fingertips clamping the pelt to the palm or heel of the hand. The fist can be used to force the carcass away while the fingers pull the hide. The knife is used to cut the skin from the carcass, right over the knuckles underneath. The knuckles are used as a feeling device to make sure the

CASE SKINNING A BOBCAT

1. (Left) The author prepares to case skin a bobcat by first cutting up the back of the hind legs to the vent, near the base of the tail.

2. The cut is extended up the back of the leg to the vent. The same cut is made up the back of each leg. These are the only cuts that are made, with the exception of the cut extending from the tip of the tail to the vent, before further skinning.

pelt is being skinned clean. It's important to have the pelt as clean and free of meat and fat as possible.

I once saw a skinner use two large barbless fish hooks attached by heavy cord to a table opposite where he was sitting. The beaver carcass was hooked by the two fish hooks to offer pelt-pulling resistance. The hooks could be repositioned as needed while the skinner cut around the carcass.

The important thing is to take your time — don't be in a rush. Probably one of the most conducive things to taking your time is to first be comfortable. If you're out in −10-degree weather trying to skin a beaver pelt which is lying on the pond ice, it's a bit difficult to take your time. If possible, get inside a garage or basement where it's warm and dry or possibly in a shed with a wood heating stove.

In "case" skinning most animals, the first step is to cut around the hairline or "ankles" of all four legs. Some trappers simply whack off the front feet with a hatchet. Don't whack off the hind feet, or if you do, be sure you don't chop so far up that you destroy the utility of using the skinning gambrel in the hind legs. I make the cuts around all four feet just through the hide with a sharp knife. Next, I cut up the back of the hind legs to the anal opening or vent.

It helps if you acquire a knack for cutting only through the hide — not going too deeply and cutting into the meat or tendons. When you cut into the meat, it has a tendency to cling to the hide instead of separating from it when you begin pulling the hide from the legs.

Once the hind leg cuts are made, hang the animal by the skinning gambrel, if this is the method you're using, and work the hide off each hind leg. Actually, skinning most animals involves more pulling or peeling than cutting. In most instances after the initial cuts are made, a hide can be pulled from an animal without the use of a knife, except around the head. About all a sharp knife serves to do is to cut holes in pelts when it's used where it isn't needed. There will be difficult spots in separating the hide from the carcass and when a trapper meets this resistance, it's generally better to use your fingers than to use a knife.

Once you've worked the pelt off the hind legs, you'll have the tail to contend with. If the tail is bare, with no hair on it, it can be cut off at the hairline. If the animal has a furry tail, such as a fox or a raccoon, you'll want to leave it attached to the rest of the pelt. However, the tail bone has to be removed from the fur.

A commercial tail stripper is made for this purpose. It

3. (Left) The skin is now worked free of one hind leg, as shown here. Then, stout nylon cord is looped around the single hind leg of the cat just below the hock, as shown here. When the loop is tightened below the hock, it will hold the cat securely while the hide is pulled off.

4. Here, the bobcat is hung in a juniper tree for skinning. The author continues to work the pelt from the hind legs and tail prior to pulling it down off the body.

consists of two pieces of wood or metal 3 or 4 inches long, hinged at one end and with a groove in each piece mid-way down. When the two pieces are brought together, the grooves form a small hole to accept the tail bone. Once the skin is worked away from the base of the tail, the grooved sections of the stripper are placed on either side of the bone and the two halves are held tightly together with the fingers. Pull the root of the tail in the opposite direction with the other hand. If enough pressure is applied and the stripper is held very tightly next to the bone, the entire bone will be stripped right out of the skin.

Instead of using a commercial tail stripper, some trappers use two sticks, a clothespin, or nothing but their fingers. I use only my fingers and find that this works quite well even on animals as large as coyote. Just pinch the tail bone between two fingers and pull.

After the tail bone is removed the tail skin must then be slit the length of its underside all the way to the tip. If you don't slit the tail all the way to the tip, fluids will be trapped inside and the tail could spoil rather than dry.

After the pelt is worked off the hind legs, and the tail bone is stripped out, the pelt can generally be separated from the carcass in one smooth pull down to the back of the head. It's much like pulling off a tight fitting sweat-er. There will usually be some resistance around the forward portion of the front legs and, again, this is the place to use finger pushing and pulling pressure rather than a knife. Sometimes, a blunt instrument such as a sharpening steel can be thrust between the forward part of the shoulder and the skin. After the steel is pushed clear through, it can be grasped with a hand on either end and the leg separated entirely from the pelt in a downward pulling motion.

Then continue pulling the hide off the head. You'll have to cut the ears off next to the skull when you come to them. Feel for the base of the ear and then cut each ear through the cartilage next to the skull. Don't cut through the pelt. Continue pulling the hide downward whereupon you'll encounter the resistance around the eyes. Skin carefully around the eyes, being careful not to cut the eyelids but to leave only eyeholes in the pelt — not making them any larger than they already are. When the skin is pulled below the eyes, you'll have to separate the pelt from the mouth section. Cut through the inside of the *lips* — not the fur. Keep pulling the hide and when you come to the tip of the nose, simply cut the nose cartilage underneath so that the entire pelt is left intact, complete with nose and ears.

The head area is generally what gives most beginning

5. With a single swift pull, the bobcat pelt pulls down the entire length of the body, off the shoulders, and down to the legs and base of the skull. The pelt must now be worked free by pulling each foreleg through. Though no cuts are made around the front feet, the pelt will pull cleanly if a trapper puts a lot of strength into it. A skinning knife must be used to free the pelt around the eyes, ears and mouth.

Two bobcats and four grey foxes—all done in one hour.

trappers problems. Quick and easy (but good) skinning requires experience and it can only be gained by trial and error — I don't know of a better teacher. Just take your time.

I'll never forget the first animal that I ever skinned. I was fortunate to grow up on a farm where there were plenty of good trapping areas — both for large animals such as coyotes and foxes, and small ones such as muskrats, raccoon and 'possum. I had become interested in trapping primarily because my father had done a lot of it. He had trapped for most of the water-dwelling furbearers in northeastern Kansas when he was growing up. Though he was willing to tell me some of the tales of bygone days, milking a lot of cows and taking care of a large dairy farm didn't leave much time for first-hand instruction.

My primary education regarding skinning a furbearer came through a booklet, "Johnny Muskrat's Tips to Trappers." My first attempt at skinning a furbearer, as would be expected, was with the ubiquitous 'possum. My father had described, in detail, how to do it though I felt totally inadequate when, with knife in hand, and "Tips to Trappers" placed on the haybaler, I began peeling my first 'possum behind the corn crib.

I didn't have a skinning gambrel but hung it up by tying baler twine around its hind legs. I imagine that it took the better part of an hour and a half to separate that hide from the carcass, and when I was finished, there was an inch of fat over most of the hide. How that hide could have an inch of fat and seven big holes in it I still haven't figured out.

My father had said to slip the hide on a piece of wood skin-side out. I tried everything we had in the scrap pile from a 2x4 through a 2x12 and, as I recall, nothing seemed to fit that hide. Finally, I got a piece of 1x6 and, with the aid of a rusty old keyhole saw, I shaped out a stretcher as nearly resembling the drawing in the booklet as I could. I stuck the board in that first hide, tacked it down with four nails, and hung it up to dry, fat and all. Boy, did I ever have a lot to learn.

There is an alternative to skinning an animal. It's called selling it "in the round," meaning that it is sold unskinned. However, the trapper must first have a local buyer who'll take it like this, and it must be sold before it spoils. Generally, it has to be sold the same day it is caught. If you aren't adept at skinning, fleshing, and stretching pelts, you'll probably get more money for the pelt if it is sold in this manner. However, you'll certainly be paid less for it than you would if you were to skin and flesh the animal yourself and do a good job of it. Fur-

CASE SKINNING A COYOTE

1. Clarence Wales, a furbuyer in Kansas, prepares to skin a coyote. Circular cuts are made around each hind leg and then a cut made up the back of each to the vent. Note how the pelt coloration changes to very light on the inside of the hind leg compared to the outside. The cut should be made along this color line.

2. Wales hangs the coyote from a skinning gambrel.

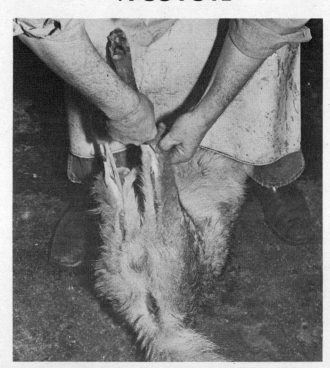

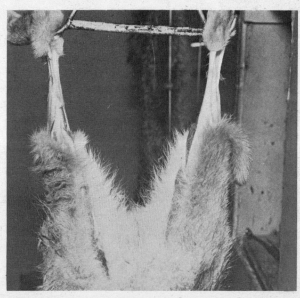

thermore, every trapper has to start somewhere, and the only way you're going to learn how to do a good job of skinning is to get some experience at it. Sure, you're going to mess up some pelts, put some holes in them, cut the tail off, cut the face off, and who knows what, before you learn how. But you can chalk it up to experience, and once you get the hang of it, it won't be the awful task that you had once envisioned. In fact, a great sense of pride generally results in the trapper who handles his own fur and is able to do a good job of it. There's not much that can match the sense of satisfaction received when a fur buyer comments, in front of a half-dozen other trappers, "This trapper really knows how to handle his fur."

This is a "tail stripper." Once the skin is partially removed from the base of an animal's tail, the tail bone is placed between the U-shaped notches and then the device is scissored together, tightly around the tail bone. Held in this manner, it is then pulled to strip the bone out of the inside of the tail in a very quick, easy motion.

3. At this point along the body, more pulling and less knife work generally serves the skinner best. Excess use of the knife generally results in too many holes in the pelt.

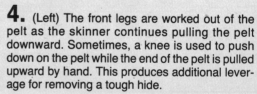

4. (Left) The front legs are worked out of the pelt as the skinner continues pulling the pelt downward. Sometimes, a knee is used to push down on the pelt while the end of the pelt is pulled upward by hand. This produces additional leverage for removing a tough hide.

5. (Left) Here, Wales passes the pelt between his legs, and wraps it around one of his own legs so that a backward motion will exert a lot of pull on the coyote pelt to free it from the carcass. It is easy to use the knife while he is pulling the pelt in this manner.

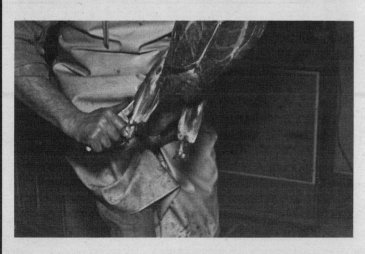

chapter 16

FLESHING BEAMS AND STRETCHERS

ONCE A trapper has skinned out an animal he needs equipment to take care of the pelt. This means a good fleshing beam and stretchers for the various animals that he has trapped.

Fleshing Beams

There are two different types of fleshing beams — a permanent setup and a portable one. The permanent beam is secured to the floor or a bench inside a shed or wherever the pelt fleshing will be done. Some consist of a bench-like affair wherein the beam and legs are not attached but are somewhat portable, if only in a cumbersome way. Probably the most portable types consist of nothing more than the beam itself.

The fleshing beam may vary in size, depending upon the types of animals you intend to trap. However, to give you a rough idea regarding the size, a beam for coyotes, large raccoons, and large bobcats would be about 6 feet long, and 3 inches thick with a base about 10 inches wide. The beam is tapered, much like a wooden stretcher would be and is generally rounded on the top side. A fleshing beam can be purchased though constructing one for yourself is easy and much more cost effective.

Beams for smaller animals can be somewhat smaller although one size is usually standard for fleshing any pelt. The dimensions are really not critical as long as you can slip the green pelt over the beam easily, skin side out, and can rotate the pelt, without it fitting too snugly. The beam should be wide enough to afford the trapper ample working surface and the curved topside smooth enough to prevent any danger of cutting holes in the pelt when passing the fleshing knife under pressure over it.

Some trappers prefer the beam be angled slightly up and away so that the knife is pulled toward the user, and the fat and flesh removed in a downward pulling motion. Others like the tip to point toward them and the flesh and fat removed in a downward pushing motion. The fleshing method chosen is totally up to individual preference. I prefer the push over the pull method, pushing the greasy stuff away from me into a container rather than pulling it toward me. Also, my arms tend to tire more when reaching upward than when stretching downward.

To hold the pelt in place when fleshing, a nail or simple clamp at the point end of the beam can be used. I like to lean against the tip of the beam, clamping the pelt between beam and my waist to keep the skin in place while it's being fleshed.

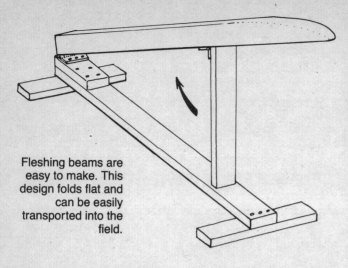

Fleshing beams are easy to make. This design folds flat and can be easily transported into the field.

This is another type of portable fleshing beam. The pelt is slipped skin-out over the upper end of the beam and the trapper leans against the beam with his stomach and scrapes the pelt in a downward-pushing motion.

This is an excellent pelt-fleshing beam design and is readily portable. It can easily be transported to the trapping camp in the field.

This close-up shows the top end of a fleshing beam which is fitted with a piece of serrated metal used to hook and hold the noses of smaller pelts for scraping. The smaller pelts will not slip over a beam of this size, therefore the hooks.

Ed Steffen, owner of Maas and Steffen Fur Company in St. Louis, has been in the fur business for many years and recommends the use of sycamore wood for a fleshing beam because it doesn't splinter like most of the other woods do. That's something to keep in mind when making one.

If the beam is used with no supporting framework, it is readily portable and easily stowed in the pickup or trailer for transporting to the trapline base camp. To jury-rig a base for my portable beam, I generally rest the base against a solid object, such as the side of a building, and place a wooden or metal milk carton container underneath the mid-section for support and angle the tip upward, to about waist level. With this setup, the beam angle can be adjusted upward or downward as desired by repositioning the supporting box.

Actually, the construction of a fleshing beam is so flexible and dependent upon personal preference, that perhaps we should merely say, "if it works for you, use it." I have seen all sorts of beams, some blunt not tapered, made of smooth wooden fenceposts, with a gripping device at one end. Others have been flat and not quite so rounded but in both instances, the trappers using them, were doing an excellent job in a short time. So who's to say what the "proper" shape of a fleshing beam might be. There are those who even use solid wooden stretchers for fleshing beams and do their pelt fleshing right on the stretchers. However, I find a fleshing beam to be more convenient and efficient.

Stretchers

Besides a fleshing beam, the trapper will need a good supply of stretchers or fur frames. There are three different types of stretchers from which to choose — solid

184

wooden forms, two-piece wooden forms, or commercial wire or spring-steel stretchers.

The wire or spring-steel type have come into wide use only in recent years and are a real boon to the trapper. It once required many hours of work to carefully shape and finish homemade wooden stretchers of various sizes. Now, spring-steel models are available at a very reasonable price — for much less than what it would cost a trapper to make wooden ones.

When I began trapping, I made a complete set of wooden stretchers. If I were to do it over again, I think I would make the solid or two-piece wooden ones only for a few furs and would use the spring-steel type for the rest. For the trapper who packs all of his gear into a remote area, the spring-steel jobs are much lighter in weight and more portable than the others. In addition, pelts dry faster on wire stretchers because there is less surface area in contact with the pelt, allowing air to circulate more freely inside. However, it is important to keep the steel units free of rust and corrosion by covering them with a thin coating of Vaseline. If this is not done, the pelt will stick to the rusty surface and be ruined. If the stretcher does rust, the rust can be removed with fine steel wool.

The author holds two basic types of stretchers. The one at left is a homemade wooden-type, the other a commercial spring steel version. These particular stretchers are used for coyote-sized animals.

The solid wooden stretcher is a flat board, shaped to fit inside a case-skinned pelt. The dimensions of the board are governed by the pelt species and standard stretcher size for that species. In addition, a wedge is almost always used in conjunction with a solid form. After a pelt is placed on the form, a long slender wedge, frequently resembling a long splinter of wood, is inserted between the pelt and the board on the belly side of the fur. This allows air circulation between the skin and the wood, speeding the drying process.

Once the pelt is completely dry, the wedge is pulled, causing some "slack" in the pelt so that it can be easily slipped off. If this were not done, the pelt could shrink tight to the form, and the trapper might not be able to pull it off. I had this happen to me in my early trapping experiences. I carefully followed the instructions for making a solid wooden stretcher for red fox though the instructions somehow failed to mention the wedge. I ruined several prime red fox pelts just trying to get the boards out of them.

The two-piece stretcher consists of two slender boards hinged at the "nose," allowing them to be spread at the base once the pelt has been slipped on. To use it, a cased skin is slipped onto the stretcher, pulled down for length, tacked in place, and then the two "legs" of the stretcher are pulled apart until the pelt is stretched firm. The two "legs" are locked apart to hold this position.

In the case of the new spring-steel stretchers, the wire frame is slipped inside the pelt and the legs of the pelt attached to one "gripper." The gripper is pulled down tight, putting tension on the legs, and then is locked into place. The other gripper is attached to the base of the animal's tail then pulled down tight and locked. With some pelts, such as raccoon, the gripper is attached about 2 inches from the base of the tail to help hold it flat, and give the pelt a better shape.

Spring steel stretchers are quick to use because all that's necessary is to slip it inside a pelt, sink a gripper into the legs and backside and pull them down tight. Just make sure the pelt is centered, and it's then ready for drying. With the wooden stretchers, on the other hand, the pelt must be pulled down and carefully tacked into place with either tacks or push pins. Push pins have come into vogue in recent years, and in some respects are an advantage over tacks. I prefer push pins when tacking the pelts of smaller animals to small, thin stretching boards because they may be made from thin crating wood, or even from a wooden shingle. Here, push pins are easier to work with because they won't split the wood. However, for larger animals such as coyote stretched on heavy stretching boards, I have had problems with the push pin heads pulling off, particularly the aluminum ones, when taking the pelt off the frame. When this happens, the pelt rips where the pin was still holding to it. Sometimes, the pelt pulls easily away from a single pin, but now the sharp pin is left in

Kent Dederick (left) holds a homemade beaver stretcher, consisting of nothing more than slender steel rod bent into a circle and held at the joined ends by two hose clamps (right). In use, the clamps are loosened and the hoop is made very small for attaching a beaver pelt. Dederick uses hog rings to hold the pelt to the hoop. Then, the hoop is pushed apart and the clamps tightened when the pelt is taut.

the stretcher board to catch on the trapper's finger later when he's least expecting it.

There are some advantages to wooden stretchers. For example, a pelt can be pulled down and stretched more thoroughly and flatter than it can on wire. In addition, it's easier to tack the tail out open and flat on a solid wooden form, thus improving the appearance and increasing the drying quality of such tailed animals as the mink and raccoon. Tails can be tacked down if you are using wire stretchers by inserting a small flat piece of wood, such as a shingle, underneath the hair side. Then, using push pins, it can be flattened out and held to the shingle much as it would be on a wooden stretcher. All in all, however, using a wooden frame and carefully tacking the legs, edges of pelt and lower lip into position results in a pelt with a much more pleasing appearance.

I use both stretcher types, and the fur buyers that I have dealt with don't seem to prefer one stretcher type over the other as long as the pelt is properly fleshed, stretched, and dried. However, the number of positive comments from fur buyers regarding the excellence of my pelts when stretched on wooden forms, far outweigh those about spring steel forms.

One important factor frequently overlooked by most beginning trappers is stretching the pelt squarely on the form before it is tacked down or the grippers pulled down tight and locked into place. The centerline of the pelt's belly side should go directly up the centerline of the stretcher; and the lower lip should also be centered, as well as the legs, both front and rear. If everything doesn't look properly spaced and centered after it's slipped onto the form, remove the pelt and reposition it.

It's amazing how many trappers slip a pelt onto a stretcher, pull it down tight, fasten it and forget it without even checking to see that everything is properly lined up. This can make a whale of a difference in the appearance (and ultimate price) of pelts. If a trapper goes to so much time, trouble and expense in order to

trap, skin, flesh, and stretch a furbearer, it only makes sense to take an extra 30 seconds to make sure that everything is stretched properly so that it will be a pelt he can be proud of.

Making Wooden Stretchers

There are all sorts of minor variations in the construction of two-piece wooden stretchers. Mine are made of 1 × 4 lumber, are properly shaped and are hinged at the nose with a leather strap. The base portion of my stretchers have two base boards that sandwich the stretching board between them at right angles in a loose-fitting manner. Nail holes are drilled crosswise so that a nail can easily be slipped into any pair of holes to lock the stretcher into any open position.

One disadvantage to making solid wooden stretchers is that the trapper has to have several different sizes to match the various animals encountered on the trapline since these stretchers aren't adjustable for width. The two-piece stretchers, on the other hand, have quite a bit of leeway, the boards scissoring apart or together to fit nearly any pelt size. The same holds true for the commercial spring steel stretchers — one size fits many different sizes of animals quite well because the sides spring outward. In many instances, I've stretched such animals as raccoons, and even skunks, to quite a nice shape on No. 6 wire stretchers intended for coyotes. I've also stretched skunks on No. 4 fox stretchers with excellent results. This couldn't be done with solid wooden stretchers, or even with two-piece stretchers for that matter.

Some people prefer wooden stretchers on the short side, hanging the pelt by the nose in the drying shed. I don't have an overhead drying rack for my pelts and, consequently, I prefer to have my forms long enough so that when leaning them against a wall the tails don't touch the ground. This really comes in handy when trapping away from home — it's not uncommon to camp near a ranch and use the rancher's barn for the storage of my pelts until I return home. The long two-piece stretchers easily lean against the side of the barn, and the tails are far enough off the ground that mice and other rodents in the barn can't reach them. This is something to consider if you do decide to make your own stretchers.

The table below outlines which commercial spring steel stretcher size is best suited to each animal. If you decide to go the wooden stretcher route, I've also included illustrations with the dimensions of stretcher boards to fit most of the common furbearers.

Recommended Commercial Wire Stretcher Sizes

Coyote — 6	Skunk — 2,3,4
Red Fox— 4,5	Badger— 5
Grey Fox — 4,5	Marten — 1½
Bobcat — 5,6	Mink — 1½
Racoon — 3,4,5	Muskrat — 1
Opossum — 2,3,4	

When I began trapping, I was warned by other trappers to stay away from spring-steel stretchers. Due to this caveat, plus the fact that I was really trying to be thrifty, I went to the local sawmill and got all the rough-sawed stretcher lumber I needed. I then had to shape the curves on the boards.

Fortunately, I had a saber saw and it worked very well for this purpose. When one side of the stretcher nose was cut to the proper shape, I used this as a pattern for the rest of the stretchers. The "template" was sim-

ply flopped over to make the boards for the other side. This way, the halves matched perfectly as long as I worked carefully.

Once the curves were cut, the rough lumber had to be sanded down, the edges of the boards rounded with a wood rasp and sanded further. Then the base pieces were made and the holes drilled. Finally, the leather strips were tacked to the noses.

In all, it was a lot of work. I spent an entire summer, working in my spare time on evenings and weekends after a regular job, just building stretchers and preparing other trapline equipment. If I had it to do over again, I'd probably use spring steel stretchers since they can be bought at moderate cost. In fact, the lumber alone cost almost as much as the spring steel stretchers would have. My time has to be worth something, so I don't think I saved any money by doing it myself.

If you make your own stretchers, it's important to find clear lumber, that with few or no knots, particularly when building two-piece stretchers. If a knot happens to be in the curved nose of the stretcher and then falls out later, the stretcher is ruined. If the knot is further toward the base, the board will be weakened and will probably break before your first season is over.

Make certain that you've got proper stretchers and a good fleshing beam before the season begins, and you won't have those headaches during the season. Trapping season is the time to be out in the woods, going after the fur, and enjoying it all. The trapper who prepares his equipment well, and makes certain that he has everything that he needs before the season opens, will find a lot more pleasure from running a trapline.

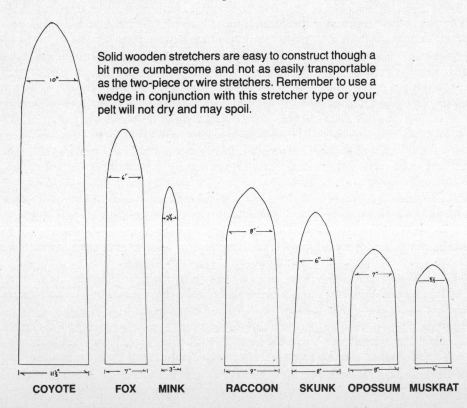

Solid wooden stretchers are easy to construct though a bit more cumbersome and not as easily transportable as the two-piece or wire stretchers. Remember to use a wedge in conjunction with this stretcher type or your pelt will not dry and may spoil.

COYOTE   FOX   MINK   RACCOON   SKUNK   OPOSSUM   MUSKRAT

chapter 17
FLESHING

AFTER THE pelt is removed from the animal, the next thing is to remove all the fat, flesh, and gristle from it. This is done so the pelt will dry properly, without spoiling, and if well done, it will fetch a higher price at the buyer. Improper or inadequate fleshing is one of the major reasons for the trapper getting less than top price for his fur.

Some animals require very little fleshing; others need a lot. In the same vein, some animals are easy to flesh with the fat and flesh separating readily from the hide, while with others the flesh is very stubborn and clings tenaciously. It's best if most of the fat and flesh can be left on the carcass, particularly with animals that are extremely difficult to flesh.

Generally, a device known as a fleshing beam, is used for this purpose. The fleshing beam offers a surface to support the underside of the hide while a scraping device is used to remove the fat and flesh from the skin. Some trappers, those that use heavy wooden stretchers, prefer to scrape the skin right on the stretcher. In fact, beaver pelts, which are sometimes tacked down flat onto a hard wooden surface can be scraped after they're stretched. The only problem is that when the pelt is tacked, the pushpins make scraping the flesh and fat off

the edges of the skin more difficult, increasing the possibility of pelt spoilage at the edges.

A fleshing knife is usually used in conjunction with a fleshing beam. It's important to make sure that the pelt is completely free of burrs because a fleshing knife can easily cut a hole in the pelt when it hits them. The burr forms a little bump in the hide and when the fleshing knife hits this bump it cuts right through the pelt.

A skilled flesher can work over a pelt in just a few seconds with the use of a fleshing knife and beam, scraping the fat off right down next to the hide without leaving any holes or thin spots. Basically, what it takes is experience, getting the hang of the angle at which to use the fleshing knife. Most inexperienced trappers tend to use too much of an angle, resulting in more of a cutting motion. For the beginner at least, it's best to keep the knife nearly vertical in relation to the work surface. As the name implies, the fat and flesh is "scraped" off of the pelt rather than being cut or sheared off. Once a section of pelt is scraped, the pelt is rotated on the fleshing beam to expose an unscraped portion. This area is then scraped and the process is repeated until the pelt is completely cleaned. It's best if a container is placed underneath the fleshing beam to

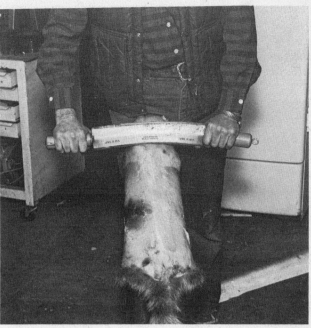

(Left) This is a muskrat pelt being fleshed with a special fleshing tool. You don't need a fleshing beam to do a muskrat pelt—a table top works great. It is important not to scrape muskrats too thin, leaving a thin layer of membrane lying next to the skin.

Here, Clyde Tryon is scraping a raccoon pelt with a fleshing knife and fleshing beam. This holds the pelt and forms a hard work surface.

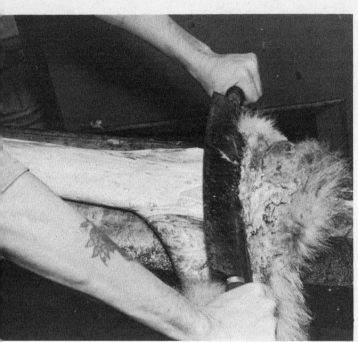

(Left) Here, a coyote pelt is being scraped with a fleshing knife. It is important to have all burrs removed from a pelt especially when using a fleshing beam. If a burr is in the fur, it will form a bump under the skin and the fleshing knife will cut through it, making a hole in the pelt.

This trapper is fleshing a raccoon on a beam and with a different type of knife. An experienced pelt flesher can do a raccoon in a matter of seconds.

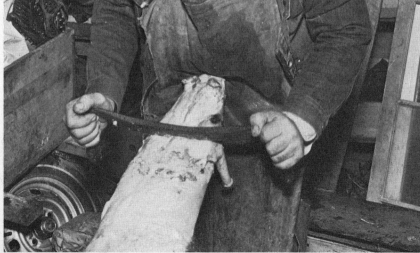

189

catch the scrapings, otherwise the work area can become pretty messy.

You don't need a store-bought fleshing knife for this purpose. In fact, an excellent fleshing knife can be made from a carpenter's draw knife. However, it's best to dull the sharp edge of one of these a bit for this purpose. A paint scraper also makes a good fleshing knife. There's been a good many muskrats and other animals scraped with nothing more than a spoon with a sharpened edge, but some trappers prefer to file tiny notches into the edge to grip the fat and flesh more efficiently.

With some pelts such as coyote, there is a thin membrane which lies next to the skin. It is sometimes better and generally quicker to pull the membrane off with the fingers rather than using a fleshing knife. Some trappers refer to this as "peeling."

Some animals like bobcat and grey fox require almost no fleshing at all. Not all of them, to be sure, though most of them will be free of fat.

The raccoon, opossum and skunk are very greasy. They have a lot of fat lying next to the skin and must be scraped clean. It sometimes helps to place one of these pelts on a stretcher for a couple of days before fleshing, allowing the fat to break down so that it can be scraped off easier. Then the pelt can be removed from the stretcher and scraped clean.

Don't keep the fleshing knife too sharp, for it can cut the roots of the hair, damaging the pelt and causing the hair to fall out. The fleshing knife should be just sharp enough to scrape cleanly.

Once the pelt has been cleaned of all loose fat and flesh, any remaining grease can be wiped off the pelt with a coarse burlap bag. Just before selling the pelts they should again be wiped free of grease with a rag or burlap bag. An old towel also works well for this purpose.

Raccoon, skunk, and opossum are the *only* three animals that are scraped quite like that described above. Other animals, such as mink, muskrat, marten, etc., should *not* be scraped right down to the skin. It is preferred that the thin membrane be left on the pelt because it tans when the pelt tans and is said to strengthen the hide.

Muskrats are commonly over-scraped; there should be a distinct membrane layer left on the pelts. On mink, there should be a "saddle" of thin fleshy membrane on the pelt which should not be removed. It lies all around the animal's mid-section and is shown in one of the photos nearby.

Beaver need to be scraped right down to the leather, and this is another one that can be scraped even after it's stretched. Beaver pelts, stretched open on a barn or piece of plywood, unlike other pelts, can be scraped anytime, without removing the pelt.

Here's a properly fleshed muskrat pelt. Note that there is a thin membrane remaining on the pelt and that there are grease droplets as well. Muskrat pelts should not be scraped too thin.

This is a properly fleshed and stretched mink pelt. Note the "saddle" of membrane around the mink, where its mid-section would be. This should not be removed.

chapter 18

STRETCHING

AFTER THE necessary fleshing is completed, the next step is to "stretch" the pelt. In order to do this, you'll need some form of stretcher if the animal is "case" stretched, or a flat surface for tacking the hide out flat if it is to be stretched "open."

Animals that are case stretched are not always done in the same way. Some are commonly sold on the market with the fur on the outside of the stretched pelt; others are sold with the fur on the inside.

However, at least at the beginning of the drying process, all case-skinned pelts are put onto the stretcher or fur frame skin side out. It doesn't really matter whether a wooden or spring-steel frame is used — both work fine. The important thing is to put the animal on the frame properly.

Most home-made wooden stretchers consist of a solid board for the smaller animals and a two-piece stretcher for the larger ones. All stretchers work on the same principle. When a commercial spring-steel frame is used, the spring action of the steel keeps the pelt stretched taut on the form. With the hinged two-piece frame, the form is scissored apart until the skin is stretched taut, and then locked in place. With the non-adjustable solid board, the match of pelt to stretcher is

much more important with the wedge taking up any slack and keeping the skin stretched tight. Then, with the pelt dry, the wedge is pulled out so the fur will slip off the board. Otherwise, it'll shrink so tight around the board you may not be able to get if off.

It really doesn't matter whether the case-skinned animal is a muskrat or fox, the important thing is to slip the stretcher up into the fur side of the pelt and then pull the skin down snugly for the full length without over-stretching. Make sure that the pelt is positioned symmetrically on the frame. The eyeholes should be centered on the back side of the pelt near the nose, and the base of the tail centered at the other end. There should be a straight hair line running between the two with no twisting or curving in between. On the reverse side of the stretcher the animal's lower lip, as well as the front and rear legs, should be centered.

Once everything appears in line, pull the skin down tight again and lock into place. With the spring-steel frames, both back legs are generally hooked into one of the pelt grippers on the belly side of the pelt and then pulled down tight. The other pelt gripper is hooked into the base of the tail on the opposite side of the pelt and it, too, is drawn tight. When the commercial pelt grip-

Clarence Wales begins working a muskrat pelt onto a commercial spring steel fur drying frame. It's important to have the eye and ear holes properly centered on the frame, as shown here.

(Right) Wales continues pulling the muskrat pelt down onto the frame. The next step is to attach each of the two grippers to the pelt. One goes onto the base of the tail at the backside of the pelt, the other in the leg skins at the front side. Then, the pelt is pulled taut.

per is released it locks in place.

Some trappers attach pelts on commercial stretchers another way. Each hind leg may be hooked into each of the pelt grippers, instead of using one gripper on the back side of the pelt. This way, the tightness of the legs is depended upon to prevent the back side of the pelt around the base of the tail from rising up too far.

With the homemade wooden stretcher, the basic principle, insofar as getting everything square, is just as important as it is on the spring-steel type. However, instead of pelt grippers, the trapper generally tacks down the legs with tacks or push-pins.

If the stretcher is solid, make sure you select the proper size. The pelt should slip onto the board easily — if it doesn't, use a smaller size. If there's any question, use a smaller stretcher so that you can pull the pelt a bit longer. Pelts are frequently graded by *length,* not width.

Once the pelt is on the form, I pull the legs down taut then tack them first. If it's a solid stretcher, the next step is to tack the base of the tail. From that point on, you can tack the edges of the pelt down as much or as little as you want. I usually end up putting more tacks in a pelt than necessary because I like the way it looks when all the edges are lying down flat and uniform. In fact, I even go to the trouble of tacking the lower lip out on a coyote, using six tacks in it.

The wedge used with solid forms is nothing more than

a long slender stick, running the length of the belly-side of the pelt. It takes up slack and holds the skin away from the board so that air can circulate better, drying the pelt out faster. If there's doubt about a pelt drying fast enough, it doesn't hurt to place a wedge in the back side of the pelt as well.

If you're stretching on one of the two-piece frames don't lock the two stretcher halves apart until the pelt is pulled down taut for length. Pull the legs down taut, tack them and then scissor the halves apart for width and lock them in place. I made this mistake when I began using the two-piece stretcher. I hinged the two boards apart to stretch the pelt as wide as I could before pulling the legs down for length. I thought coyotes looked bigger if they were wider. As a consequence, my pelts were much wider than they should have been and lacked the length needed for being highly graded. I listened to the fur buyer's constructive criticism when I sold them and wised up quickly to get a better price next time. As with coyote, bobcat pelts are frequently graded according to length, as measured from the tip of the nose to the base of the tail. When the pelt is properly proportioned — stretched for length before width — it is generally graded higher and will fetch a slightly better price.

In general, if you're working with fatty animals, the pelts are left skin out and sold in this manner when dried. These animals include the weasel, mink, musk-

(Right) Here's a properly handled grey fox on a homemade wooden stretcher. This backside view shows how the eye-holes, ears, and tail are well centered on the stretcher frame. Note also how the dark portion of the upper part of the fox's back is centered.

(Left) Like the backside of the pelt, the belly must also be centered on the stretcher frame. Note how the hind legs, front legs and lower lip are all centered on the frame.

rat, opossum, skunk, otter, and raccoon. With other long-haired and less fatty animals, they're generally started on the stretcher skin side out and then turned to fur side out for the remainder of the drying process and sold fur side out. These pelts include those of the marten, wolverine, bobcat, coyote, wolf, fox, and lynx.

If an animal is to be sold with the fur side in and skin side out, the legs are generally pulled out on the skin side so that they dry rather than spoil. Though the legs will shrivel up and become twisted, this really isn't all that important for they'll usually be cut off flush with the skin later anyway. If the animal is to be turned fur out later, tuck the legs inside the pelt while the fur is drying with the skin out.

Animals that are sold fur out, are initially placed on the fur frame skin side out until a dry glaze forms over the skin. This steps up the drying process. Later, with the fur out and the skin side next to the stretcher, the drying process progresses more slowly. The dry glaze will now help to prevent the skin from sticking to the wood.

The length of time a pelt is left skin out to acquire the glazing varies depending upon humidity and temperature so that no flat statement can be made. Some thin-skinned animals dry very quickly while other thick-skinned types with more grease in the hide tend to dry more slowly. It may require only a couple of hours or it could take all day. However, be careful not to leave a

Clyde Tryon shows off a fine collection of well-handled musk-rat pelts. The trapper who treats his furs well will not only be justifiably proud, but he'll be well paid for his efforts when he presents them to the furbuyer.

193

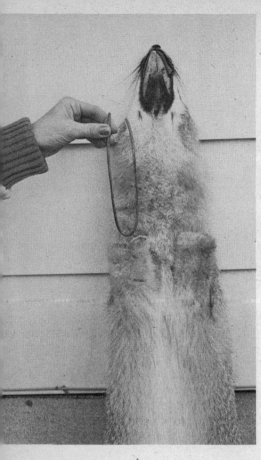

(Left) The author uses wire bent into a U-shape to hold the legs of fox pelts flat and open so that air can circulate inside them.

(Right) This illustrates how the author inserts two U-shaped wires into the leg skins of a bobcat pelt. Two wires inserted in the same leg at right angles to each other hold the leg skins open in a tube fashion. This allows air to circulate freely down inside the leg skins allowing them to dry quickly.

fur that has to be turned fur side out on the stretcher too long. The skin can become so stiff and hard that it can't be reversed to a fur-out position.

If a pelt takes more than a day to acquire the glaze when it's skin-out, it's time to evaluate the drying process. The skin simply isn't drying fast enough and may eventually spoil. Even if it does acquire the glazing and the pelt is subsequently reversed, if drying is progressing no faster than this, it could spoil before it's completely dry.

After I've turned a pelt hair-out, I then hold the legs open in a tube fashion by inserting two wires, each bent into a longish U-shape, into each leg. The wires are crossed at right angles to each other, holding the leg open so that it'll dry faster. The secret to the whole thing is air circulation.

A friend of mine, Ralph Simpson, welds the leg wires at the apex of the two "U's" so they can be quickly inserted into the leg skins. There are some trappers who don't pay much attention to the front legs, and there are others who even tie them off, closing the opening. It's true that the fur dresser may not use much of the upper legs, but I like to give him plenty to work with. Also, by propping the legs open in this manner, I believe that it allows air to circulate down inside the pelt and make it dry faster. After they're dry, the legs can either be folded flat against the pelt, or tucked inside out of the way. This, of course, is not done on pelts sold fur-in. Again,

this is my own thinking and your local fur buyer may have different ideas. He's the fellow you're selling to and need to please, and if he has different ideas and wants you to do it differently, it pays to listen to what he has to say.

The tails of animals like raccoon, mink and otter should be spread open and tacked out to dry, just like the rest of the pelt. This is no problem with a solid stretcher, and is one reason why some trappers prefer these types. However, tails can be tacked out flat, even with two-piece wooden and spring-steel stretchers by slipping a small, thin piece of plywood under the fur side to serve as backing for tacking.

When it comes to "open" stretching, a beaver is the only North American furbearer that is skinned and stretched this way today. It used to be common practice to stretch raccoons and badgers open, but now even these furbearers are generally preferred cased.

There are two basic methods of open-stretching a pelt — either tacking it onto a flat surface such as the side of barn, or a sheet of plywood, or lacing the pelt inside a hoop made from a sapling or steel rod.

For tacking a beaver pelt out flat, a half sheet of plywood, 4 feet by 4 feet, is about the right size. There are varying opinions regarding the shape the finished beaver pelt should have. Some say that it should be oval; some that it sould be egg-shaped; and others that it should be as round as a dollar. Again, your fur buyer

Here are two well-handled raccoon pelts. This is not only the proper overall shape of a raccoon pelt, but the proper general appearance, front and rear.

This is how a pelt gripper on a commercial spring steel stretcher is attached to the leg skins of a raccoon pelt. The upper gripper holds the leg skins while the lower one is attached to the tail. Note that the gripper on the backside of the pelt is attached about halfway down the raccoon's tail. This holds the tail skin out flat and open so that it will dry quicker.

Today, beaver is the only pelt which is preferred open-stretched and round. All other pelts are "cased," either fur-in or fur-out. The other single exception is badger which is acceptable either way.

will dictate which way you should stretch your beaver pelts. For the most part, however, they're stretched in something of a circular pattern, and each half of the centerline should have approximately the same shape. A beaver pelt looks like heck if it's lopsided — stretched larger on one side than the other — or if it has a lobe at one hind-quarter.

One way to keep things uniform is to, first of all, find the centerline of the pelt — a line running from the base of the tail, to the tip of the nose. Tack the tip of the nose down and the center of the tail base, but don't stretch the pelt to do this, just open it up. Next, I prefer to put a tiny tack directly in the center of the pelt. Determine the exact midpoint along each side of the pelt, opposite the center tack, and tack these out, pulling snugly. Now, you have four tacks around the perimeter of the pelt in a square pattern, and one in the center.

The next step is to split the distances between all of the nails and add tacks at these midpoints around the pelt. Continue doing this, being certain to stretch the pelt in a uniform manner all the way around and taking care to make it symmetrical, and you'll end up with a good looking pelt. When you finish, the tacks or push-pins should be spaced about 1-inch apart. Some trappers draw concentric circles on the sheet of plywood to serve as a blueprint for keeping the pelt perfectly circular or symmetrical. This is a good idea and can serve as an excellent stretching guide.

The author's wife, Mary is holding a properly stretched bobcat pelt. Note how the hind legs, tail, ears, and fur coloration are centered on the home-made stretcher boards. At right is the spotted belly side of the same cat.

The alternative to tacking is lacing the pelt onto a hoop. This is the method used in olden days. A willow or alder sapling was cut, bent into a hoop, and tied at the joined ends. Then, a strip of rawhide was used to lace the beaver pelt inside the hoop. The same methods that were used for tacking the pelt out flat — starting at opposite ends and opposite sides — may help keep the pelt shaped more uniformly on the hoop.

Kent Dederick, the beaver trapping expert from Kansas, uses a unique stetching system that appears to work quite well. He uses a hoop made of slender steel rod, joined at the ends with two small hose clamps, which makes the hoop adjustable by loosening the clamps. Rather than lacing the pelt onto the hoop, Dederick uses a hog ringer.

For those of you who didn't grow up on a hog farm, a hog ringer is a plier-like device which uses a type of heavy staple. The "staples," called "hog rings," are clamped into the snout to keep the hog from rooting under fences or barns. The rings are of different designs although most of them are a circular or triangular metal staple about ½- or 1-inch in diameter. Dederick uses hog ringers to attach the beaver pelt to the stretching hoop at close intervals all the way around the pelt's circumference.

Since the hoop is adjustable for diameter, it can be made very small for attaching the pelt. Then everything is stretched taut by pulling the wires apart and clamping

them for the final stretching. The hog rings are then spaced evenly apart until everything is symmetrical

Those who stretch beaver pelts on a hoop generally say that the pelts dry faster since both sides are exposed to air and that the hair doesn't have a tendency to be mashed down flat as it does when being stretched skin-side-out on plywood. Also, the hoop stretchers are lighter and more portable than are sheets of plywood.

On the other hand, tacking probably makes it a little easier for the novice to produce a symmetrical pelt. Also, a tacked pelt can be scraped while it's being stretched.

The amount of time it takes for a pelt to dry is dependent upon the climate. However, the careful fur handler will monitor the drying conditions almost daily, making sure it is progressing as it should. If the weather is rainy and wet, it's particularly important to watch the pelts closely. Just because they're on a stretcher, doesn't mean they're going to dry before they spoil. If the pelt begins to spoil or rot, the hair will pull out quite easily and the pelt takes on a foul odor. Fur buyers don't even want to look at such pelts and they shouldn't have to. It is a shame that many pelts, otherwise well skinned and stretched, end up spoiling because they weren't dried fast enough.

Another time for caution is during periods of freezing and thawing temperatures. Frequently, temperatures climb well above freezing during the day yet get well below freezing during the night. When a pelt is subjected to fluctuating temperatures, it takes much longer for it to dry. After the pelt freezes at night, it takes a good part of the morning for it to thaw out. It's thawed out only for a couple of hours when the temperature drops and it begins freezing again. All this freezing and thawing without much drying taking place does to a pelt what it would to a beefsteak — eventually spoil it. One way to prevent this is to keep the pelt from freezing.

When we have this kind of weather, I generally put the pelts on the shady side of the house during the daytime so that breezes can circulate around the fur without exposure to the sun. I then place the pelts inside an insulated pumphouse where temperatures don't hit the freezing mark at night.

If there's a long wet spell, I bring the pelts into my heated laundry room and turn a fan on, allowing it to run day and night until the pelts are dry. If pelts are subjected to a fairly warm temperature, say in the 60-degree range with a fan continually blowing across them, they can be dried in just a few hours. This is also something to remember if you're trying to dry pelts quickly so they can be sold.

If a pelt such as that of a coyote has a lot of blood on it, I'll generally wash it in cold water after skinning the animal out. This quickly removes all traces of blood, and then I hang the coyote nose-up and allow it to drip-dry before placing its still-wet pelt on the stretcher.

When the skin is reversed, fur-side-out, on the stretcher, the hair is still wet. However, it will quickly dry when exposed to the air. A word of caution: Never put a wethaired pelt on a stretcher if it is to be left and then sold fur-in. In other words, what works fine for a coyote won't work for a raccoon or mink,

It's important to leave pelts on the stretchers until they are thoroughly dry. You can never leave a pelt on a stretcher too long though you can take it off too soon. When you pull a pelt off of a stretcher it should be somewhat stiff and bend with a crackling sound. If the pelt goes limp anywhere, it's not completely dry. Grab the pelt by the snout and give it a hard flip. If it has spoiled anywhere, hair will fly out in chunks.

Once the pelt is off the stretcher it's almost ready to sell. But first inspect it thoroughly then comb or brush the fur to get rid of any dirt or hidden burrs. In short, make the pelt as presentable to the fur buyer as possible. If he's feeling the belly of a coyote while admiring the thick white underfur and runs a sand burr into his finger, it changes his whole outlook on the pelt. Besides the burrs, make sure the pelt is free of mud and blood. A small amount can generally be removed with a cat comb and a brush once it becomes dry and brittle.

When packing furs for the trip to the buyer, don't stack the skin of a pelt next to the hair side of another pelt. Keep them skin side to skin side and hair side to hair side. No one wants grease in the hair of a pelt.

chapter 19
REPAIRING PELT DAMAGE

TRAPPERS after large predatory furbearers such as coyote and fox, will frequently have the opportunity to add extra pelts to the fur shed in the course of checking the trapline each day. It's not uncommon in good coyote or fox country to spot a couple of these "extras" each day. If the trapper has an accurate, flat-shooting rifle, he'll be able to collect a good many of these furs, even when the animals are at some distance.

I prefer one of the high-velocity .22-caliber centerfire rifles for coyote or bobcat shooting. A .22-250 Remington or .220 Swift is ideal for nailing coyotes at long range. For fox a .17 Remington is a better choice because it is less damaging to the pelts.

With any of the high-velocity .22-caliber centerfires, and with proper bullets, the projectile won't exit a coyote if a solid hit is made. They usually go inside, do what's necessary, and drop the animal in its tracks. However, on some occasions, the trapper will bag one of these long-range predators and will end up with a good-sized hole in the pelt. Sometimes a coyote must be taken at a quartering angle wherein a long rip in the pelt results. At other times, if the trapper doesn't have a suitable pelt-hunting caliber (meaning too big) a large exit hole is the result.

I have shot coyote-sized predators with all sorts of calibers and have even nailed a good many of them with a .300 Winchester Magnum. There's no question that this caliber is over-kill for coyotes, but this might be the only one that a trapper has, and it's better to shoot a coyote with a big one than not shoot it at all.

Many trappers disagree for they've blown extremely large holes in coyotes. I've sewn up a good many such holes myself. However, the skin on the opposite side of a predator is not necessarily blown *away*, it's just blown outward. A trapper will find that once the animal is skinned, if the skin is all folded back over the bullet hole, it all fits together for the most part. I have taken coyotes that were discarded by other hunters and trappers who thought they were too damaged to warrant messing with. After a 30-minute sew-up job, the pelts sometimes net top prices — in the $50 – $60 range. Including skinning, stretching, washing and sewing up, I have perhaps an hour of time invested in some of the pelts. At $50 an hour, I'll do it all day long.

The point I'm making, is that a pelt really can't be damaged beyond the point of repair, contrary to what most people believe. As long as pelts are fetching a high price, it is worth the trapper's time to repair them.

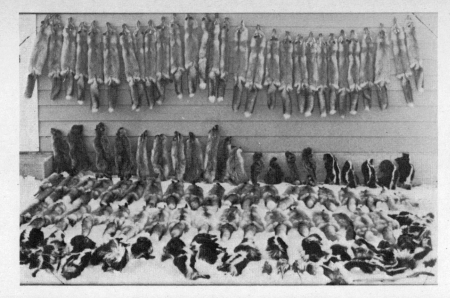

Pelts which have been not only properly skinned, fleshed, and dried, but repaired as well, can make any trapper proud. Those which are carefully repaired can net top dollar while pelts with holes, bare spots, etc., can depreciate up to 50% of the normal price. It pays to repair these damaged areas. (Photo courtesy of Tal Lockwood.)

There's no question that a trapper won't be able to get much, if anything, for a pelt with a grapefruit-sized hole in it. However, spending a little time sewing when the pelt is freshly skinned, can net top price.

I want to make it clear that by sewing up a hole we're not trying to pull the wool over the fur buyer's eyes. Buyers themselves are the ones who suggest sewing up the holes. Every one I have talked to recommends the practice. Sewing up a hole allows all the hide around the hole to dry in a taut, flat position without spoiling so that it will take a tan later. According to the buyers, pelts are so cut up in manufacturing that holes, in a small percentage, are acceptable.

Skinning an animal with a good sized hole is a bit more difficult and messy. A trapper needs to be careful in skinning around the hole to make certain he separates all parts of the hide from the carcass without tearing it. Since a bullet exit hole weakens a pelt considerably, you'll have to skin carefully around the hole without the normal hide pulling. Just separate the flesh from the skin by using your fingers to pull the two apart around the bullet hole.

Any time a large hole is shot into an animal, there's going to be a lot of blood. There may also be pieces of flesh and fat on the hair around the edges of the hole. The first thing I do whenever I skin an animal with a bloody pelt is to wash it in cold water. In the case of the coyote, I believe that washing its pelt improves its appearance. This is a dingy, dirty animal, and a good bath not only cleans the blood out but a lot of dirt as well.

When washing, I use a bucket and do it under the water faucet out back of the house. Fill the bucket with cold, clear water and dunk the freshly skinned coyote pelt into it. Swish it up and down and then dump the water out and refill the bucket. I do this repeatedly, changing the water seven or eight times during a 5-minute washing. When the pelt is free of blood and the water remains relatively clean, it's time to stop.

If you wash the pelt before the blood has dried, it comes out quickly and easily. If the blood has dried, it will help to soak the pelt in cold water for an hour before washing it.

After all the blood and dirt is washed out of the pelt, hang it up by the nose to drain the excess water. Hang it fur side out so that the water drains faster. If there is a breeze the fur side of the pelt will dry in a bit. You don't want the inside of the pelt drying until you get it on the stretcher.

After the excess water has drained off, take the pelt down, and examine the fur side of the hole closely. Make certain that all the pieces of flesh and fat have been picked out of the hair and that none of the hair has been blown away around the hole. Sometimes, a high velocity rifle bullet destroys hair around the hole, leaving it short around the edges. Some of the strips of hide around the hole may also be missing hair. Any area that has hair missing should be cut out of the pelt. I know that cutting an even larger hole in the pelt is a hard thing to do since you're working to *preserve* it, but believe me, you'll be making yourself money in the long run.

Now, turn the pelt skin side out. It's a good idea to hand-flesh the pelt around the edges of the hole with a pocketknife or with a pulling motion of the fingers. Removal all excess flesh from around the edges of the hole for an inch in all directions because you won't be able to scrape over it with a fleshing knife later. There should be nothing but healthy skin right up to the edge of the hole; anything else should be trimmed away.

I generally sew up the pelt with a conventional sewing needle with 4 to 6-lb. test monofilament fishing line. I've found this to work very well although other trappers prefer to use dental floss. I usually place a plastic garbage bag across my lap to keep from getting wet because, at this point, the pelt is still soaked.

Get a length of the fishing line, thread the needle and tie both ends together into a knot. Generally the hole of

a high velocity bullet consists of long rips radiating about a central point with flaps of skin in between. Sometimes there will only be two or three rips. Try to arrange the skin over the hole so that it fits together the way it was before it was blown out. Once you've got everything in place, start sewing at the outside edge of one of the rips toward the center of the hole.

Always punch the needle through from the skin side and pull it out the hair side, alternating sides of the separated skin. Repeat the process until the hole is entirely closed. It's usually best to sew only to the middle of the hole and then tie off the thread. Then go to the opposite side of the hole to another radiating rip and sew it toward the middle. When all the rips are sewn together, do the central hole separately, drawing everything neatly together. The two edges of skin should meet smoothly, without puckering. Some puckering or gathering will come out of the hide once it'a placed on the stretcher though ideally, when the sewing is finished, everything should lie flat.

If you have a perfectly round hole that is not very large, it can sometimes be closed to lay flatter if the ends of the hole are cut to form an eliptical or football-shaped hole. This way there isn't such a tendency for the edges to pucker when sewing. Stitches about an ⅛-inch apart generally result in a good job though I have taken even larger stitches on occasion.

After you've finished sewing, the pelt will be a little bit drier and the fleshing can be completed. Just be careful that you don't rip the hole open again while you're fleshing the pelt. In the case of a coyote, there won't be much fleshing to do — just a little hand pulling of membrane will sometimes be enough, depending upon the individual pelt and how fat the coyote was.

After a pelt is washed, and on the stretcher check it daily to make sure it's drying well. First leave it on the stretcher skin-side-out as long as possible. Let it get just as dry as you dare, but don't let it get so dry that you can't turn it fur-out for final drying. The reason for leaving the pelt on the stretcher skin-side out as long as possible is so that the overall drying time is reduced. There is greater risk of a pelt spoiling after it has been washed.

Once a pelt is dry enough, it's put on the stretcher fur-side-out in the conventional manner. The hair will still be wet, and at this point it helps to brush the hair opposite the direction it lies to make it fluff out and dry faster. This also makes the hair puff out more when it's dry, much like a hairdresser might back-comb a person's hair to make it stand out. Once the pelt is dry, brush it again in the normal direction. You may well find that the washed coyote pelts with the bullet holes will end up looking better than the unwashed pelts.

This bobcat trapper is presenting his pelts to the furbuyer, who in turn carefully scrutinizes every pelt for holes, bare spots, etc. Wise trappers repair these damaged areas before selling them.

Bullet holes aren't the only reasons for repairing a pelt. You may even accidentally cut a hole in one while you're skinning. The pelt can be repaired in the same manner except it won't have to be washed.

Sometimes, there are instances when you may get a higher price for a pelt by cutting a hole in it! I once caught a coyote which had the hair rubbed off the top part of its shoulders, exposing bare skin. I did nothing to repair the damage and, when I took it to the fur buyer, he said that he would have to knock 30 percent off the price due to the bare spot. He told me to take the pelt home, soak it in cold water to soften it, cut out the bare spot, sew up the hole, restretch it, and return it to him. I did that, and 2 weeks later the pelt netted $20 more than it would have originally!

If you encounter a situation such as this, just remember to cut the hole in the shape of a football or an ellipse rather than round because it will sew together better.

Once a pelt has dried on the stretcher or fur frame, it can be re-soaked and re-stretched, as mentioned. Just put the whole thing in cold water for about 3 hours. It'll then be pliable but not as soft as a freshly skinned pelt by any means. If for some reason you end up with a bad looking pelt that was not properly stretched, it too, can be soaked and restretched. However, any pelt that has been soaked and re-stretched, or one that has been washed is more prone to spoilage, so beware.

chapter 20
MARKETING FURS

THERE'S A LOT of excitement involved in running a trapline. Finding sign, outwitting the animals and just being in the out-of-doors is a satisfying experience. Skinning and fleshing the pelts also gives a lot of satisfaction that is culminated when you present them to the fur buyer.

Basically, there are two ways that a trapper can market raw fur. The first method, and no doubt the one used by most trappers, is to take the furs to a local buyer. He'll look them over carefully, eye-balling the length and density of the guard hairs. He'll brush the fur with his hand to look at the soft fur underneath the guard hairs. He may grab the pelt by the snout and the hind legs and give it a flip or pop to see if it's dried properly. At the same time, he'll be looking at the primeness of the pelt, and for holes or any other damage that shouldn't be there. Through all these evaluations he'll apply some sort of a mental grade to the fur, and based upon this, make you an offer.

You have the option of either accepting or rejecting the offer. If it isn't suitable, you can take the furs to another buyer and get a second opinion. If you're satisfied with the original offer, the buyer will write you a check on the spot and you're done with it. This same process can take place by mail and/or by phone if a fur buyer is too far away to deal with face-to-face.

The second alternative involves shipping the fur to one of the major auction houses. There are several types of auctions throughout the United States and Canada that are readily accessible to the trapper through the mail. These places operate in different manners. In some cases, a trapper can specify a bottom dollar that he's willing to accept and, if a potential buyer doesn't bid higher than that figure, the furs aren't sold but are held for a later auction or returned to the trapper.

In other instances, when an individual's furs are received at a large auction, they're graded and separated, and placed into large lots with other pelts of the same quality. There is some form of record keeping at the auction house so that they know where each trapper's furs went, though, from this point on, there's no separating out a trapper's individual furs. The furs are then sold in those large lots. In this case, the trapper may not have the right to refuse the price but rather receives a blanket or average price for his pelts. If a very low price is offered, the auction house may sometimes "buy back" the fur, not allowing it to be sold at the low price.

Some fur-buying companies have agents who travel to small towns all over the countryside, like this one operating out of a pick-up with a camper shell. Here, a trapper presents his furs for evaluation and possible sale. Meeting the furbuyer face-to-face is an excellent way to find out why you may not be getting top dollar for your furs. He can explain to you, first hand, if you're making any mistakes in the way that your pelts are handled.

On the surface, this latter method may not sound ideal to most trappers, but it should be kept in mind that the larger auction houses operating in this manner frequently attract some of the best potential buyers from overseas. Keeping in mind that a good portion of our fur is exported to Europe, Japan, and other countries, this is a factor to consider.

In all cases, the auction house gets a commission for selling the fur, usually about 6 percent, and that's how they make their money.

There are advantages and disadvantages to selling fur both ways. For the beginning trapper, there are definite advantages in selling pelts to a local buyer. Most local buyers are helpful to trappers and are willing to take the time to explain what is wrong with an individual fur or lot of furs. If they aren't well fleshed or if they're stretched improperly, most fur buyers will tell the trapper what's wrong with them and how he might improve his handling methods in order to receive top dollar. After all, it is to a buyer's advantage to receive good quality, properly handled furs. I know of no better way to get a good fur-handling education, because this type of first-hand information can't be gained through selling them at an auction.

Some local buyers sell furs at the larger auctions, hoping to buy them locally and sell them at the auctions for a net profit. On the other hand, there are other local buyers who have contracts with manufacturers and know exactly what they're going to receive for the pelts before they're purchased. Since the large auctions do

(Left) B&M traders of Mesa, Arizona, is one of the major fur-buyers in the southwestern United States. Here, one of their fur handlers prepares pelts taken during the 1982-83 season. They will be hung in cold storage for safe keeping.

attract major buyers, a trapper can sometimes receive a higher price. However, on a number of occasions, the local buyer may beat that price. You never know for sure where you're going to get the best price.

Generally, there is a delay between the time a trapper sends his furs to an auction and when they're sold. Sometimes the larger houses request that furs be sent a month in advance of an auction. Since the fur business can fluctuate considerably, the prices may rise or fall during this period. Again, there are advantages and disadvantages to selling either way. The only suggestion I

These grey fox pelts are being sorted by grade in preparation for shipment to a major processor. They have come from trappers all over the southwestern United States.

have is for the beginning trapper to sell his furs to a local buyer — the information gained by doing so will be invaluable to him later.

There's no real problem in shipping fur today. It can be sent either by parcel post or UPS. If the trapper is really concerned about getting his pelts to an auction on time, the various air freight services can be an advantage and, for the most part, they are reliable.

Furs can be shipped in cardboard cartons. They don't necessarily have to be laid out flat as they come off the stretcher. If you don't have a long flat box, say for the longer pelts, just take a bunch of them, stack them on top of each other and then roll up the entire stack so that it will fit into a rectangular or cube-shaped box. Be sure that you place fur-out pelts together and skin-out pelts together. Don't put fur-out pelts next to skin-out pelts — make it hair to hair, skin to skin.

Also, pack the pelts so they can "breathe," allowing air to get in and out. An air-tight box could conceivably cause the pelts to spoil or for an excessive amount of grease to run out of them if they get warm. You never know when the plane that your pelts are on might have a lay-over in Phoenix where the temperatures can climb quite high, even in the winter. If the pelts are properly dried and fleshed, however, there should be little problem. The important thing is to insure them for an adequate amount in case they come up missing.

You don't have to sell your fur the same winter that it's trapped. It's possible to hold it until the next year though, in most cases, I don't recommend it. Sometimes, a trapper may suspect that prices are going to rise, for one reason or another, and he may think he'll be able to get a better price next year. If you have just a few pelts, and they're thoroughly dried, they can be stored over the summer in a freezer. Don't think that

just because the pelts are dried that they can be left at ambient temperature over the summer. All sorts of things can happen to them. They may dry-rot when exposed to warm temperatures, and may even fall apart when being tanned. Frequently, the skin will turn a yellowish color when stored over the summer. Some pelts, such as mink, may lose the luster of the fur, or even fade. Perhaps worse, is the danger of them getting infested with "bugs." For these reasons, a dry pelt must be stored in the freezer if it's to be kept over the summer. It's not recommended to keep pelts longer than a single summer, for like meat, they will eventually deteriorate even in the freezer.

If your pelts fail to sell at the final auction sale that winter and the auction house suggests keeping them until next year, don't be alarmed. These sizable operations have excellent methods of keeping them in long-term storage under carefully controlled conditions, free from insects, or the various types of molds and fungus that can also attack them.

Possibly the best insurance a trapper has that he's getting top dollar is to keep in touch with a lot of other trappers. Find out what they're getting for pelts. Friends in various parts of the country can also be of some help, but keep in mind that pelts from other sections of the country vary considerably in value. Also, if you're relying on information from local friends, it's best if you have an opportunity to see their furs to see how they've been handled and what quality they are. This way, you have a better basis for a price comparison. By keeping on top of the pelt prices any way you can, you'll get a feel for what yours should be worth.

However, I know of few, if any, trappers who can grade pelts as well as experienced graders. Pelts that might look great to you may have some major flaw that

Furs are sometimes tumbled in large drums such as this in order to clean the dirt and blood out of them. A tumbled pelt comes out much softer. Also, a type of powdered detergent or other cleanser is sometimes placed into the drum in order to make the fur appear more glossy to the manufacturer.

(Right) After the pelts are removed from the drum they're stacked and bundled in preparation for shipment.

Here's a good-sized load of coyote pelts after they've been tumbled in the drum. They're now ready for shipment to either a manufacturer or possibly one of the major fur auction houses.

you never saw. For example, a pelt can look quite nice, even when it has very little underhair or nat down the middle of its back. To the unknowing trapper, a pelt without guard hairs over a large portion of the fur is hardly noticeable yet a fur buyer spots it immediately. For these reasons, any trapper should approach only those buyers who have a reputation for honesty and fair prices.

Several years ago I had the opportunity to visit the Maas and Steffen Fur Company in St. Louis. This name will no doubt be familiar to many trappers for Maas and Steffen has been in St. Louis continuously since 1914. This company began with the Hudson Bay Company, when that firm sent Art Brown here from England. Brown and Steffen became partners and opened shop in New Orleans and Minneapolis in 1904, before moving to St. Louis 10 years later.

Ed Steffen, son of the original Steffen of "Maas and Steffen," is one of the few buyers who purchases fur from individual trappers over all of the North American continent. I had the opportunity to visit with Steffen and to record some of his tips and comments on fur handling, and fur buying:

" When I open a package of fur, I look for size, handling, and the overall quality — they're all important. There are only three furs that are scraped in the fur industry — skunk, 'possum, and 'coon. If the other pelts have a little grease on them it doesn't matter that much. They say that muskrat, mink and the ringtailed cat tan better when they've got a little grease left on them. With these furbearers it's important to leave some grease; the tanners don't like 'em fleshed off too much. Of course, you can't leave *too* much on them because they're put up in bales under pressure and you'd squeeze the oil right out of them.

If a fur is real greasy you can always take it out with hardwood sawdust or oatmeal or something like that. Just rub it in real well and shake it out. Cornmeal also works well. But, if a skin is a little bit greasy, nobody pays any attention to that because when it's tanned, it's all going to come out. Once in a while, I get a fur that's absolutely soaked in grease so you can't tell whether it has any underfur. I dock heavy for that.

Don't try to sell frozen furs. We get people coming in with skins that have been rolled up in a bag and thrown in the deep freeze. Every one, to them, is a Number One Extra Large. For all I

The Mass & Steffen Fur Co., taken in the early 1940s. This building was a center of activity for trappers traveling to St. Louis to sell their furs.

ED STEFFEN
ON MARKETING FUR

know, they could be full of holes, or tainted, or who knows what. I can't sit around for 4 or 5 hours waiting for them to thaw out to grade them, so I have to buy cheap.

It's the same thing with buying a skin on a carcass, unskinned. Like a 'coon, for example, hells bells! If he's frozen, you don't know how long it's been since he was killed, whether it's 2 days or a week old. On the carcass is a poor way for a trapper or fur hunter to sell anything. He just can't get as much. There's labor involved for a dealer to skin, flesh and stretch the thing, and some dealers are in a city like St. Louis where you're not allowed to buy things like that.

A lot of trappers don't realize that a pelt that's an Extra Large in one section isn't necessarily an Extra Large in another section. In other words, an Extra Large mink in Missouri might only be a Medium or Large in some sections of Alaska, but he would be quite a bit bigger than a mink from the Great Lakes region. Muskrat also differ like that, and coyotes are bigger in some areas, than others. When you buy fur you get to know all those different sections. For instance, I can tell clear across the room where some foxes came from just by looking at them.

Sew up holes when the skin is green before it's stretched. Make sure it's sewed up strong enough so it'll hold together during tanning. When pelts have too many holes in them, or sometimes one big hole, and they tan them, it means problems. That's a pretty tough process and the tanners aren't too gentle. It's like a fur without a head on it — the head is really tough skin and it holds the whole pelt together. Knock the head off, and the skin tears like tissue paper. Sew up holes with nylon thread or monofilament and sew them as close together as you can without puckering them up.

It's very important on skunk to slit the tails full length and don't cut the tails off short. They must have a good tail on them. A fox's tail is also important, not so much for the price of the skin, but just for the good looks. A fox pelt without a tail looks like hell; in fact, it doesn't even look like a fox. You should be careful with the tails, and if you happen to tear one off, it looks better if you sew the thing back on. Be sure to slit the tail because if a tail rots it stinks up the fur baler. The manufacturers can smell that and then they get suspicious. They think that some of the fur bodies are tainted. You don't want an old rotten tail hanging on 'em.

My father always said that if every trapper used a really stiff curry comb on a 'coon or a coyote it would really help. With that you get rid of golden-rod seeds, cockleburrs, beggar lice and stuff like that. It makes a lot of difference. A fur buyer doesn't want to jam his hand into something that's full of holes, matted with weed seeds, mud, blood and stuff like that.

You don't have to put any preservative on those skins. You can forget about salt and alum and tanning lotion or anyting like that because they don't need that. Just air dry them in a cool place where the air can circulate. Keep them in a room at 50 or 60 degrees but don't get them up next to Grandma's old wood stove and put them between the stove and the wall where it's about 90 or 95 back there. That would be all right if they were scraped right down to the pelt but otherwise they get grease-burned and brittle and they'll break and snap like a dry stick.

Don't let your pelts freeze and thaw. It's just like taking a piece of meat out of the freezer and letting it thaw and freezing it again — it'll spoil.

Don't keep furs over the summer. Usually, too much fat is left on a fur, like a 'coon or 'possum.

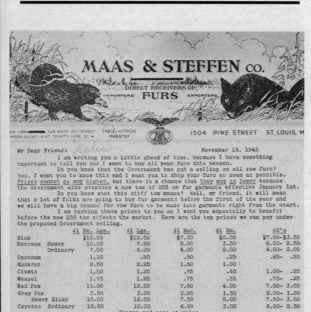

It's interesting for today's trapper to compare the prices offered 40 years ago (left) to a current price list. The 1943 price list was also a folksy newsletter and commented briefly on the war and the economy. This year's list (above) is much enlarged, showing more animals, but it, too, comments on economic conditions.

Right away I know they're old skins, because they get that yellowish-orange color to the pelt side. All wild mink, regardless of whether they're shut in a completely black room or in a freezer, oxidize, and mink don't keep worth a damn. The first year they fade rather badly and held-over mink always sell at a discount. Usually when I grade fur, if a guy has some fresh stuff and some old stuff, he'll get about a third or half again as much for the fresh stuff as for the old. It just doesn't dress out as well; it's usually too dried out; they get moths and beetles in them; the larvae drill holes through the leather and the moths get in the fur.

Some things are caught too early and the skin side is not white, but has a blue cast to it. Those are inferior furs. Sometimes the color might be all right but the density of the hair isn't there. Any fur, when it's prime, has a real nice bright white pelt or, like a muskrat, has a nice bright reddish color to it. If a pelt was taken too late in the spring, the hair is rubbed. In other words, it has lost the guard hair. On beaver, the edges of the fur get a reddish color when it's taken too late.

All the water animals prime up later than the land animals. A muskrat or beaver swims around but it can't swim in water that's colder than 32 degrees. It could be 32 degrees and the poor old coyote or fox has to live out in it, and he has to get prime quicker. The water animals don't get prime until after the first of the year, even up North.

You would think that the best fur would come from Alaska but that's not always true. For example, the best muskrats come from upper New York state and parts of New England; even local Missouri and Illinois muskrats are better than the Alaskans. They're bigger, and have thicker leather on them, which is important.

There's really about four different kinds of mink in Alaska. There are the upper Yukon mink which are pretty good, and you have the lower Yukon mink which are probaby the best in the world; there's the Kenai mink that's equivalent in price to those from Michigan or Northern Ohio, and you have one from Southeast Alaska, down in the rain forest. That one has a lot of white on its belly, and these aren't worth any more than mink from Missouri or Arkansas.

Even though fur prices have risen in the last few years, I think the overall take has been pretty much the same. There's just so many amateurs trapping now. In the old days, there were a few trappers, long dead now, who could catch a hundred mink the first night of the season if the Alabama weather was decent. Those guys were real mink trappers. After the first night their catch would fall to maybe 10 or 15 a night for a few nights. We don't have any mink trappers like that any more.

Gee whiz, in the old days we got furs in here that we didn't have to touch. They were handled beautifully. You still get that once in a while, but mainly from the older generation, the guys in their 60's and 70's.

Today, I get pelts from southwest Texas and northern Mexico that look like they've been pulled over a fencepost and left there to dry. I've gotten otters from Florida that have been stretched on a 4×4 hunk of lumber. We even get stuff shipped to us and we can't get the stretcher out!

A buyer's first impression is always important. When you open up a package of fur and see a bunch of junk on top, even though the rest of it might be handled okay, it gags you right away and it doesn't set very well. But when you open up a package of fur that has been fleshed nicely, combed out well, and is all handled the same, like cigarettes in a package, that impresses a buyer. ”

chapter 21
SNOW TRAPPING

TRAPPING IN country where there's snow most of the winter requires entirely different trapping techniques. I learned how to trap in the snow first-hand from ex-government trapper Jim Nolan. Nolan is from Wyoming and has extensive trapping experience in snow from a few inches, to many feet deep.

I thought you might find his techniques as interesting as I did. Here they are, first-hand:

JIM NOLAN
ON SNOW TRAPPING

❝ As far as equipment goes, the same things that you use for trapping in dry country can be used for snow sets too. However, the means for getting around the countryside may be considerably different. For example, snowshoes are a basic item, necessary for working a trapline in deep snow country. The snowshoe that you use depends upon the terrain. I use a long shoe up here because there's not a hell of a lot of brush. If you're in brush country, you'd use a shorter shoe.

You're going to be limited in the amount of ground you can cover on foot in deep snow. If you've got a creek, where you can run a few beaver sets on the way in, you can travel a frozen creek like a highway going in and out. This makes it a lot easier to cover ground than if you're running a deep woods line. The ease with which you can get around determines how far you're going to go in a day. It may take you several days to get out a complete trapline, but you don't want to go where you have to over-extend yourself physically.

A hand-pulled sled can help if you're on snow-shoes in deep snow. It's a bunch easier to pull something than it is to carry it because the snow — not you — supports the weight. I've got a pack basket that I use for traps and other equipment and I can carry six or eight No. 3's in there. By the time you get the drags and everything else that goes with trapping in the basket, that's all you'll want to carry on your back. The sled allows you to carry more.

Snowmobiles are probably the best shot you've got in deep snow. The distance and the ease with which you can cover it is extended quite a bit with these machines. Most of the guys I know who use snowmobiles up in this country usually have a sled behind for towing gear. They also have a buddy with a second machine going with them for safety. The likelihood of both machines breaking down is slim but just in case they both carry snowshoes.

A lot of the snow trapping technique depends upon how much snow is on the ground. If the snow is not deep, say less than 8 or 10 inches, you're better off to clear it down to the ground and plant the trap in the dirt or mud. Otherwise you don't have enough snow on top of the set to keep the trap from freezing; if you get a sudden thaw, that'll bind everything up.

For setting in deep snow, it's best if the weather stays cold constantly so that the snow stays granular. Then it's about like setting in sand. If the snow is crunchy or squeaks when you're walking on it, that's cold enough weather to trap in deep snow and you don't have to worry too much about it.

When making a set for predators, such as a flat set or dirt-hole in shallow snow, use your boots to kick, scrape and stomp the snow down in a 3- or 4-foot circular pattern. Clear the center of the circle down to bare dirt around the intended trap bed. Beyond this, stomp a basin out of the snow so that there's perhaps a 6-foot diameter pattern in the snow.

Coyotes might be suspicious of this area at first, but they'll eventually enter it. The old timers, up in Wyoming where I come from, used to make this same type of set, but instead of clearing it all the way down to the dirt, they left about ½-inch of packed snow on the bottom. They would then squirt blood from a cow or sheep around on the snow in the tramped-down circles. You'd be surprised how far this would spread by capillary action through the snow. It makes big red splotches on the snow and it looks like you killed a cow out there. That's a great call for predators.

When you're setting in the dirt, for a low snow situation, you try to avoid moisture where the trap is set. There are two or three different ways of doing this. One is to dig out an excavation for the trap, chain and drag. Put the chain and drag down and cover them with dirt. Then put in a piece of canvas, or double wax paper if it's a real wet situation, but don't crinkle it up, because then it loses some of its moisture resistance. Lay the waxed pa-

per in the hole and up the sides of the excavation but not so far that it's going to stick out. This provides a moisture barrier for the trap. Now, set your trap in, and top if off with dry mulch or dry dirt mixed with calcium chloride.

When bedding in the ground when the snow is not deep you have to use an anti-freeze of some type like calcium chloride. It's fairly cheap, and you can find it at most cement plants. They use it as a slurry mix in tractor tires to keep the liquid in them from freezing and that's its primary function when you're using it around your trap. When using calcium chloride it's important to wax your traps heavily, because the stuff is highly corrosive. Calcium chloride takes moisture out of the air, and becomes moist. I like to mix it with the dry dirt at the site in a small bucket. I use pre-sifted dirt or mulch because sticks or rocks can jam the trap.

After I mix the dirt and calcium chloride, I put it around the trap. Sometimes I use a foam pad under the trap pan, rather than a trap cover.

I boil the foam rubber to decontaminate it. While the foam rubber pieces are boiling, I put in a bit of cedar or some pine needles to give the rubber a little natural smell. With the foam rubber underneath, it takes more pan pressure to spring the trap, so it won't get triggered by rabbits and rats. It also keeps debris out from under the pan.

The trapper going after furbearers in deep snow will, of necessity, become thoroughly familiar with snowshoes. Here, Jim Nolan straps on his snowshoes in preparation to "string steel" in furbearer habitat.

These foam pads do get contaminated easily if you don't keep them in a plastic bag. I just cut them to the shape of the trap pan and store them in the bags. Next, I use a cup-shaped tool, called a Trapper's Cap, that fits over the pan and around the sides of it to keep the trap from springing while I bed it. Now I use my fingers to pack the dirt in and around the trap jaw — inside and out, right up to the foam rubber. This way, there's no loose material around the trap. When you get to the point where you're ready to cover the top of the trap, the last ¼- or ⅜-inch is sifted on. It'll be loose so that the jaws can come up through it. The cover dirt won't freeze because of the calcium chloride, and yet it retains that hard ground feeling. The only place there's any "give" is right on the trap pan.

If I'm making a flat set or scent post set, a chunk of rotted wood or a small rock or bush can be moved into place and lure placed upon it. I like to use three flat cow chips for backing. I first stack two on top of each other, place scent on top of that, and then place the third chip on top of that.

This way, the top cow chip protects the scent from the elements, and the predators can't find it right away. They'll generally circle the cow chips, looking for it. I place a trap on either side of the chips and, when using grapnels, I've taken doubles with this set.

For coyotes and cats I set the trap back aways, the pan center being about 8 inches from the cow pies. If you're going for foxes, set it back no more than 6 inches.

A dirt hole set is made basically the same way except that there is a hole by the trap. The hole, in a wet, freezing situation, is made a little differently than in most land trapping, for it's prone to get water in it that will freeze. The best way to eliminate that problem is to dig the hole deeper than you normally would and then put some grass, or crumpled up leaves, in the bottom of it, then put the bait in. That holds the bait up so that there's a little sump at the bottom. Moisture filters through the grass, collecting at the bottom of the hole.

Predators, as mentioned earlier, are a natural for trapping in deep snow. One reason is that they have a habit of following snowshoe trails broken through deep snows, and it's relatively easy to make sets right along your own trail.

However, you still have to follow the basics in snow trapping. If there's no natural trail originally, there's a good chance the animals won't travel in your tracks. You have to look for sign the same way you always do. The trail that you break will be the one that they'll follow, but your trail has to follow an area that is feasible to them.

Follow a deer trail or something like that, one that an animal would normally take. The bottoms

MAKING A SCENT POST SET IN DEEP SNOW

1. (Left) Once Jim Nolan finds a good site, he prepares to cut out a crust of snow over the top of the intended trap bed. He is using a small spade to cut the crust.

2. Lifting the plug of snow out of the trap bed, Nolan will now continue to further excavate the hole. When trapping in deep snow, traps are placed quite a ways below the surface of the snow. The reason is that the trap must be placed below the "crust line" to prevent freeze-up or clogging.

of ravines, if they're not brush-choked will be a normal travel route; the lip or top edge of a ravine is another one. If there's heavy snow they'll follow the lip rather than the bottom.

They run creeks and rivers like highways. You'll find more tracks up and down the creek ice than you will anywhere else because it's kept pretty well cleared by the wind.

Coyotes, foxes and bobcats are ideal for trapping in deep snow because they're out hunting regardless of conditions. They may lay up for a day, but no more than that usually. Raccoons, on the other hand, will hole up. They've got enough fat to live on, and they're not that voracious of an eater. A coyote is a little different. It doesn't have the fat surplus that other animals do — same for fox.

When you get into deeper snow, you've got a couple of problems that you don't have with shallow snow. One, you can't use calcium chloride to keep the set from freezing and any warming temperatures can cause a frozen film to form over the top of the snow that would support a coyote. You have to continually check the set for this. If there is a frozen crust on top of the snow where the trap is, use a stick to punch through the snow above the trap. In snow trapping for predators, you set traps 6 to 8 inches under the snow — not right near the top. For this reason, it's easy to clean the crust off without springing the trap.

To set a trap in deep snow you first determine if there's a crust on the snow. If so, take a trowel and cut out a square or circular section right over the intended trap bed. Try to get this crust out in one piece without breaking it, and carefully set it aside. Then, dig on down in the snow about 8 to 12 inches. Coyotes, bobcats and foxes are long-legged animals and they're going to punch down through the snow. The idea of setting the trap down that far is that the temperature is more constant there. There's less chance of a trap freezing up because the snow above insulates it.

Once you have the trap bed dug to the proper depth, carefully place the crust in the bottom of the hole. This serves as a hard base for the trap.

Like the low snow situation, you need a bottom cover as well as a top cover, and about the easiest thing to carry for both is waxed paper. Contrary to what many trappers think, the crinkle of the waxed paper when a furbearer steps on it does not give the set away because it's too late then. They've already got their foot in the trap. The waxed paper does work to keep moisture away from the working parts of the trap that can freeze it up solid. Lay the waxed paper on top of the crust, followed by the trap, then another sheet of waxed paper.

Now, use ¼-inch wire mesh screen to sift the excavated snow into the hole over the trap. It's im-

4. Here, Nolan sets a Montgomery trap before placing it in the bottom of the hole. Coil spring traps such as this are an advantage in that they're small and compact and will fit into a small hole conveniently.

3. After the snow has been excavated for the trap bed, Nolan packs the bottom of the bed down with his hands. After the bottom and sides of the bed are smoothed out, the next step is to carefully replace the plug of snow crust which was initially removed from the site. This forms a solid base for the trap. It also offers firm resistance when an animal breaks through from above, putting downward pressure on the trap. With the solid footing underneath the trap, it will spring rather than simply be pressed deeper into the snow. Nolan next lines the bottom of the hole with waxed paper.

portant to sift the snow because otherwise it has a tendency to pack. When you get the snow sifted back into the hole about level with the top, you can make it look natural by brushing over it with a little stick. Don't agitate this covering too much because the more it's agitated the more it tends to pack and freeze again.

Now, the only thing you have to worry about is fluctuating temperatures that thaw and freeze the snow, forming a crust down to where your trap is. If your trap is down deep, it won't get there. But the top will crust over, and you'll have to remove it on your next visit. If you make the set in the shade, where the sun's rays won't melt the surface of the snow, it may keep working longer.

The easiest way to lure a set in deep snow is to dip a stick in scent and then just stick it up in the snow near the trap. This set is just like a flat or scent-post set made in dirt only deeper.

You can even dig a "dirt" hole set in snow. The only problem with that is rabbits because they have a tendency to go down and inspect the holes, though they rarely get caught. That's another reason for setting the trap deep; a rabbit doesn't have the weight to spring the trap if you've got enough snow between rabbit and trap. Another advantage to trapping in deep snow is that animals aren't as likely to smell the trap when it is buried in 6 inches of covering.

The cubby set is another good one to make in deep snow. The best cubby sets in snow country are frequently under a tree, where they're protected. All you have to do is knock a couple of evergreen limbs out of the way to get right under the tree. This protects the trap if more snow falls, and the bait is protected as well. You have an opening from under the dense branches coming out onto the deeper snow. Your tracks will lead right up to this entrance and this will lead the animal in. Remember, they'll follow your tracks, and that's all you need. They follow tracks out there like you wouldn't believe. Snowshoe trails become regular expressways for furbearers, once they get started using them.

If the cubby is made for cats, it's better if the cat can see through it — a double-opening cubby. Hang the bait in the middle where it can't be seen by raptors. Make snowshoe tracks right up to both openings so that you've got two trails coming into it. Now, you've got twice the likelihood of something approaching. And if they can see through it, there's no fear.

I build quite a few artificial cubbies, mostly around rocky areas. Cats like to run the bases of rocky cliffs because there's a lot of rodents living in the rocks at the bottom. They'll patrol those areas pretty regularly, and it's an ideal spot to make a cubby out of rock. It's very easy to throw a

6. The snow must be sifted back over the top of the trap to camouflage the set. Snow has a tendency to pack whenever it's moved from one place to another and packed snow over the top of the trap may slow the trap's action or even prevent it from working at all. Here, Nolan sifts snow through a standard dirt-type sifter back into the hole over the top of the trap.

5. After the trap is carefully positioned in the bottom of the hole, another layer of waxed paper goes in on top. Some trappers wrinkle the waxed paper up to prevent it from making the crackling sound, but once it has been folded or rolled between the hands it loses its ability to form a moisture barrier. Again, when snow trapping like this noise is no problem. There's just too much snow on top of the trap.

few sticks up to form a "roof" between two boulders and cats don't seem to notice that it's been constructed; they'll go into it with no hesitation.

For cold snow country lures, you should use a lot of glycerine in them; mine are about 25 percent glycerine. Glycerine won't freeze, and it'll carry the scent a lot better.

The gland lures work the best for a predator like a coyote. They keep it in the area, but you should also have a strong call lure to get it interested in the first place. The gland lures aren't that strong. They're short-distance stuff.

If you're setting in a snowshoe trail where you've broken deep snow, furbearers will follow in your broken trail — every place you go, they'll go because it's the easiest route. This isn't true if there's a crust on, but if it's powder snow, the easiest way is to follow the path of least resistance, and that's the trail that you made. Make your sets just off this trail and, in this case, a gland lure without a call is fine.

If it's a low snow situation, where you're making sets in the mud or dirt, or in mulch, then you need a call lure because they won't necessarily be following in your footsteps and the set might be a ways from where they are coming from.

It's also important to pay attention to prevailing winds and not just from the standpoint of scent-drifting qualities. Watch the snow drifts to see

Jim Nolan makes a set in a "low snow" situation. Sometimes, when the snow is not sufficiently deep, it's actually easier and better to simply remove the snow down to the dirt to make a set.

7. Once the snow over the trap has been sifted to fill the hole level with the surrounding snow, it's necessary to smooth everything out so that there's no visible sign of any disturbance having taken place in the area. Make it look as natural as possible. Here, Nolan adds scratch marks for authenticity.

8. (Right) Any excess snow should be carried away from the trap-setting site and scattered to further eliminate suspicion.

(Right) One very popular set is a scent post, in this instance formed by a couple of sticks. The scent is placed on top of the sticks and the traps covered. The traps will be bedded with waxed paper top and bottom as shown for a deep snow situation. Two traps are used on either side of the scent post just in case a predator doesn't walk all the way around it.

The sun beating down on a rock causes the snow to melt around the rock before it melts in other areas.

which way the heavy snow piles up on which side of the trees. That tells you the prevailing direction of wind. Set the trap to the lightly drifted side so that it doesn't cover over if it snows again.

If you're making the low snow set in the dirt, make it on the southeast side of the bush. That's the side that will melt and dry out first when it starts to clear out. The warmest sun is in the morning, before noon. The afternoon sun doesn't give much heat. That's why you set it on the southeast side of the tree."

10. This is the way the set appears after everything is complete. As you can see, there is little sign of any disturbance. The snowshoes form a trail of packed snow that will be naturally traveled by predators, leading directly to the trap site.

9. Nolan decides to put his lure on a stick pushed into the side of the old tree stump. This should attract any animals passing by the set.

Here, Jim Nolan prepares a set in adverse conditions. First, he decided to make a scent post set beside this small pine tree stump. The first step is to remove the layer of snow and chop down into the frozen turf underneath.

(Right) Here, Nolan uses a hatchet to chop the frozen soil out from under the snow. It's simply too hard to dig out with a shovel.

Preventing Trap Freeze-up

Since most trapping is done during the cold winter months and because traps will be subjected to freezing temperatures, trap freeze-up is one of the major problems confronting fur harvesters over much of North America. There are a good many trappers who do fine early in the season, taking a number of pelts, but when the conditions get tough, they pull up and quit fighting the elements.

The persistent, hardy trapper who is willing to tough it out and put up with adverse conditions is the one who takes the most and some of the best furs during the weeks when trapping is toughest. Furthermore, severe weather eliminates a lot of the trapping competition.

Here in Arizona, the state actually isn't all desert, as some people think. A lot of country in the northern part of the state is at elevations higher than 5,000 or 7,000 feet, and gets its share of cold, snow, and freezing rain during the winter. Trappers are generally out working this high country early in the season when conditions are nice. Later in the year when the snows come to stay, and battling the freezing and thawing conditions becomes tough, a good many trappers pull out and move south to the desert where they don't have to contend with it all. A trapper who is willing to tough it out up north can have a lot of that section of the state to himself during severe winters.

Foul weather doesn't *have* to stop the trapper completely. Trapping under adverse conditions does take a lot more effort, in most cases, although the trapper who is willing to put forth the effort can generally keep his traps working. There are some conditions where it's next to impossible and some regions do have much more severe weather than others. Furthermore, the methods required to keep the set working will vary considerably, depending upon the weather in a particular area.

I'm referring here to land trapping rather than water trapping. Water trapping becomes a cold, hard business during winter as well, but it involves setting traps in non-frozen liquid. In land trapping, on the other hand, the trapper is forced to expose his traps to freezing conditions.

In many instances, one of the keys to keeping traps working during freezing and thawing conditions begins long before the trapping season. Let me explain. Many sets made in the West, particularly for bobcat and grey fox, are made in areas of dense brush, frequently in a juniper forest. Junipers are a type of evergreen that litter the forest floor with 2 inches or more of needles. It is quite easy to make a set under a juniper tree for the trap can be concealed beneath the duff with little or no digging. Furthermore, this duff serves as an excellent trap covering material. When it is sifted free of rocks, it is very lightweight, and the trap comes through it very quickly and easily.

When the rains and later the snows come, along with the freezing conditions, the juniper duff naturally gets water-logged and any trap underneath it will be frozen

(Above) After the trap bed is excavated to the depth needed, it is lined with a double thickness of waxed paper as shown here. This forms a moisture barrier, preventing moisture from coming up from the soil and condensing on the trap. It also prevents melted snow from puddling around the trap. (Right) The trap is shown here in position in the trap bed. It is ready to be re-covered though you shouldn't use the material that came out of the trap bed.

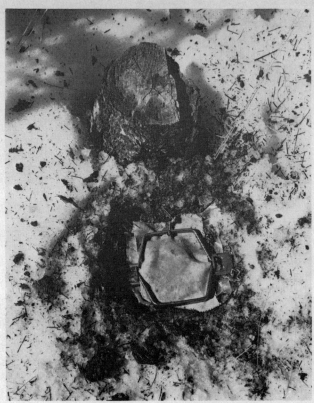

solid. However, if one has collected a quantity of this juniper material and kept it dry, it's a simple matter to dig out the frozen trap, replace the wet or frozen juniper duff around the trap with the dry material and re-bed the trap.

Long before season, when everything is still dry, a trapper may go into the juniper forest and collect garbage bags full of the stuff. Use the heavy-duty bags (3-mil thick) to prevent holes and leakage. Again, this stuff isn't difficult to collect for it may lie a couple of inches deep under many of the trees. By having someone hold the bag open for him, the trapper can shovel it in and fill a lot of bags in no time if there are a lot of trees around.

This works great for trapping bobcat because they like to scratch in the juniper duff under the trees. Foxes are also found in these same areas. As mentioned in the earlier chapters on foxes and bobcats, the same set will take both animals. Sometimes even wary coyotes get into sets under juniper trees.

The juniper duff can be conveniently carried on a trapline in a wide-mouth plastic gallon jug. The trap bed is dug out, the bottom lined with the dry duff, the trap positioned and then completely covered with the pre-sifted duff. If another rain comes, the tree protects the trap for a short while although if the rain is of any quantity, it will eventually soak the duff and it will re-freeze. Hence it will have to be replaced again, just as before.

However, there is one method of preventing mois-

ture from falling upon the trap springs themselves. In this instance, I'm talking about a double long-spring trap. Basically, it involves placing a large flat cow chip (dry, of course) on top of each trap spring next to the trap jaws. The cow chips will not only protect the springs from moisture, but they serve as an excellent insulating material to prevent freezing-up if the freeze isn't a hard one. This simple trick keeps traps operating for several hours or perhaps even the entire night until you're able to get to the sets and remake them the next morning.

A simple remedy to keep a trap working in freeze/thaw conditions, one overlooked by most trappers, is getting out to the sets early in the morning and brushing the new fallen snow off the top of the traps so that it doesn't melt and run down into the beds. A simple whisk broom is great for this purpose. Once you get the hang of it, the snow can be quickly whisked away without springing the traps. It just takes a second and it'll keep the traps working the following night whereas they would otherwise be frozen in.

Junipers aren't the only trees that deposit usable duff for the trapper to use. Evergreen duff from trees farther east or, in some instances, oak leaf litter can be the answer. However, a trapper must use material indigenous to his local area so that the animals won't become wary of foreign matter. When using oak leaf litter, the leaves can be gathered in early fall, again, when they're perfectly dry, and run through a shredder and bagged, just like the juniper duff mentioned earlier. In fact, nearly

Jim Nolan is careful to cover the trap with dry pine needles taken from the surrounding area. It is also important to cover the trap lightly—don't get too many needles over the trap itself.

Nolan scraped a small amount of snow and ice back over the top of the needles to camouflage it somewhat. He was careful not use too much snow because it would melt and cause a frozen crust to form over the top of the trap. The last step is to dispense scent on the tree stump to attract predatory furbearers.

any type of deciduous tree leaves can be treated in this manner.

The type of shredder to be used can be left to the imagination. If you don't have access to a shredder, you can bag up the leaves and crumple them inside the bags by squeezing and rubbing the outsides of the bags together. Be sure to bag up enough of the material, particularly deciduous leaf litter, for it's fluffy and trap-bedding may take a lot of it. This is one of the best and most natural precautions for keeping traps working in the winter. Remember, it takes moisture for traps to freeze. All you have to do is keep things dry, and they won't freeze.

Sand can also be used for a trap bedding material. It can be covered with a thin camouflage of nearly any material from the surrounding area. Even if the leaves or grasses around the set are damp, a very light film can be sprinkled over the trap. Just keep it light enough so that when the material does freeze it won't be enough to jam a double-spring trap.

I mention the double-spring trap for it is generally thought to be one of the best for coming up through frozen material. Those large flat springs have a lot of power, and they're second to none for trapping during freezing and thawing conditions.

If the freezing and thawing conditions come before you're able to collect leaf litter or juniper duff, there are other alternatives. One is to collect dry dirt which can frequently be found underneath bridges. A lot of times rain and snow don't reach under bridges or over-passes

and many a trap has been kept working by using it.

As Jim Nolan pointed out earlier, it is a good idea when using dirt on top of the trap, to mix calcium chloride with it to absorb any moisture inherent in the dirt. I generally buy it by the 50-pound bag and carry some of it in a plastic 1-gallon jug. The flakes are small enough that they'll pour out of the small mouth of the jug. It's not a bad idea to mix it in with dirt around the trap as well, unless, of course, you've been experiencing only thin crust-type freeze-overs during the night. Though the calcium chloride is white it quickly dissolves becoming invisible.

There are some problems in using calcium chloride, though. For one, it has a moisture-attracting characteristic, meaning it causes traps to rust severely. It is important, when using it, to make sure your traps are thoroughly waxed. Secondly, since the calcium chloride attracts moisture, a wet spot may develop around the trap where it's used. This is no problem insofar as trapping is concerned as long as there are other wet spots in the surrounding area. However, there are times when most of the ground, at least on the surface, is relatively dry and the spot right where the trap and calcium chloride are, is wet. Most predators probably wouldn't hesitate to put their foot in a muddy spot for they do it all the time, but to a trap-wary coyote, it might be suspicious.

Another method of keeping traps from freezing down involves the use of grasses. In nearly every case, grasses dry out long before the dirt. These dry winter grasses

One trick used by some trappers to prevent trap freeze-up is to simply line the trap bed and cover it with dry, fluffy vegetation. As long as the vegetation is completely dry, it won't freeze into a crust over a trap. The dried grass is simply cut into small pieces and packed underneath and over the top of the trap. As long as it doesn't rain on top of the trap, this will prevent it from freezing and will keep it operable.

can be clipped and placed on the bottom of the trap bed with more clippings, chopped up in shorter lengths, placed on top of the trap — over the springs, around the outside of the jaws, inside the jaws, and over the pan. Then, a sprinkling can be scattered over the entire set, being careful not to block the trap pan underneath. Using this method a trap cover is not needed. These grasses are frequently found in meadows inhabited by foxes in the winter, so here you have a natural freeze-up preventative right at the site where you're making the set. What could make a set more natural looking? Farmers frequently bale up brome grass and leave it in the pasture during the winter and, naturally, field mice gather around these large circular hay bales and burrow underneath. These spots, as might be expected, are favorite mouse hunting grounds for red foxes. They almost always investigate areas around these hay bales when traveling through any such meadow or brome grass pasture. There's no better place to make fox sets and the brome grass is an ideal bedding and insulating material around the trap.

Some trappers in the Dakotas excavate a sizeable hole in the prairie where they intend to trap for foxes, then fill it with dry peat moss which, though the ground around may be frozen, keeps the trap dry and working.

If it rains, or freezes and then thaws, the moisture drains underneath the trap.

Another type of set that can work quite well during freezing conditions is the spring or running water set. Even when temperatures become quite cold, there are usually places around springs, or flowing creeks, which don't freeze. Furbearers come to these places to drink, and it's an excellent place for making a set.

Find a place where there is a rock projecting above the water level 3 feet or more away from the bank. If you can't find such a rock, put one in the stream or spring so that the top of it remains dry. On top of the rock place some type of small bait with a food scent designed to attract the animals you're after. Next, about halfway between the rock and the bank, place a trap. If possible, adjust everything so that the trap pan is almost level with the surface of the water. Next, put a small flat rock on top of the trap pan — one that's not heavy enough to cause the trap to spring, of course. When your quarry comes to drink at the spring, it'll smell and see the bait out on the large rock. The small rock above the water (and on top of trap) looks like a stepping stone to the bait on the large rock, and will more than likely be used as such. This is an excellent way for catching the predators.

chapter 22

SNARING

THE USE OF snares in trapping furbearers and other animals goes back even farther than the foot-hold trap itself. In fact, the Indians had been snaring animals long before the white man came to North America. Those used by the Indians and early white men were extremely primitive by today's standards. Today's snare is an efficient trapping device that, in my opinion, is grossly overlooked and underrated by the average trapper.

I suppose the primary reason it is overlooked is tradition. The steel foot-hold trap has become the standard and generally accepted method of catching furbearers. Furthermore, the techniques for successful trapping are widely known and a large number of trappers, educated in the "how-tos" of foot-hold trapping, have had a high degree of success. Besides tradition, I don't believe that today's trapper is aware of the techniques involved in snaring nor does he know just how effective a properly set snare can be. Most have the mistaken assumption that snares have only very limited applications. Actually, I can't think of any animal which cannot be snared nor can I envision any terrain where a snare won't work.

Basically, a snare is a specialized steel cable that has a sliding lock on it to form a loop. The loop closes very easily when an animal places pressure upon it, and once it closes, the slide lock prevents the loop from opening up. It only tightens when it's pulled. An animal is usually caught around the neck, body, or legs, restraining it, sometimes alive, until the trapper arrives.

To be effective, a snare has to be positioned so that the furbearer walks, runs, slides, or swims into it. The most natural place is along a trail. In nearly any type of country there are a great many trails — both game and cow trails. Predators and other furbearers habitually use these, making them a natural place for snare setting. However, the trapper must be cautious regarding their use and avoid areas where livestock, deer or pets could possibly get into them. With these precautions in mind, snaring can be a very effective, safe, and humane way of taking furbearers.

Due to their light weight and relatively low cost, snares have definite advantages over steel traps. First of all, they can be carried in quantity into the backcountry. For the trapper after the larger predators such as coyotes and bobcats, which require the use of the large No. 3 or 4 foot-hold traps, the trapper is really limited regarding the number of traps and other paraphernalia he can carry into the backcountry. Due to their light

This photo illustrates a snare at the entrance to a culvert where grey fox had been passing through. Note how much of the pipe is blocked by sticks to force the fox through the largest opening where the snare is located.

(Left) Snares don't always kill the trapped animal though they can be made to do so. One way is to attach a snare to a fence so that when the animal jumps through the fence it hangs itself. (Photo courtesy of A.M. Grawe.)

weight, snares, on the other hand, can be carried for long distances and in great quantities, leaving plenty of room for other set-making materials.

Their use simply requires a lot of common sense for nearly anywhere that an animal travels regularly, a snare can be used to trap it. Culverts and dens regularly used by furbearers are other examples of excellent snare sites. Setting snares in these places simply involves forming a loop of the proper diameter and height in the path of the animal.

In some instances, a trapper can make the loop more effective by blocking other travel routes around it with brush or other natural materials in the area. The wire can also be easily camouflaged by using fine sticks or grasses to break up its outline.

When snaring animals such as coyotes in a cow trail, where there is nothing but short grass all around, the trapper is better off not even attempting to make a fence to direct the coyote into it but rather setting the bare snare on the barren cow trail. It'll stick out like a sore thumb, but you'll be surprised how coyotes will walk right into it. As a rule of thumb, block alternate routes only if you can make the route-blocking appear natural. Otherwise, wary animals will walk way around it to avoid the suspicious-looking area.

Though snares can be homemade, I strongly recommend buying them from reputable manufacturers. I have used several types and am completely satisfied

with snares produced by A.M. Grawe at Box 704, Wahpeton, ND 58075. Grawe makes a relatively inexpensive snare which has a very smooth-closing slide-lock and cable. In addition, they market a support system, making the snare entirely self-contained. It can be set right on bare ground with no tree branch or anything else around for support or attachment. Another reputable maker is the Raymond Thompson Co. at 15815 Second Place West, Alderwood Manor Station, Lynnwood, WA 98036.

Snares should be handled and set much like steel traps but with some important exceptions. Don't boil snares in lye water or vinegar for both of these will corrode the cable. Grawe suggests boiling them in baking soda water for ½-hour using ½-pound of baking soda per 3 gallons of water. After that, common sense dictates they should be handled with clean gloves to prevent imparting any more human odor than necessary. On the other hand, if you're working in heavy brush country where you can't avoid brushing against the vegetation, the scent on the snare may not be that much of a deterrent to a predator entering it. It'll simply be a little more human scent right in the trail where the rest of it is anyway.

My experience in snaring is limited compared to my steel trap experience. However, the number of sets I've made, even with my limited experience, indicates that my success with snares is as great as with foot-hold

Snares are an advantage during freezing and thawing conditions in that they are not as susceptible to inclement weather as steel traps are. In other words, foul weather doesn't put snares out of commission as readily as it does steel traps. This red fox was snared by A.M. Grawe. (Photo courtesy of A.M. Grawe.)

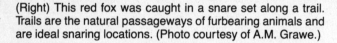

(Right) This red fox was caught in a snare set along a trail. Trails are the natural passageways of furbearing animals and are ideal snaring locations. (Photo courtesy of A.M. Grawe.)

traps. Actually, I think that a trapper would be wise to become adept at using both and choosing whichever one works best for the situation at hand.

One very important advantage to snares is that they continue to work even during periods of heavy snowfall or extremely wet weather where freezing and thawing occurs. Unlike the steel foot-hold trap, the snare is set above ground level and is not as susceptible to freeze-up.

Once a trapper becomes adept at using snares, he usually finds it's faster to set a snare than it is to set a foot-hold trap. The major difference, however, is that each snare setting situation is different, requiring the trapper to analyze and adapt the snare to the specific site. Steel trap sets, on the other hand, are basically the same wherever you set them.

Some trappers have the mistaken idea that a snare has some sort of a spring-loaded trigger to jerk the loop tightly about the animal's neck. In truth, a snare is little more than a lasso with a locking device on it, utilizing the animal's own pressure to tighten the loop. Generally, the loop tightens about the animal before it realizes what's happening. The animal will struggle somewhat at first but when the loop doesn't slack off, it generally quits struggling. Unless a killing-type of snare setup is devised, the animal will usually be alive when the trapper returns. Sometimes, a snared animal will jump over a fence and kill itself.

A trapper can devise several types of snare killing devices. One is by simply driving a second stake solidly into the ground a few feet away from the snare-securing stake. When the animal is snared, it wraps around the two stakes and strangles itself. Another killing device is one of the old Indian tricks wherein a sapling is bent over the trail where the snare is to be set. A rope is tied to its tip and a triggering device is rigged to hold the rope and sapling in a bent position. The snare is then attached to the sapling or rope, and once an animal is snared it struggles and triggers the secondary device releasing the sapling, causing it to spring upward, pulling the animal off the ground.

In conventional use, snares can either be staked solid or attached to a drag. The loop can be suspended from a tree branch, a wire at the bottom of a fence, a hole in a culvert, or some sort of artificial attachment devised by the trapper for the sole purpose of supporting the snare. For example, a tree limb can be leaned against another tree and the snare suspended from the limb. In other instances the trapper may use some type of auxiliary support system such as a stiff wire to hold the snare loop over a trail. The Grawe system, in fact, uses a very excellent self-supporting snaring device called the "figure seven." This device makes it possible to quickly set the snare anywhere without having to depend upon some natural form of support. The vegetation in the area serves as camouflage to break up the outline of the snare.

This coyote was snared where it had been passing underneath a fence. Any spot that forces an animal into a tight place can be snared very effectively. (Photo courtesy of A.M. Grawe.)

This red fox was caught with a snare positioned in a trail frequented by these valuable furbearers. In this case, a small tree was used to the trapper's advantage to dispatch the animal. (Photo courtesy of A.M. Grawe.)

The snare can be used on animals of any size, up to and including bears. This timber wolf was caught with the use of a snare. As you can see, it is quite large. (Photo courtesy of A.M. Grawe.)

Besides trails and culverts, snares can be set along fencerows, or in the "dead furrow" at the edge of a plowed field. Where a log crosses a stream or ditch is an excellent place for snaring animals using these areas as crossings. Snares can be set where animals go through a fence or around a cattle guard, or along the edge of a stream where raccoons and other furbearers travel. Generally, the creek bank is bare for several feet next to the water. However, the trapper can usually find a natural opening through driftwood for snare placement. If not, it's a simple matter to pile brush or sticks along the bank to force a raccoon or other furbearer through the opening next to the water. Raccoons are so used to walking around such sticks, brush, and even human trash that they'll readily walk through a snare opening.

As a rule of thumb, a person using a snare should remember that animals will generally take the path of least resistance. This is why animals travel on trails the way that they do — because the going is so much easier. If the trapper using snares makes the alternative routes more difficult for the animal to go through than the opening where the snare is, the animal will likely go where the snare is.

There are a number of trappers who have become adept at snaring beaver. Beaver snares can be placed on top of dams, in slides leading into water, dens, both in the bank and in huts in the water, or they can be placed in the middle of a stream with sticks blocking alternate routes. Dangling snare sets for beavers can be made under the ice simply by hanging snares on either side of

These red fox were all caught with snares. Used in the proper manner, they can obviously be very effective. (Photo courtesy of A.M. Grawe.)

bait sticks such as poplar, aspen, or willow, or placing a bait stick in the center of the snare loop. Some beavers are snared by dangling the loop next to feed beds. All that's necessary is to cut a small hole in the ice, form a loop in the snare, lower it into the water, and attach the snare's free end above the ice, possibly to a log or limb laid across the hole.

On a particularly well-used game trail it may pay to set several snares in succession. The same holds true when snaring well-used log crossings.

One important aspect to being effective with snares is to have a proper size loop the right distance off the ground. This all depends upon the animal you're attempting to snare, and its physical attitude — nose-down or nose-up — when entering the area of the snare.

For fox, raccoon, and bobcat, a loop about 8 inches in diameter and 8 inches off the ground is about right. For coyotes, the loop should be about 10 to 12 inches off the ground and 9 to 12 inches in diameter. For beaver snaring on dry land make the bottom of the loop only 2 inches off the ground and 10 to 12 inches in diameter. For the small grey fox, make a loop about 5 to 6 inches off the ground and about 6 to 7 inches in diameter.

In some instances you may want to put a small stick under the snare loop to make the animal raise its head and stick it through the loop. If a canine predator such as a coyote or fox is expected to be hunting, his nose will generally be next to the ground. Therefore, if you're setting these snares in rabbit thickets, you may want to make the loop a little closer to the ground than if it's on

a cow trail where they will be traveling with their heads in a more raised position.

To prevent deer from getting into snares, be careful about where the snare is placed. For example, deer use game trails regularly. If a snare is placed on a game trail in an attempt to catch coyotes or fox, you may want to place the snare underneath a sizable limb hanging low over the trail. A good many of these limbs are much easier for a deer to go over yet are more practical for a furbearer to go under. Hence, the deer is prevented from getting into a set.

Some makers also produce a snare with what is termed a "deer guard." This is a metal stop placed about 7 inches from the end of the lock which allows the snare to close down and still leave a 2-inch free space, thus allowing the deer to shake off the snare after it steps into it.

You never know when some unique trapping situation might suggest the use of a snare as being more efficient than a foot-hold trap. I ran into this situation this past winter when a friend of mine who had some livestock, including hogs and sheep, first began losing rabbits. The animal, (I didn't know what it was at the time) had to jump over a fence to get inside a pen where the rabbit hutches were, then rip the wire mesh bottoms out of the hutches and kill the rabbits. My friend lost six rabbits the first night, then, a short while later, one of his pigs was killed, then three more rabbits.

No one had seen what the animal was, though the owner had seen a coyote standing near the pen one

This red fox was snared during a snowfall, proving that they work very well, under most any condition. Since they're positioned above ground level, they aren't as susceptible to adverse weather conditions as are traps which are placed below ground. (Photo courtesy of A.M. Grawe.)

morning. Other neighbors also began reporting losing livestock to the animal, whatever it was. The ground was frozen and no tracks could be discerned.

When the pig was killed my friend called me and told me the whole story, and asked if I would come over and see if I could catch the critter. At first, I was a bit reluctant for my friend is at the edge of town and I knew there were dogs around. However, I decided to at least go have a look for I was curious about what was doing the killing.

The pig, which weighed only about 30 pounds, had been bitten behind the head in the neck area. There were very deep gashes in the sides of the neck about 3 inches long.

My friend had earlier called a local game warden who supplied a live trap and several foot-hold traps to catch the whatever-it-was. So far, they had had no luck.

When I looked at the pen where the rabbits were I could see that there was a high fence all around the perimeter except for one gate about 5 feet high and 8 feet long. There were still some rabbits left in the hutches and I decided that whatever it was must have leaped over the gate to get inside the pen for this was the lowest point in the fence, and it would be the natural place of entrance. There were no holes of any sort in the pen for an animal to squeeze through.

Foot-hold traps couldn't be placed around the pen due to pets in the area. Yet, anything that went over the top of that gate was up to no-good and deserved to be nailed, dog or beast. I decided that the thing to do was to set snares along the *top* of the gate. The state and local laws were clearcut — any stock killer could be immediately dispatched.

The first thing I did was stretch a piece of heavy wire from gate post to gate post, about a foot above the top of the gate itself. I tied the wire so that the owner would still be able to go in and out of the gate—he'd just have to duck a little to get under it. Next, I attached a series of six snares to the wire and with the use of clothespins, hung the snares downward from it. I figured if anything came over the top of the gate, such as a coyote or bobcat, or even a dog, it would hit one of the snares. Hopefully, the mere presence of the dangling snares wouldn't prevent the animal from trying to jump the gate again.

I used a 6-foot length of snare cable so that if caught, the animal wouldn't hang itself but would most likely be alive. About 2 weeks later, we caught the stock killer by a right front leg, high up on the shoulder. It was a Great Dane which had been running loose in the area and was little worse for the wear.

This is one instance where a snare was ideally suited to the situation and I don't think any sort of a foot-hold trap or live trap (which had been tried) would have done the job like the snare had. In short, your effectiveness in snaring animals is dependent upon your ability as an outdoorsman—your knowledge of the animals and their habits, and being able to adapt the snaring setup to each individual situation. If you haven't tried using snares, I suggest you do. It'll be an education, an exciting sidebar from foot-hold trapping, and you'll soon begin visualizing sets where snares play an increasingly important role in your trapping operation.